"A cogent study of hip-hop's outsized influence on fashion trends. The link between hip-hop and high fashion is so tight that many consider them part of the same package. In this fast-paced, deeply researched history, Krishnamurthy chronicles how and why that deep bond continues today. . . . Exciting and exhaustive, this fun hip-hop history explains what your favorite rappers are wearing and why."

—*Kirkus Reviews* (starred review)

"Readers are lucky that this brilliant, shining gem of a book exists. . . . Along with its many nuanced arguments and observations, the book is a stunning historical record of years, people, places, runway shows, brands, and evolutions that should be studied. An essential book about U.S. culture."

—*Booklist* (starred review)

"The first comprehensive anthology of the marriage between hip-hop and luxury fashion, mapping out well-examined evidence of the two entities being inextricably linked."

—*The Cut*

"Krishnamurthy cements herself as a necessary historian for the culture."

—*Paper*

"*Fashion Killa* is a love letter to hustlers, innovators, and people who didn't abide by the rules. Krishnamurthy's comprehensive work gives the history of hip-hop its due, recognizing the elevated contributions of the icons, designers, and rappers who came together to claim a place in a culture."

—Dapper Dan, fashion innovator

"*Fashion Killa* is super important because we are the culture that transcends into fashion. Rappers motivate designers to make something dope. Hip-hop and fashion is a perfect marriage!"

—Raekwon, rapper and author of *From Staircase to Stage*

"A sharp and engaging contribution to fashion, art, and storytelling. A must-read for anyone who adores and respects fashion's contribution to mankind."

—Slick Rick, storyteller and fashion icon

"Sowmya Krishnamurthy's powerful and meticulously told deep dive into hip-hop's culture of showing out is a vibrant and historic telling of a groundbreaking story. *Fashion Killa* captures the visionaries, misfits, and rule breakers who revolutionized the worlds of fashion, innovation, and luxury. This is not just the American dream but a global story."

—Vikki Tobak, author of *Ice Cold: A Hip-Hop Jewelry History* and *Contact High: A Visual History of Hip-Hop*

"*Fashion Killa* is a luxury quilt of hip-hop journalism sewn with gilded floss. In Sowmya's skillful sartorial hand, the stories of fashion icons and upstart rappers appear in a two-way mirror, revealing the line between haute and street as a fabrication born out of aspiration, and the thread tying hip-hop to fashion as inevitable and durable indeed."

—Dan Charnas, *New York Times* bestselling author of *Dilla Time* and *The Big Payback*

FASHION KILLA

HOW HIP-HOP REVOLUTIONIZED HIGH FASHION

SOWMYA KRISHNAMURTHY

G

GALLERY BOOKS

New York   London   Toronto   Sydney   New Delhi

G

Gallery Books
An Imprint of Simon & Schuster, LLC
1230 Avenue of the Americas
New York, NY 10020

First Gallery Books trade paperback edition September 2024

GALLERY BOOKS and colophon are registered trademarks of Simon & Schuster, LLC

Simon & Schuster: Celebrating 100 Years of Publishing in 2024

For information about special discounts for bulk purchases, please contact Simon & Schuster Special Sales at 1-866-506-1949 or business@simonandschuster.com.

The Simon & Schuster Speakers Bureau can bring authors to your live event. For more information or to book an event, contact the Simon & Schuster Speakers Bureau at 1-866-248-3049 or visit our website at www.simonspeakers.com.

Interior design by Davina Mock-Maniscalco

Manufactured in the United States of America

10 9 8 7 6 5 4 3 2 1

Library of Congress Cataloging-in-Publication Data is available for the hardcover.

ISBN 978-1-9821-7632-7
ISBN 978-1-9821-7633-4 (pbk)
ISBN 978-1-9821-7634-1 (ebook)

For Mom and Dad

Contents

BACK TO SCHOOL

Before hip-hop was the arbiter of culture—the most dominant music genre, supplanting pop and all-American rock and roll—influencing the way the world walks, speaks, and wears its jeans, it was one teenager's means of raising money for new school clothes. August 11, 1973, was the hot summer day when DJ Kool Herc (born Clive Campbell) spun a party for his sister in the rec room of the family's nondescript brick apartment building at 1520 Sedgwick Avenue in the Bronx. The sixteen-year-old Jamaican American had been experimenting with his father's speakers and tinkering with new ways to spin records. With two turntables and a mixer, he could play without interruption and seamlessly transition from one track to the next, keeping the party going. He loved to spin James Brown's "Give It Up or Turnit a Loose." He saw how break-dancers, B-boys and B-girls, got wild during "the break," the part of a song when the instrumentals faded and the beat took over. "And once they heard that, that was it, wasn't no turning back," Herc said. "They always wanted to hear breaks after breaks after breaks after breaks."

Meanwhile, Cindy Campbell didn't wax poetic about esoteric sounds; she just wanted to look good. "When you go back to school, you want to go with things that nobody has so you could look nice and fresh," she said. "I was saving my money, because what you did for back-to-school is go down to Delancey Street instead of going to Fordham Road, because you can get the newest things that a lot of people don't have." At the time, her paycheck from working at the Neighborhood Youth Corps was $45 a week. There's no way she could look *fly* on that budget. "So how am I gonna turn over my money? I mean, that is not enough money!" The entrepreneurial teenager decided to throw a party to crowdfund her wardrobe. She bought Olde English 800 malt liquor, Colt 45 beer, and soda in bulk, and advertised on index cards handwritten in big block letters: A DJ KOOL HERC PARTY: Back To School Jam. To pay the $25 in order to rent the rec room of Herc's family home, she charged an entry fee of a quarter for girls and fifty cents for the guys.

What happened that day was magic: the confluence of youth, innovation, self-expression, and creativity against the backdrop of New York City. Herc originated a technique called the "Merry-Go-Round," in which he worked two copies of the same record, back-cueing one to the beginning of the break just as the other reached the end, creating one long loop. The "get-down" was the beginning or middle of the song, giving dancers a pocket to bust their freshest moves. "The music was just, it was slammin'!" said partygoer Jean Stickland. "I remember going to Herc parties that started in the community room. It grew so big that we couldn't fit in the community room anymore." Parents just didn't understand this new music—and that increased its appeal. "This was a breath of fresh air," Herc said. "Turned out to be a success."

Despite the mythos around the August 11 party, hip-hop's origin cannot be pinpointed to one moment on a timeline. Its lineage traces to oral traditions from Africa, the Black experience in America, and the invention of jazz and the blues. "Rap music is rooted in the Black oral tradition of tonal semantics, narrativizing, signification/signifyin', the dozens/playin' the dozens, Africanized syntax, and other communicative practices," wrote Professor Geneva Smitherman in "'The Chain

Remain the Same': Communicative Practices in the Hip Hop Nation," commending rappers as the "postmodern African griot, the verbally gifted storyteller and cultural historian in traditional African society."

During hip-hop's infancy, the urban decay of crime, police brutality, and white flight had left the South Bronx ravaged and on fire. From these ashes, hip-hop rose with break-dancers and street gangs that were succeeded by rap crews that traded physical fighting for verbal sparring while maintaining the same element of competition. Hip-hop was centered in the Black American experience in New York City, but integral contributions by Puerto Ricans, Caribbeans, and rappers who were immigrants from these communities cannot be forgotten. Hip-hop reverberated through the five boroughs—the Bronx, Brooklyn, Queens, Manhattan, and Staten Island— with early innovators like Grandmaster Flash and Afrika Bambaataa.

It was a holistic culture that touched upon all aspects of life, often delineated by four basic pillars: MCing (words), DJing (sounds), Break dancing (movement), and Graffiti (visuals). "Hip-hop is the study of self-transformation and the pursuit of self-expression," explained veteran rapper and scholar KRS-One in a lecture at Harvard University. In his definition, hip-hop encompassed nine pillars, including Knowledge and Street Fashion. An early inflection point from house party to mainstream success came with the Sugarhill Gang's "Rapper's Delight," released on September 16, 1979. The song was the first hip-hop single to break into Billboard's Top 40 chart, and also charted in Canada and across Europe. "Basically, it's a record that created an industry," said Dan Charnas, author of *The Big Payback: The History of the Business of Hip-Hop*. "Nobody thought the stuff that was in the streets was even music. It was stuff that people did at parties."

Hip-hop was the voice for the voiceless. A bildungsroman of life in America's inner city—predominantly told through the lens of young Black and Latino men—that went beyond feel-good dance tracks. These were perspectives of life, more complex and nuanced than the headlines:

poverty, racism, drugs, police brutality, and humanity embedded in verses of sixteen bars. The hyperlocal perspective offered a sonic passport that transported listeners to the concrete streets of New York City, gang lands in Los Angeles, Detroit trailer parks, and trap houses in the South. Explicit lyrics would cause ongoing controversy from parents' groups and law enforcement, and hip-hop would become a bellwether of First Amendment rights. As hip-hop transcended the block, it was usurped by Madison Avenue to sell products and to give brands the cachet of cool.

In 2017, hip-hop became the most successful music genre in America, surpassing both pop and rock, in terms of overall consumption. Six of the top ten artists that year were rappers, with Drake and Kendrick Lamar taking the top two spots, respectively. Hip-hop had outlasted the critics that said it was just a fad, ephemera, noise. As rappers became the new superstars, they made the dress code. Like preachers, they propagated luxury to the hungry and poorly dressed masses. Their music was the primer to learn about international brands: Versace, Balenciaga, and Balmain. As Kanye West said in 2004's "All Falls Down," "*I can't even pronounce nothin', pass that Ver-say-see.*" By 2013, A$AP Rocky's "Fashion Killa" was a crash course in erudition, as he name-checked some twenty-seven luxury brands. Wanting to see their names on those tags, some rappers launched their own clothing lines, and a few even disrupted fashion in the process.

Growing up in middle-of-nowhere Kalamazoo, Michigan, my introduction to hip-hop happened around 1995 through copious hours of MTV and BET; glossy magazines like *Vibe*, *The Source*, *Blaze*, *Word Up!*, and *XXL*; and spending my allowance at Record Town and Sam Goody every Tuesday. The only radio station that played hip-hop was in another town and came in as mostly static.

It was 1997 and I desperately wanted . . . nah, I *needed* some Tommy Hilfiger. Aaliyah's *One in a Million* album was playing out of my Sony Discman and I had to cop some small piece of the singer's street-but-sweet visage: dark sunglasses, bangs swept over one eye (an homage to silver-screen siren Veronica Lake), and Tommy Hilfiger crop top. Tommy's red, white, and blue was way too expensive at retail, but for $25, there was a knockoff from the bargain store. The stitching was a bit off-center and the designer's name was definitely misspelled (but only if you were close enough to read it). Gauche, yes. But that "Tommy Hilifiger" was a tangible way for a first-generation teenager to connect to hip-hop. No counterfeit could blow my high.

———————

Twenty-five years later, Kendrick Lamar sat back, cross-legged, holding the microphone. His diminutive five-foot-five frame was dressed in a slate-gray Louis Vuitton suit and silver-tipped cowboy boots. Naomi Campbell, the most successful Black supermodel of all time, captured everything on her phone nearby. The rapper performed "Savior" while wearing a blinged-out crown of thorns, one of the most recognizable symbols of Christian iconography. According to scripture, Jesus Christ was forced to wear a crown of thorns to humiliate him before his crucifixion. But Kendrick's headpiece was one of glory. The custom titanium–and–pavé diamond headpiece from Tiffany & Co. featured 50 thorns—made of 8,000 cobblestone micro pavé diamonds totaling more than 137 carats—and cost $3 million.

Kendrick Lamar was the rap messiah of his generation. In 2022 he released his fifth studio album, *Mr. Morale & the Big Steppers*, and tackled ambitious and taboo topics like masculine fragility, generational trauma, sex addiction, and gender identity. His performance at Louis Vuitton's Spring-Summer 2023 Collection show in Paris—in honor of the house's late designer Virgil Abloh—integrated rap and fashion into a singular live-art installation. A tableau vivant of Black excellence years in the making.

Hip-hop wasn't always on the runway. Or even in the room. For most of its history, gatekeepers sequestered it behind the velvet rope. Hip-hop fashion was categorized as "urban," which was essentially coded language for "Black," and was not afforded the same respect as its white counterparts.

For hip-hop to influence high fashion en masse, it was more complicated than the nouveau riche rappers simply being able to afford a luxury price tag. There were significant barriers that had to be overcome involving race, class, and the very notion of who *deserved* to wear luxury. Luxury brands could argue that they were discerning and cautious about preserving their history and pedigree. "It wasn't protective. It was classism. It was racism," said June Ambrose, renowned stylist and costume designer for Jay-Z, Missy Elliott, and Sean "Diddy" Combs. "Now they can say, 'protective.' Before, they were just like, 'No. Who? What? They're from where? I've never heard of them.'" At its heart, there was a cultural schism. The heritage houses of Europe like Chanel, Balenciaga, and Gucci were founded in Europe over fifty years before DJ Kool Herc ever touched a record. As time progressed, these institutions, fashion media, and runways remained overwhelmingly white in contrast with the young and diverse voices of hip-hop. The high fashion decision-makers were either ignorant or blissfully naive. "Hip-hop embraced fashion before fashion embraced hip-hop," Kyle Luu, a stylist and creative director who has worked with artists like Travis Scott and Young Thug, said to me. "It's a bunch of rich white people who work in fashion . . . Fashion people are always late to the party."

That's not to say that hip-hop didn't inspire high fashion. The genre's look, élan, and slang would be incorporated—and more accurately, appropriated—by luxury brands. Hip-hop was young, cool, and profitable—and when designers saw it as a lucrative commodity, things shifted. "When something is hot and makes money, people want to now figure out how to do business and get down with it," said stylist Misa Hylton. Hip-hop being aspirational and desiring material success resonated with luxury brands that sold the same dream. "The change [in branding] for luxury goods is very simple," said Steve Stoute, author of *The Tanning of America: How Hip-Hop Created a Culture*

That Rewrote the Rules of the New Economy and an early connector in bringing hip-hop and brands together. "The generation of hip-hop music has done a lot to influence mainstream culture by really driving it home. It became part of the aspirational dimension of America."

Unlike artists in other genres, rappers were unapologetic capitalists. They not only wanted to look good, they wanted to get paid handsomely for it. Clothing lines like Sean John and Yeezy, fronted by Sean "Diddy" Combs and Kanye respectively, garnered commercial success and acceptance among the fashion cognoscenti. By the aughts, the pendulum had swung fully and it was common to see rappers sit in the front row of fashion shows in New York, Paris, and Milan; walk down runways; and cozy up to *Vogue*'s powerful editor in chief, Anna Wintour. Rappers overtook movie stars, athletes, and supermodels as influencers. It was not far-fetched for a rapper to sign a deal with a fashion brand before having a hit record.

Institutional change became a reality when hip-hop protégé and streetwear maven Virgil Abloh was appointed as the first African American artistic director of menswear at Louis Vuitton in 2018. Now there was actual representation in leadership, and hip-hop had a seat in the boardroom. "The days of the gilded cage, and everything happens behind sealed walls, those days are over for the time being," said Michael Burke, CEO of Louis Vuitton. It was a landmark moment that hip-hop had its own plug at one of the most renowned fashion houses. "I now have a platform to change the industry," Virgil Abloh said. "So I should do that." Hip-hop had the microphone, and high fashion was listening.

FASHION KILLA

Chapter One

ACROSS 125TH STREET

I knocked them up. I didn't knock them off.
–Dapper Dan

I n the early twentieth century, the Black community of Harlem grew in the Great Migration as millions of African Americans fled the rural South for Northern, Midwestern, and Western states in search of economic and educational opportunities and to escape racial oppression, Jim Crow laws, and violence. Rudolph Fisher's 1925 short story, "The City of Refuge," explained the vast difference of living in the Black enclave: "In Harlem, Black was white. You had rights that could not be denied you; you had privileges, protected by law. And you had money. Everybody in Harlem had money. It was a land of plenty."

Harlem is located in upper Manhattan and bounded by the Hudson River on the west; Fifth Avenue on the east; the Harlem River and 155th Street on the north; and Central Park North on the south. Colloquially called "Uptown," the area is divided into regions: West, Central, and East Harlem (also known as Spanish Harlem or El Barrio). The names of some neighborhoods reflected the elite residents. Sugar Hill was home to prosperous Black residents who lived in prominent town houses and mansions. Its moniker was a nod to the "sweet life" residents enjoyed there. Strivers' Row featured stately homes and brownstones for white-collar professionals and notables like pianist Eubie Blake, entertainer Flournoy Miller, and composer Noble Sissle.

Between 1910 and 1930, the African American population in Harlem increased by over 40 percent, from fifty thousand to more than two hundred thousand, with the Great Migration. The culture, energy, and prosperity in these 1.4 square miles would be a magical alchemy. White flight created a Black majority population in the decade following the end of World War I. Immigrants from the Caribbean—countries like Jamaica, Antigua, and Trinidad—and later, Puerto Rico, arrived in large numbers, fleeing economic hardships and pursuing the promise of a better life.

The Harlem Renaissance was one of America's most significant cultural movements of Black music, literature, theater, art, and critical writing. This golden age (approximately from the end of World War I to the mid-1930s) of artistic and social life flourished. Jazz and blues migrated into the city and legendary artists like Louis Armstrong, Billie Holiday, Josephine Baker, and Ella Fitzgerald performed at famous venues like the Cotton Club and the Apollo Theater (originally "whites only"). Jazz artists were musicians as style icons, performing in dapper attire like double-breasted suits, elegant bow ties, and collared shirts.

During this time, literary luminaries like Langston Hughes and Zora Neale Hurston rose to prominence and showed the depth and complexity of Black life in America, along with intellectuals and activists including W. E. B. Du Bois, Marcus Garvey, and Cyril Briggs. The ethos was one of pride, political awareness, and being unapologetically Black. As Langston Hughes wrote in "The Negro Artist and the Racial Mountain": "We younger Negro artists who create now intend to express our individual dark-skinned selves without fear or shame. If white people are pleased we are glad. If they are not, it doesn't matter. We know we are beautiful."

The Harlem aesthetic reflected this deep sense of self: elegance, dignity, and style. Economic mobility allowed residents to embrace formalwear and cocktail attire that was usually relegated to whites. Women wore lavish furs, flapper dresses, and cloche hats. Men donned bowler hats, newsboy caps, wingtip shoes, and suits, like zoot suits. The supersized suits, with huge shoulder pads and lapels and peg leg pants, became a symbol of civil disobedience during World War II rations on fabric, which for some added to the appeal. Dancer Josephine Baker represented social defiance against racial and gender norms when she popularized short skirts—nearly forty years before the term "miniskirt" was coined by Mary Quant—by swiveling her hips onstage in a skirt constructed of bananas at Folies Bergère in Paris in 1926. *Vogue* looked back on the significance of her attire ninety years later: "Aside from these surface-level interests, there was a much deeper and disturbing fascination with the widely accepted belief in Black people's inherent primitiveness . . . Baker brilliantly manipulated the white male imagination. Crossing her eyes, waving her arms, swaying her hips, poking out her backside, she clowned and seduced and subverted stereotypes. By reclaiming her image, she advanced her career in ways unprecedented for a woman of that time."

The Harlem dandy was the quintessential sartorial rebel. A self-consciously stylish man was not a new concept (French poet Charles Baudelaire defined the dandy "as one who elevates aesthetics to a living religion" in 1863), but the Black dandy was more complex. "The Black dandy is this African diaspora man who cleverly manipulates and appropriates western fashion, menswear in particular," explained Shantrelle P. Lewis, author of *Dandy Lion: The Black Dandy and Street Style*. With his dapper wardrobe (e.g., double-breasted blazer, pocket square, and fedora), he was a rebel who defied stereotypes of Black masculinity such as hyper-aggression and subservience. "In a society that sought comfort in clearly defined social and spatially predictable landscape, the Black dandy's audacious appearance on American streets upset the white majority's assumption of racial homogeneity and cultural superiority," noted art historian Richard J. Powell in *Cutting a Figure: Fashioning*

Black Portraiture. "The Black dandy's two greatest sins—visibility and indiscretion—made sense only in the context of a society where Black people (and specifically Black men) had clearly demarcated positions."

The Black church was the community pillar and the pinnacle of fashion in civilian life. The oldest congregation in Harlem was formed in 1796. The neighborhood was home to several historical houses of worship like Mother AME Zion Church, Mount Olivet Baptist Church, Mount Morris Ascension Presbyterian Church, and Abyssinian Baptist Church. These were holy runways. Dressing in one's "Sunday best" had origins dating back to slavery, when masters required slaves to dress up and attend church or special occasions. After emancipation, this meant congregants replaced weekday uniforms with their finest attire of matching colors and prints, suits, and for women, ornate hats. Sportswear pioneer Willi Smith once said, "Most of these designers who have to run to Paris for color and fabric combinations should go to church on Sunday in Harlem. It's all right there." Easter Sunday, in particular, was the annual stage for worshippers to show up and show out. Churchgoers planned outfits ahead of time to ensure that they were conspicuous among the flock. André Leon Talley, Black fashion icon and former *Vogue* editor, remembered modeling his finest spring gray suits and Italian loafers on Easter. "We [my grandmother and I] weren't poor, but we weren't rich. We sometimes had hard times," he said. "But church was very important, so everything was invested in beautiful church clothes. So church was where we decked out and put on our finest clothes."

In all aspects of life, both public and private, Harlem was synonymous with sartorial excellence. And the neighborhood's future hip-hop progeny would take great pride in being the descendants of these giants. Growing up and witnessing firsthand the rich history, prosperity, and style, they would be risk-takers and iconoclasts. Harlem was perpetually the best dressed. Call it swagger, confidence, or just plain *fly*.

43 East 125th Street was always open. Day or night. The site of a brownstone church a century earlier, the cheery storefront on Harlem's main drag was discernible by a bright yellow awning emblazoned with its name—Dapper Dan's Boutique—in cursive font. In the window on this particular day was a full-length woman's fur coat, a nod to the owner's origins in fur. "When I opened my shop, my dream was to become a big-time furrier and cater to the underworld, where I knew the real money was in Harlem," said Dapper Dan in his autobiography *Dapper Dan: Made in Harlem*. "The numbers runners, the grifters, the drug dealers." He was described as many things: a designer, haberdasher, or, simply, the blueprint. In his own words: "I can't sew at all. I'm not a tailor. I'm an observer and a people person."

Dapper Dan was born Daniel Day on August 8, 1944, in Harlem, New York. Before his fashion hustle, he was a literal hustler, running numbers and credit card scams, and playing dice. The spirit of his surroundings permeated his psyche. He understood the importance of having that Uptown swagger. Dap, as he was known, explained: "Were you fly? Flyness wasn't about how handsome you were, although that helped, or how expensive your clothes were, although that helped, or what brand they were . . . It was about something intangible." He opened his first boutique on 125th Street in 1982. The manufacturing was eventually expanded to a building nearby on 120th Street between Second and Third Avenues.

Dap began selling fur but the seasonality of it led him to expand into leather. He saw the $1,200 leather jackets with possum lining that A.J. Lester (also referred to as A.J. Lester's), the popular retailer in Harlem frequented by drug dealers, musicians, and athletes, was selling and created his replica—only 33 percent cheaper! He made a killing but knew that he needed to go beyond being a copycat to stay relevant. His first attempt at DIY and bespoke design came after customers requested leather jackets with fox fur lining on the inside *and* on the outside. "It was my first attempt at customization, and a learning experience in how to make clothes with the particular tastes of my customer in mind," he remembered.

Customization was paramount to hip-hop fashion as a way to stand out. In the beginning, street gangs like the Ghetto Brothers and Savage Nomads put their crew names on motorcycle jackets and "cut sleeve" denim jackets. This was a warning shot to anybody, especially rivals. Graffiti inspired custom airbrushed designs on T-shirts, jackets, and denim. Break-dance pioneer Richard "Crazy Legs" Colón donned a denim jacket emblazoned with his Rock Steady Crew and the names of his cohort who had passed away, turning clothing into a walking memorial. Jewelry was a status purchase, and adding the wearer's name to nameplate necklaces, gold medallions, four-finger rings, and bamboo earrings made pieces truly unique. "Custom apparel has always had a special place in the hearts of hip-hop loyalists," wrote Elena Romero in *Free Stylin': How Hip Hop Changed the Fashion Industry (Hip Hop in America)*. "It is no surprise that part of the infatuation developed as a means of standing out for the ladies, in the crowd, at the club, in a battle, or on the streets." Custom pieces were one of one and ensured that no two people were dressed alike.

Dapper Dan saw the opportunity to combine customization with luxury branding the first time he saw a Louis Vuitton leather clutch held by a drug dealer's girlfriend: "It was a beautiful bag made with amazing craftsmanship. I could tell it was expensive. As someone who knew all about leather, I marveled at the stitching and the way the ink rested on the skin. Most of all, I was fascinated by the excitement it was creating among my customers." He offered to make the drug dealer a "knock-up"—an upgrade not to be confused with an imitation or knockoff—with the same print, which meant going to the Louis Vuitton store to source material that he could extract the logo from, like, say, a jacket. Shopping downtown involved experiencing firsthand racial bias and microaggressions in luxury retail. "I was the only Black person in there, and I felt the place tense up when I walked in," he remembered. "The doorman's eyes never left me. No wonder none of my customers liked to spend their money down here."

Harlem spent money at Dapper Dan's Boutique or A.J. Lester's locally, but big-name luxury was located below 96th Street. Lord & Taylor, the oldest department store in America, became the first department store on Fifth Avenue in 1914. The mecca of fine shopping was Fifth Avenue: Bergdorf Goodman, Henri Bendel, and Saks Fifth Avenue—all within walking distance—and boutiques like Cartier and Tiffany & Co., whose flagship became a shopping and cinephile destination after 1961's *Breakfast at Tiffany's*. The corner of Delancey Street and Orchard Street was a haven to spot early hip-hop street fashion. Madison Avenue, a stone's throw away from Fifth Avenue, became a draw when Barneys New York moved into the area in 1993. The beloved playground of fashion insiders was the first store to feature Giorgio Armani stateside. Barneys specialized in curating emerging designers—Comme des Garçons, Martin Margiela, Dries Van Noten, Ann Demeulemeester, Yohji Yamamoto, and Rick Owens—and every shopping trip ended with $30 chopped salads and French fries at the in-store restaurant, Freds.

After realizing that Louis Vuitton didn't have what he needed, Dapper Dan went next door to Gucci to buy garment bags to make the jacket. Perusing the racks, he was astounded by the Italian house's subtle logos. "Crests and logos stayed on the inside of the clothes those days, tucked away like a secret." It was a sharp contrast from his clientele who didn't want *quiet* luxury. They saw logos like a royal coat of arms, something to display proudly. Visible logos signaled prestige and meant that the wearer could afford to spend a small fortune on clothing. What the statant guardant lion wearing the St Edward's Crown meant to the British monarchy, Gucci's interlocking double Gs or Louis Vuitton's monogram represented for his customers. The logos symbolized power, strength, and authority. Reputation was paramount for those in precarious lines of work like drug dealing and hustling. The sheer act of wearing expensive clothing—without getting robbed—meant that the wearer was someone respected and not to be fucked with. Being able to flex that kind of machismo was worth the price.

Dapper Dan became the self-proclaimed "father of logomania" and created bespoke pieces with ostentatious branding that appealed to his young Black customers. He taught himself the process of silk-screening, so that he could fabricate the logos of every luxury label: Louis Vuitton, Gucci, Fendi, MCM. What flipping samples was to hip-hop music, Dap did with luxury insignia. Mixing, cutting up, and making something both familiar but fresh. The store was open 24/7; perfect for underworld denizens or the late-night crowd leaving a party, nightclub, or show at the nearby Apollo Theater. Even before they were famous, rappers like Jay-Z and Fat Joe made their pilgrimage to Dap's store.

The quintessential Dapper Dan piece was the reversible Louis Vuitton coat that was soft mink on the inside. His sizing was inclusive (you didn't have to be a sample size or a model) and he often added special accouterments that appealed to his clientele that the heritage houses would clutch their pearls at, like stitching bulletproof lining into hats and garments or putting in extra-deep pockets to hold a firearm. "My customers wanted to buy into that power, and didn't have to wear something done in colors they didn't like, with sizes that didn't fit them right, made by someone who hadn't taken the time to know them and understand the specificity of their lives and experiences. At Dapper Dan's they didn't have to compromise. Not only did the clothes make them look good on the outside, it actually made them feel good when they wore it."

A custom Dapper Dan 'fit could run into the tens of thousands of dollars, so price was a barrier to entry when hip-hop was still young (and broke). "My clothes were expensive, and in the early days of hip-hop, rappers didn't have money like the hustlers and athletes," Dap explained. "In the early days, the rappers were like all of us in the neighborhood, looking up to hustlers on the corner. They wanted to dress like the hustlers." Notable clientele included drug dealer Alpo Martinez, who purchased a custom Louis Vuitton snorkel that was later replicated for future rappers like Cam'ron and French Montana. Boxer Mike Tyson brought a pre-fame Naomi Campbell to the shop. As the lore of Dapper Dan circulated—accelerated when Tyson famously beat up Mitch Green outside the shop in 1988—and hip-hop became more lucrative, rappers became devotees who could afford to shop. LL Cool J was one of Dap's biggest supporters, with pieces like a red-and-white Gucci jacket he got in 1986. LL Cool J remembered Dap's store being a welcoming haven for rappers. "Sometimes you bang on the gate in the middle of the night, or like halfway up, you'd just go up yelling, 'Yo, Dap! Yo, yo, yo.' He'd come out of nowhere," he said. "We were paying in cash, giving him the money to get it done quick. It was a heck of a vibe, something like Brand Nubian's 'Slow Down' playing in the background. We felt really safe there, in a dangerous world."

Eric B. & Rakim wore custom Gucci jackets Dap created for the cover of two of their albums, 1987's *Paid in Full* and 1988's *Follow the Leader*, which amplified the Dapper Dan brand beyond the in-the-know clientele. Kelefa Sanneh, author and writer at the *New Yorker*, said: "These were Gucci jackets that look like no Gucci jackets you've ever seen. And in fact, they look like no Gucci jackets that anyone at Gucci had ever seen." There was no better endorsement than Rakim at the time. The lyrical virtuoso had complex rhymes delivered with samurai-like precision. *"I came in the door, I said it before / I never let the mic magnetize me no more,"* he rapped on "Eric B. Is President," one of hip-hop's most famous openers. "A song like that only comes along maybe twice a decade, and few of them stay with you like the duo's master tome," lauded Brian Coleman in *Check the Technique*. Rakim's wordplay and smooth cadence, likened to velvet or molasses, upped the ante for all rappers. Forget party songs, let's see your rhymes. Eric B.'s bombastic production and use of funk samples, specifically on "I Know You Got Soul," kick-started hip-hop's infatuation with using James Brown samples. *Paid in Full* would be celebrated as one of hip-hop's most seminal albums. Real hip-hop had skill and style—and wore Dapper Dan.

Dap's creations were especially attractive for artists who wanted to market their stage names alongside the luxury logos. Big Daddy Kane got a custom Louis Vuitton velour suit from Dap with "KANE" across his chest. Eric B. & Rakim's jackets had their names across the back in gold lettering. These customized looks were theatrical and perfect for artist photoshoots, live shows, and music videos. Salt-N-Pepa wore matching polychrome leather jackets—one with "SALT" and the other with "PEPA" in the "Push It!" music video in 1986—designed by Christopher "Play" Martin of Kid 'n Play at Dapper Dan's studio. With its funky synthesizer line and sexual innuendo, "Push It!" was the group's foray into a smash party anthem. As such, Sandra "Pepa" Denton remarked that the jackets became as associated with the girl group as Michael Jackson's glove.

Dapper Dan would be immortalized in well over one hundred hip-hop songs from the 1980s onward and propagated his name to those far outside his purview. One early reference was in 1989, when Kool G Rap name-checked Dapper Dan on "Men at Work," a lyrical onslaught with wordplay, metaphors, and attitude accentuated by DJ Polo's record-scratching: *"If I was Gucci, then you would be Dapper Dan."* This was followed by Showbiz and A.G.'s laid-back groove "Diggin' in the Crates" in 1991: *"Get upset like Buster did to Tyson / That wasn't the plan and he's still my man / Since he beat up Mitch Green outside Dapper Dan."*

Hip-hop's love for Dap went beyond clothing. The designer merged high fashion with cars—it was not uncommon to see Bentleys, Mercedes-Benzes, and Rolls-Royces parked up and down his block—and he upholstered car interiors with luxury fashion logos. "Luxury cars had always been a part of the hustler repertoire, expensive status symbols of wealth and power," Dap said. "I wanted to upholster the interiors of these status symbols with even more symbolism." He parked his burgundy Benz (with beige-on-beige and burgundy-on-burgundy Gucci print) and a cherry-red Jeep Wrangler (upholstered in white leather with cherry-red MCM print) outside the store as advertising, and it was perfect for photo-ops. In 1988, Big Daddy Kane posed by the Jeep with a group of customers wearing custom Gucci and MCM jackets. In 1989, LL Cool J borrowed the Jeep Wrangler for his "Big Ole Butt" music video. The song, a cheeky number about pursuing women with ample assets, had several "jeep" references in its lyrics, and in the visual, the rapper and his friends pull up to a playground of voluptuous hotties in the custom ride.

Just as hip-hop was initially dismissed as a fledgling music genre, Dapper Dan's fashion received backlash from the older generation. He explained: "Middle-class Blacks didn't buy. They snubbed me. I remember in Morningside Park, we had the biggest block party in the city, period. Everybody from everywhere came. And I was walking by and heard someone on the microphone say, 'Dapper Dan with that fake Gucci'—like I was a laughingstock. It was humiliating. A lot of people didn't understand what I was doing."

The luxury houses didn't understand what he was doing either, but they knew they didn't like it. Louis Vuitton was the first brand to raid Dapper Dan's Boutique over counterfeiting. "One day, a bunch of armed investigators just walked right in and started taking clothes off the racks like they belonged to them," he said. "A lawyer handed me their documentation, explaining that this was a seizure due to infringement of the Louis Vuitton trademark . . . They started putting everything I made that had Louis on it into trash bags and carrying them outside."

What constitutes theft in the fashion industry is a gray area at best. There's a lot of parsing of words and nuance between a loving homage, inspiration, and shameless bootlegging. According to *Women's Wear*

Daily, "In the fashion world, and even with other products, there are fine—very fine—distinctions . . ." Generally, a counterfeit is essentially identical to the original product and is illegal. A knockoff resembles the original item but is not identical. The key is whether the knockoff is so close to the original that the buyer will be misled as to who made the goods.

Dap's work could arguably fall somewhere between the counterfeit and knockoff, but his designs were unique and oftentimes more expensive than the luxury original. Any fashion aficionado should be able to discern a Dapper Dan creation from the austere source material. His designs were far more flashy, with exaggerated logos and silhouettes that the luxury houses were simply not producing. Nevertheless, he knew that legal ramifications were possible. "Did I think I might catch hell from the brands for co-opting their logos? Yeah, the thought crossed my mind. I was aware of the risks, but you gotta understand, I'm a gambler at heart. The whole time I was in business, I was rolling the dice."

The raids became a regular occurrence: Louis Vuitton, Gucci, MCM. "They just kept raiding me and raiding me. They were raiding me broke." The final coup de grâce was dealt from an unlikely source: future associate justice of the Supreme Court Sonia Sotomayor. In 1992, Sotomayor was a lawyer at Pavia & Harcourt and represented Italian luxury house Fendi. Dap remembered her as "very cordial" and professional as she documented evidence and watched investigators confiscate his wares. But one piece caught even her eye: a full-length black-on-black plongé leather Fendi coat with a shawl created for rapper Big Daddy Kane. She admired the buttery soft, regal design. "Wow, this guy really belongs downtown," she said. Still, Fendi took Dapper Dan to court and successfully won its trademark infringement case despite his assertion that his designs were "interpretative homages." In all, it cost him some quarter million dollars' worth of merchandise and equipment. He was financially decimated and emotionally depleted. "I was fighting a war with myself about what I had achieved with the boutique. I knew I had made an impact, but was I any closer to whatever it was I was truly searching for?" he wondered. "I was tired of fighting. I didn't want to own a shop no more." He shut down Dapper Dan's Boutique in 1992 and went underground for several years. It would be decades before he would return and bring his luxury back to Harlem.

Chapter Two

LUXURY LAW

uxury has no one definition. Over time, the etymology evolved from one of excess and sumptuousness to forbidden, sensual pleasure to its modern-day definition of coveted extravagance, exclusivity—and a high price tag. The word "luxury" originally comes from the Latin word *luxus,* meaning "abundance," and *luxuria,* meaning "rankness" or "offensiveness." The French *luxe* added "wealth" and "indulgence" to the meaning. And the English *luxurie* referred to lasciviousness and sexual wantonness. Luxury has an inherent duality as it shape-shifts through time and culture. It represented wealth and socioeconomic success—ideals greatly desired and celebrated in modern American capitalism—as well as hedonistic consumerism, highly wasteful spending, and gross decadence that far exceeded the basic levels of need.

Since ancient Greece and Rome, societies have tried to regulate access to luxury goods with sumptuary laws—any regulation designed to restrict spending on food, drink, clothing, and personal items—to prevent extravagance and, more important, to differentiate the royalty and one percent from the commoners. Before designer labels and logos, social stature could be conveyed by something as simple as the fabric or even hue of a garment. In 1363, the parliament of England introduced A Statute Concerning Diet and Apparel, one in a series of apparel proclamations, setting the price and type of fabrics for each class of society, including servants, artisans, clergy, and knights. Social climbing was strictly prohibited. Under Edward IV, specific laws restricted the wearing of finery like sable fur, "cloth of gold," and purple silk to those of the stature of knight or lord and higher. "Color's link to luxury originally stems from its connections to royalty," wrote Véronique Hyland in *Dress Code: Unlocking Fashion from the New Look to Millennial Pink*. "Nearly every civilization had some form of dress-based sumptuary laws, many of them centered around color and reserving brighter shades for higher-class citizens. Naturally, this only made certain colors more desirable and stirred up status anxiety around them."

Purple has long been associated with royalty. If ancient Rome had a Pantone Color of the Year, it would be Tyrian purple. Emperor Julius Caesar wore togas in this deep reddish-purple hue, made of a pricey dye tragically derived from the desiccated glands of sea snails, and outlawed others from biting his color palette. As the legend goes, King Ptolemy of Mauretania was put to death after daring to wear purple to visit Emperor Caligula in Rome in 40 CE. A literal fashion killer. It's no wonder that American designer Ralph Lauren reserved his most upscale offerings for his Purple Label collection. As Jay-Z celebrated his grown-man metamorphosis from rapper to president of Def Jam Records on 2005's "Dear Summer," he rapped about wearing the sophisticated line of premium fabrics and tasteful branding: "Purple label shit with the logo secret."

Sumptuary laws were often shrouded as homilies for the social good and maintained class stratification for the elites. In England, Queen Elizabeth I issued several proclamations on the subject of "excess of apparel" and how it led to vanity, overspending, and criminality by the have-nots. Her Royal Proclamation of June 5, 1574, stated in part that luxury caused "manifest decay of the whole realm." Sumptuary laws were also present in the American colonies to control clothing like silk, lace, slashed sleeves, buttons, and scarves. In 1651, the General Court of Massachusetts, the colonial legislature, declared "utter detestation and dislike" for men or women who dressed above their social standing. In 1662, an addition to the law admonished that dressing above one's rank was sacrilege and stoked moral fears about being corrupted and effeminate.

Black people in America were subject to additional attire regulations that discriminated on the basis of race before and after the country's independence. "Clothing was an important and immediately visible mark of social status," wrote textile historian and curator Madelyn Shaw in *Slave Cloth and Clothing Slaves: Craftsmanship, Commerce, and Industry.* Clothing efficiently differentiated the enslaved from free people. Enslaved workers received most, if not all, of their wardrobe as an allowance from their owners and they would sometimes cut and sew it on their own. This clothing was made from various types of textiles, based on durability, geography, and economic factors, including: *osnaburg* or *osnabrigs*, a coarse unfinished linen or hemp; *kersey*, a twill weave fabric made from wool; and *linsey-woolsey*, a linen and wool blend. Most fabrics lacked color, but osnaburg could be sold in solid colors (natural unbleached or white, brown, or blue) or stripes. Enslaved people in upper-class homes were allowed to wear better fashion, with the understanding that they had no ownership over it. As Giorgio Riello and Ulinka Rublack wrote in *The Right to Dress: Sumptuary Laws in a Global Perspective, c. 1200–1800*: "Whites retained all the defining power to determine what constituted excessive apparel—and therefore allowed regulations to be created at a whim."

These laws assumed that if Black people were dressing above their station, they had employed nefarious means to do so—a precursor to racial profiling and aggressive policing of Black shoppers in luxury retail in the future. Laws collectively known as "slave codes" aimed to control and restrict the autonomy and mobility of enslaved people.

South Carolina's An Act for the Better Ordering and Governing Negroes and Other Slaves codified dress code in 1740 and stated in part: "And whereas, many of the slaves in this Province wear clothes much above the condition of slaves, for the procuring whereof they use sinister and evil methods." The law, also known as the Negro Act, was intentionally inhumane and "authorized, empowered and required" any free person to confiscate offensive attire from the enslaved at will. Interestingly, an exception was made for "livery-men and boys." Since these enslaved people were a public-facing extension of their households—they were property and a status symbol—they had to appear presentable to keep up a reputation in society.

Dr. Jonathan Michael Square, writer, historian, and curator of Afro-Diasporic fashion and visual culture and assistant professor of Black Visual Culture at Parsons School of Design, explained to me that the connection between luxury fashion and Black identity began as early as the eighteenth and nineteenth centuries. "The kind of negative stereotypes that are attached to people of African descent—particularly people who were enslaved and their descendants—and one of a battery of litany of negative stereotypes is that we're often associated with poverty and deficit. And so, one way in which Black people in general have fought against that stereotype is by flipping the script and associating themselves, their identity, their self-representation, their brands with abundance and wealth." This is important in understanding hip-hop's penchant for luxury as a complex social and cultural phenomenon. Modern materialism could be viewed as a response to historical lack of ownership. "Fashion has always been an important part of the hip-hop identity because fashion has always been an important part of Black identity in America," said Sacha Jenkins, director of the documentary *Fresh Dressed*. "Because when you don't have much ownership over where you can land in society, your financial situation, your educational situation, the one thing you can control is the way you look."

Survival in America is predicated on appearances, and that's compounded for people of color, immigrants, and other marginalized groups who don't have the privilege of second impressions. "We make judgments about a person based on their appearance alone in under one second," wrote Dr. Carolyn Mair in *The Psychology of Fashion*. "Clothing is our second skin; it sits next to our bodies and becomes part of our identity." The job candidate in the clean Tom Ford suit has better chances than their counterpart in the ill-fitting counterfeit. Wearing a dirty pair of sneakers (actually filthy, not the tattered and trendy Balenciagas for $600) conjures assumptions about the wearer's success, self-esteem, health, and hygiene.

The adage *dress for success* encapsulates this mentality of clothing as upward mobility. "Many low-income Americans can't afford to appear like low-income Americans," explained Dr. Peter Ubel, physician and behavioral scientist at Duke University. "It is hard to attract a romantic partner if you look like a loser. It is hard to get a good job if you show up at an interview looking like someone who's never held down a job. And the more extreme income inequality becomes, the more pressure people feel to create the impression that they've climbed up the social ladder." Fashion can signal success before it materializes, and the idea of manifestation or "fake it till you make it" is popular in hip-hop. "Urban young people are always attracted or addicted to fashion because it's an expression of aspiration," said André Leon Talley, editor-at-large of *Vogue*, in *Fresh Dressed*. "A lot of people who are in hip-hop have aspirations."

––––––––––––

The term "luxury fashion" is an umbrella concept that encapsulates prêt-à-porter (ready-to-wear), custom-made pieces, and ultimately haute couture. "Haute couture" is a legally protected term that translates into English as "high dressmaking" and refers to custom and hand-made garments impeccably crafted by skilled artisans and made with the highest quality materials and fabrics. Haute couture originated in

France in the late nineteenth century and is closely regulated by the French government. According to *Vogue*, haute couture is "fashion at its most refined," with an emphasis on design and innovation. British designer Charles Frederick Worth, known by historians as "the father of haute couture" and "the first couturier," opened the first Couture House at number 7, rue de la Paix in Paris in 1858. However, the country's penchant for couture dates back to Louis XIV in the seventeenth century, who wore ostentatious and ornamental styles, including signature high, red-heeled shoes (long before designer Christian Louboutin trademarked his famous red-soled stilettos).

The self-proclaimed "Sun King" was a peacock who loved luxury. During his record seventy-two-year reign, Louis XIV transformed the Palace of Versailles from a dilapidated hunting lodge to a luxurious and ornate bastion of fashion, art, music, and lifestyle. Fashion was a source of national pride and economic power propagating France's elevated tastes. He expanded the country's clothing and textile sectors, created regulated worker guilds, and made fashion a lucrative export. As his finance minister, Jean-Baptiste Colbert, famously said, "Fashions were to France what the mines of Peru were to Spain." Louis XIV positioned France as the epicenter of high fashion, a crown it still holds today.

Haute couture was analogous to buying a one-of-one artistic masterpiece. Lineage, relationships, and money determined entry, and as such, it was relegated to the most discerning buyers—royalty and socialites. The Fédération de la Haute Couture et de la Mode is the governing body overseeing French fashion, and only houses that are approved every year by the Chambre Syndicale de la Haute Couture, which was established in 1868, may become eligible for the classification of haute couture.

A couture house is traditionally composed of two parts, one devoted to dressmaking (*flou*), the other devoted to tailoring of suits and coats (*tailleur*). Fit is paramount and there are a series of fittings with the client with minute alterations. On January 23, 1945, "haute couture" became a legally registered term. Members must fulfill criteria—which have changed over time—in order to qualify for the designation: design made-to-order for private clients; have an atelier (workshop) in Paris that employs twenty full-time staff members and at least twenty full-time technical people; present a collection of at least twenty-five original designs twice a year (January & July) at the Paris Couture Week. According to Fédération de la Haute Couture et de la Mode, there were sixteen official haute couture designers in 2023: Adeline André, Alexandre Vauthier, Alexis Mabille, Bouchra Jarrar, Chanel, Dior, Franck Sorbier, Giambattista Valli, Givenchy, Jean Paul Gaultier, Julien Fournié, Maison Margiela, Maison Rabih Kayrouz, Maurizio Galante, Schiaparelli, and Stéphane Rolland. Correspondent or guest members included emerging brands like Gauchere (established in 2013) and Koché (established in 2015).

As Robin Givhan explained in *The Battle of Versailles*, clients historically maintained close relationships with *vendeuses*, salespeople who served as gatekeepers, advisors, and project managers keeping track of garments advancing through the atelier. The vendeuse was aware of social circles and hierarchy and was the precursor to today's celebrity connector or fashion publicist. A haute couture gown could take over eight hundred hours to create, and the cost was passed on to the consumer. Made-to-measure daywear could start at $10,000, while an intricately embroidered gown ran into several hundred thousand dollars. These were valued investments. "From a rudimentary muslin to the final product, the garment is handmade, embroidered, beaded, and feathered by a group of artisans who have learned their trade over the generations," wrote Givhan. "This is not disposable fashion. Clients keep garments for years, often altering them slightly to freshen them up."

Haute couture was a truly artistic endeavor, a labor of love. "Couture is emotion. Couture is freedom. Couture is not thinking about pricing and not thinking about craziness," said Riccardo Tisci, designer for Givenchy at the time. "You can do whatever you want to do in couture."

Luxury fashion was not a singular destination but a journey. As hip-hop grew and flourished over the next several decades, so did its relationship to luxury. From buying off-the-rack to custom and, ultimately, couture, rappers would one day be the faces of haute couture. The rap nouveau riche was coming.

Chapter Three

EVERY DAY I'M HUSTLIN'

When you see these guys riding by in their cars with the girls with the furs on, it really is seductive. They were like neighborhood superheroes.

—LL Cool J

he party was in full effect and birthday boy Gerald "Prince" Miller had all eyes on him and his crew. Onstage, they were two-stepping, laughing, and enjoying life. Grandmaster Flash and the Furious Five's "The Message" filled the room: *"It's like a jungle sometimes. It makes me wonder how I keep from going under."* This was the Supreme Team, and they were far from going under. For now. In 1985, their life of crime paid . . . handsomely. The good liquor was flowing. Blunts were passed around like candy. Everyone was dressed up. Prince was in a slate-gray suit that cast a luminous sheen when the spotlight hit, and his neck was adorned with chains befitting of his namesake. Kenneth "Supreme" McGriff, his uncle and the founder of the cohort, had on a beautiful white leisure suit (à la Tony Montana in *Scarface*) contrasted by a striped burgundy shirt. In the crowd, a teenager from 'round the way looked on in awe. It was dark, but in his signature Kangol hat, he was discernible as LL Cool J. The rapper had released his breakout debut, "I Need a Beat," but in here, surrounded by legends, he might as well have been just a fan.

"I remember going to some of them parties. I also remember not being able to get near that stage at that time because it was bossed up, real heavy. So I was in the crowd playing my position," he reminisced on the *Supreme Team* documentary (executive produced by fellow Queens rapper Nas). LL Cool J would ride his bicycle from his residential neighborhood of St. Albans, Queens, to nearby South Jamaica to witness the action. It was a short stretch—ten minutes if he took Foch Boulevard and thirteen minutes via Linden Boulevard—but when he arrived, what he saw was a different world. "I would just be over there, just checking out what they was doing. They were the biggest and the brightest. Me, because I was always ambitious, I gravitated to those kinds of characters."

The Supreme Team was one of New York City's most notorious street gangs and became part of rap lore for their success and style. Founded in 1981 and operating out of the Baisley Park Houses in Jamaica, Queens, the crew consisted of fourteen core members: Supreme, Prince, Bimmy Antney, Green Eyed Born, Black Just, Baby Wise, Shannon, C-Just, Tucker, Teddy, Bing, God B, Robo Just, and Corey Pegues. The gang's business was the distribution of cocaine base or "crack." And it wasn't some flimsy operation. Inspired by the mafia saga *The Godfather*, they believed in honor and a code of loyalty. They considered themselves a blue-chip company with a formal organizational hierarchy and top-down management. They operated like a business and worked six days a week. According to the United States Department of Justice, the Supreme Team's street-level revenues exceeded $200,000 a day at its peak.

But nothing lasts forever. "The point of the game is to get out of the game," Supreme said. The denouement of this life was ending up either dead or in jail.

America has a long love affair with its gangsters both real and fictional—Al Capone, killer couple Bonnie and Clyde, New York City's five mafia families, Harlem heroin magnate Frank Lucas, *The Godfather*, *Goodfellas*, *The Untouchables*—and in the 1980s, crack dealers were the latest iteration of bad guys. They exuded wealth, power, and charisma, and had access to the kind of disposable income that poor and working-class (or even white-collar professionals) could only dream about. They drove foreign cars, wore the nicest clothing, and dated the prettiest girls. And it didn't hurt that their occupation had the youthful lure of danger and defiance for the law built in. To some, these were villains leeching off human suffering and killing their own. But for many young men in inner cities, drug dealers were role models: big brothers and father figures who threw parties, sponsored local sports teams, and handed out turkeys during Thanksgiving (a tradition dating back to the American mafia). They were heroes in the hood and a testament to how good life could be.

The 1980s were in dire need of salvation in New York City. The *New York Times* proclaimed the start of the decade as "The Worst Year of Crime in City History." There were 1,814 murders reported (which would swell to 2,245 by 1990). The city was gritty, dirty, and dangerous, with the most significant increase of crime in Queens. People did not feel safe. In 1981, robberies hit a record high of 107,495. Subway cars and buildings were tagged with graffiti. Times Square was a seedy red-light district that you kept the kids away from. Public spaces, known by ominous names like Needle Park, were hot spots for junkies and fiends.

These malaises of urban living were further exacerbated by President Ronald Reagan's economic policies, known as Reaganomics. In his term, he passed tax cuts that benefited the wealthy and reduced spending on social welfare programs like food stamps, Social Security, and job training. In 1985, 23.9 percent of the population lived below the Federal poverty level (1.8 million people), and Black unemployment rates were at least twice that of their white contemporaries. Selling drugs was a means for daily survival.

Nearly four hundred miles away, Pusha T remembered looking up to his older brother, No Malice (formerly Malice), as the drug dealer aesthete of Norfolk, Virginia. "I thought he was like *the GOD!*" the rapper told me. There was one showstopper garment that he never forgot. "He had a silk shirt. It wasn't like a T-shirt. It was maybe a three-button or two-button down. I don't remember the brand, but people who know are gonna know exactly what I'm talking about. I was fully impressed." It was hard to put into words, but trust, it was fly. No Malice also had an airbrushed T-shirt from the Shirt Kings—the legendary Queens customization outlet inspired by graffiti and known for remixing pop culture with street iconography, like Mickey Mouse in a gold chain while smoking marijuana—and his little brother was in total awe. "I was like, 'No way. LL Cool J has this!' I thought he was the absolute coolest guy in the world." The allure of the streets was strong. Although he had a stable home life with two hardworking parents, Pusha "was outside" (a euphemism for being in the streets) by the time he was in the eighth grade. "We're kids. We're trading clothes. We're stealing clothes." Selling drugs gave him the income to buy whatever fashion he wanted. "At that time, that was my only driver. I didn't want anything else."

If hustling was a gateway into fashion, sneakers were often the first stop on the path to destruction. "Fresh sneakers are important on a man. It's like a new pair of boxers or a new pair of socks," said DJ Khaled, an avid collector with more than ten thousand pairs. Sneakers added flair and personality to an ordinary outfit. For a man, it was analogous to a woman accessorizing with a nice handbag. Sneakers created first impressions, especially in pedestrian cities like New York, and looking someone up and down started from the shoes. This also made sneakers a target for getting robbed. Christopher "Kid" Reid of Kid 'n Play explained the barometer for gauging a threat: "There was one question you never wanted to hear when somebody you didn't know rolled up on you. That was: 'What's your size?'" Added B-boy Popmaster Fabel: "If you were live, you'd say, 'Your size! Why you wanna know?!' If you were live. If you were a chump or a sucka, you'd probably be quiet and get punched in the face and get vicked [slang for being robbed]."

Popular sneakers often originated with athletes such as basketball greats Michael Jordan (Air Jordan) or Walt "Clyde" Frazier (Puma Clyde, later called the Puma Suede), but hip-hop co-opted certain styles as favorites. The Puma Suede launched in 1968 and became the definitive shoe for B-boys, or break-dancers, in the 1980s because of its malleable sole and flexible upper. Groups like the New York City Breakers and Rocksteady Crew adopted the Puma Suede as their go-to footwear. Nike's Air Jordans, which first launched in 1985, were coveted among drug dealers and rappers. Early Jordan ambassadors included KRS-One, who wore the Jordan 3s in his "My Philosophy" music video in 1988, and Ice-T wore the Jordan 4s on the artwork for his "What Ya Wanna Do?" in 1989. The controversial sneakers incited national incidents of assault and robbery involving kids and teenagers trying to cop a pair. "I thought people would try to emulate the good things I do, they'd try to achieve, to be better. Nothing bad. I never thought because of my endorsement of a shoe, or any product, that people would harm each other," Michael Jordan said to *Sports Illustrated*. Nike's Air Force 1s, which came out in 1982, were known as "Uptowns" because they were a favorite of people from Harlem, but they resonated widely. Obsessives would do anything to keep their Air Force 1s crisp white—scrubbing them with baking soda and vinegar—because dirty sneakers were a sign that you could only afford one pair.

For Bimmy, having one new pair of sneakers at the start of the school year was considered a blessing. "I had a friend who came to school with sneakers. Like every other month, he had sneakers. Me? I had to buy one pair for the whole year," Bimmy said. "When I seen that, I was like, I have to get me some sneakers." His well-intentioned mother committed the cardinal sin of buying him affordable but totally wrong shoes that were neither practical nor fashionable. "She took me to the Chinese store and bought me Chinese slippers. I had to play basketball in them. I'm sliding in them. The front toe always stretched out and busted open."

Ultra-consumerism raged across the country. The new generation of spendthrift consumers were known as *yuppies* (short for "young urban professionals") and loved high-end fashion like Burberry cashmere scarves, Ralph Lauren power suits, or Panthère de Cartier watches. They were ambitious, active, and white. For the have-nots, there was no shortage of wealth porn and voyeurism into the lives of the filthy rich. Decades before MTV *Cribs* opened the doors to celebrity homes, Robin Leach salivated over extravagant manses on *Lifestyles of the Rich and Famous*. Socialites feuded in sequined gowns, lamé cocktail dresses, and exaggerated shoulder pads on *Dynasty*, which led to costume designer Nolan Miller launching his ready-to-wear line. There was no shame in being shamelessly rich. As Gordon Gecko, played by Michael Douglas, famously said in the 1987 film *Wall Street*: "Greed, for lack of a better word, is good."

The designer lifestyle needed a designer drug, and that was cocaine. Coming off disco fever, cocaine was expensive, heady, and the perfect stimulant to fuel the *go, go, go* velocity of the time. Author Jay McInerney called the substance "Bolivian Marching Powder" in his 1984 novel *Bright Lights, Big City*: "Your brain at this moment is composed of brigades of tiny Bolivian soldiers. They are tired and muddy from their long march through the night. There are holes in their boots and they are hungry. They need to be fed." It was perfectly acceptable for the rich, white, and beautiful to do a bump or two. The *Australian Financial Review* observed that snorting cocaine was so commonplace by financiers on Wall Street that "reports abound of the time when walking into the office toilets was like walking into a Hoover testing facility." The drug didn't discriminate among the sexes. Dr. Ronald J. Dougherty, medical director of an outpatient center, told the *New York Times* in 1985 that his female patients "wouldn't do heroin because it's dirty, but cocaine is clean . . . It is something the jet set does."

Hollywood pushed dopamine receptors into overdrive by sensationalizing drugs in film and television, especially 1983's *Scarface*, which made the life of a cocaine cowboy look like one hazy, sexy fantasy. The film's protagonist, Tony Montana (portrayed by Al Pacino), would become a cult hero in hip-hop and the patron saint to drug dealers with monologues about loyalty; vibrant fashions (white three-piece suit, Cuban collar shirt with at least one button undone, gold chains); and the merciless pursuit of success at any cost, famously wielding a machine gun while proclaiming, "Say hello to my little friend!"

If cocaine was the luxury drug, crack was the deadlier knockoff. The designer imposter promised cheaper thrills—just $5 to $20 for a vial versus the street price of powdered cocaine that ranged wildly from $16 to $125 per gram—but was four times stronger than cocaine. "Using it even once can make a person crave cocaine for as long as they live," Peter Jennings warned on *ABC World News Tonight* in 1989. In 1986, there were 182,000 regular cocaine users in New York City, according to New York State statistics. That number increased to an estimated 600,000 just two years later (with most being addicted to the derivative crack).

The "crack era" began in the early 1980s. Many people wanted an affordable taste of the cocaine high. "Without a steady supply of cocaine, there is no crack," David Farber wrote in *Crack: Rock Cocaine, Street Capitalism, and the Decade of Greed*. "The men who turned powder cocaine into crack and sold 'rocks' at the local level were disproportionately low-income African Americans." The crack era brought with it an extreme level of violence, crime, over-policing, and mass incarceration to inner cities.

Producing crack was easy, fast, and cheap. Powdered cocaine was mixed—or cut—with baking soda and then cooked with water until hard pellets—rocks—formed. The whole process was done with everyday items. No chemistry degree required. "When people start to analyze that street entrepreneurship, don't analyze it from your intellectual, born-on-third-base mindset. Those cats were not even born in the ballpark," explained New York City mayor Eric Adams, who was a police officer in New York City at the time. "But in the street, your

degree comes from having the heart. And that's what you saw. You saw
street corner CEOs popping up all over our city."

The negative externalities of the crack epidemic disproportionately
affected Black lives. Between 1984 and 1994, the homicide rate of Black
men ages fourteen to seventeen more than doubled. "Crack poisoned
bodies, ravaged minds, ripped apart families, and tore jagged holes in
communities," Farber wrote. The media—which did its share of fear-
mongering and race-baiting—ran stories about "crack babies" born to
addicted mothers, fiends passed out on street corners, and menacing
drug dealers wearing beepers, four-finger rings, and Nikes.

America's failed war on drugs was summed up in three words: "Just
Say No." First Lady Nancy Reagan's facile philosophy would ultimately
be remembered as a joke in the annals of history. "Drugs are menacing
our society. They're threatening our values and institutions. They're
killing our children," the president said on September 14, 1986, during
a joint address with the First Lady. "Today, there's a new epidemic.
Smokeable cocaine, otherwise known as crack. It is an explosive, destructive, and often lethal substance which is crushing its users. It is
an uncontrolled fire."

"Just Say No" permeated pop culture throughout the 1980s and '90s.
Every kid remembers the overwrought public service announcements.
"Any Questions?" was especially memorable and likened an addicted
brain to an egg cracked on a skillet with the stern voice-over: "This
is your brain on drugs! Any questions?" There was the "very special
episode" of popular sitcoms like *Growing Pains*, *The Fresh Prince of
Bel-Air*, and *Diff'rent Strokes*, where a character faced a dramatized
experience with drugs but inevitably got sober and sanctimonious by
the commercial break. Even Melle Mel's 1983 "White Lines (Don't Do
It)" was initially a "celebration of cocaine," but an abstinence angle was
added to the song to ensure commercial viability.

Drugs were so much in the zeitgeist that they made it into fashion.
In 1983, the chief of the Los Angeles Police Department, Daryl Gates,

and the Los Angeles Unified School District started the Drug Abuse Resistance Education (D.A.R.E.) program to teach children about peer pressure and living drug- and violence-free. But all we really got was a T-shirt. The famous black shirt with the slogan "D.A.R.E. to resist drugs and violence" in ominous red lettering was in every child's closet. It turned into an unintended must-have and was beloved among stoners, especially. Countless celebrities wore the shirt, including those with highly publicized substance abuse issues.

Instead of treating crack as a public health crisis or the result of systematic economic, social, and political failures, it was criminalized. New York's Rockefeller Drug Laws of 1973 increased mass incarceration with severe mandatory minimum sentences. Possession of four ounces of narcotics came with a sentence of fifteen years to life, approximately the same as a sentence for second-degree murder. President Ronald Reagan's Anti-Drug Abuse Act of 1986 included a mandatory minimum penalty of five years for possession with intent to distribute five grams of crack cocaine (while five hundred grams of powder cocaine received the same punishment). In other words, crack would be punished harsher for no discernible reason other than racism. The judicial system was merciless and punitive against low-level and nonviolent offenders and leaned harder on Black convictions. The United States Sentencing Commission found that "African Americans made up 88.3 percent of those convicted of federal crack offenses in 1993, even though federal survey data showed that a majority of crack users were white."

Bimmy began selling heroin and dope around 1983 when he was fifteen or sixteen years old. He knew what it was like to struggle. "We grew up with nothing. My moms was working jobs but there was no food in the crib and I had no clothes," he told me. Living in Jamaica, Queens, he had a large family—two brothers and five sisters—and his version of shopping was riffling through hand-me-downs. Anything he could get. "My sisters had Gloria Vanderbilt and Sasson jeans," he said. "I wore both of them shits. I wasn't supposed to because I was a boy, but

I didn't have no clothes. I didn't have nothing." At thirteen years old, he wasn't trying to break gender boundaries (and get teased at school), so he wore a long T-shirt to cover up the incriminating logos and stitching on the back pockets. He instantly felt an elevation wearing expensive denim. "The stitching of it, the texture, it was different from any clothing I had." The desire to have nice clothing—his *own* clothing—was one of the catalysts that drew him into the street life. "That was one of my motivators. Definitely."

His initiation—like for many young men—was through an older guy in the neighborhood. "I stood on the corner in front of the deli. He gave me the work. I sold it all and I gave him the money." It started slow—$20 in profit—but business got better. "When I made $500, I thought I had made it," he said. He headed straight to Jamaica Avenue and bought several pairs of Lee jeans. No more borrowing from his sisters. Bimmy joined the Supreme Team at eighteen years old, and he eventually took on a more significant role in leadership after Supreme pled guilty to engaging in a continuing criminal enterprise in 1989 and was sentenced to twelve years of incarceration.

The Supreme Team gave hustling both financial and aesthetic appeal. Their old photos were like *GQ* editorials: Supreme, handsome with those light green eyes, wearing a plush mink coat, with his hands folded like a power broker. Baby-faced Prince in a silk shirt, unbuttoned, surrounded by pretty young things eager for his attention. Bimmy giving a puppy dog look to the camera in a fedora and leather bomber. This was off-duty. When it came to business, the Supreme Team had an official uniform that was recognizable and functional—a branded sweatsuit and La Tigre joggers—especially for street peddlers who needed easy movement. "Yeah, we was known for that [fashion]. We had cars. Jewelry," said Bimmy. "We were definitely known for all that."

Hustlers and rappers were natural extensions of one another. "Street guys and rap dudes are from the same stuff," Nas explained. The rapper shouted Supreme Team out on his acclaimed debut *Illmatic* in 1994 on

"Memory Lane (Sittin' in da Park)": "*Some fiends scream about Supreme Team, a Jamaica Queens thing.*" Both hustlers and rappers had a mutual interest in escaping what they were born into, and in fact, many rappers were former "street dudes" whom hip-hop enabled to make legal money. Two early rap records that depicted explicit tales from the streets of this era were Toddy Tee's 1985 "Batterram" (a reference to the armored trucks and battering rams the Los Angeles Police Department used to raid crack houses) and Ice-T's 1987 "6 'N the Mornin'." There would be subsequent discographies about drug dealers moving weight, trap houses, out-of-town trips, and the Racketeer Influenced and Corrupt Organizations (RICO) Act.

On the business side, it was common for independent rappers and record labels to be funded by drug money. "*Partner, I'm still spendin' money from '88,*" Jay-Z boasted on "Dead Presidents II" from his 1996 debut album *Reasonable Doubt*. According to industry legend, the rapper's Roc-A-Fella Records was initially financed with the drug-dealing proceeds of co-founder Kareem "Biggs" Burke (who won't publicly confirm or deny it). Real g's move in silence. But not everyone was a certified hustler who actually lived that life. Some rappers inflated their prowess or patchworked stories from those around them. The Notorious B.I.G. exaggerated his impoverished past as a Brooklyn crack dealer. "He's telling a story," his mother said. "Some of the stories are his friends' stories." According to flashy gangster Jacques "Haitian Jack" Agnant, he inspired Tupac's thug life persona. "He loved the respect and recognition I got in New York and I think he wanted that same respect," said Jack. Meanwhile, Tupac's childhood friends remembered that he was an empath—his mother was a drug addict—and "such a nice person" that he barely sold crack for a week.

The ethos of drug dealing would pervade hip-hop's definition of masculinity. On the streets, being a man meant being strong and intimidating. Appearing physically imposing was important for survival—a gun was a common accessory—and baggy clothing was a proxy for those who weren't blessed with muscle. These rappers didn't smile or dance out of fear of appearing weak. Everybody wanted to be a tough guy.

Rappers who were around hustlers were inspired by their style through osmosis. Jam Master Jay gave Run-D.M.C. their trademark look in the 1980s—black fedoras, laceless Adidas sneakers, Cazal glasses, and leather—by seeing how his older brother in the streets dressed. "Their style was a Queens street hustler's style. Mostly people hadn't seen it before and they loved it right away," Bill Adler, author of *Tougher Than Leather: The Rise of Run-DMC* and director of publicity at Def Jam Recordings/Rush Artist Management from 1984 to 1990, told me. It was a collaborative effort with the group's manager and founder of Def Jam Records, Russell Simmons. "Russell had an eye for fashion. And what he saw was, of the three of them, Jam Master Jay had the most style," said Adler. "When they really started to make their records and tour, Russell turned to them and said, 'From now on, you're dressing like Jay.'" Run credited his turntablist for shaping the group's iconic look. "Jay was cool enough to know everything that's cool. The leather suit—Jay. Cazal [sunglasses] with the eye lenses popped out—Jay. This hat—Jay. We wore the hat because Jay set the tone. The Adidas with no shoestrings [was] Hollis. Street culture, Jam Master Jay fashion."

The aesthetic spread with the success of "My Adidas" in 1986, ironically, a song responding to *criticisms* of drug dealer fashion. "The whole Adidas record actually came about—there was a doctor in our neighborhood named Dr. Deas, and he was like this community activist dude," Darryl "DMC" McDaniels said to *Sole Collector*. Deas made a novelty song called "Felon Sneakers" in 1985 that correlated the style *inspired* by drug dealing to actual criminal behavior. "He was saying [that] kids and youth in the streets that wore Lee jeans and Kangol hats and gold chains and Pumas and Adidas without shoelaces were the thugs, the drug dealers, and the low-lifes of the community." The group recorded "My Adidas" to prove that a person shouldn't be stereotyped on style. Explained DMC: "Like, you can't judge a book by its cover. We're young; we're educated. A lot of us go to school; a lot of us have jobs. A lot of us, even though we look like our peers in the neighborhood—but you can't judge everybody by that."

Adidas Superstar sneakers (commonly known as "shell-toes") flew off the shelves thanks to Run-D.M.C. And the way to rock them properly was without laces, a nod to prison where laces were prohibited for safety reasons. It was an unpaid plug, and manager Lyor Cohen invited Adidas executive Angelo Anastasio to witness the group's influence in person. On July 19, 1986, Run-D.M.C. took the stage at Madison Square Garden, where they famously instructed the crowd to hold up their sneakers during "My Adidas." "Run went out there during the show, 'D, take it off your feet; hold it up. What's those? Everybody in here, if you got Adidas on, hold 'em up,'" DMC remembered. "So, forty thousand people in a sold-out Madison Square Garden held a sneaker up, and Anastasio was like, 'Oh my God, it's true.'" This watershed style moment, and a personal video message to Adidas, led to Run-D.M.C. securing an unprecedented endorsement deal from the sneaker brand for $1 million.

Run-D.M.C.'s look became synonymous with hip-hop. Anastasio estimated that the brand sold an extra half million pairs immediately following the endorsement. "It introduced hip-hop style to people who'd been listening to rap records for a while. Run-D.M.C. was the first," said Adler. He remembered fashion magazine *Details* noticing the impact early. "I think they named Run-D.M.C. as the biggest style influence of the '80s. It was a way of high fashion recognizing the influence of hip-hop." The December/January 1989 cover featured actress Melanie Griffith, and Run-D.M.C.'s name was placed far less prominently, in smaller font between several other names. But it was there. Hip-hop was in the building.

Chapter Four

BURY THEM IN LO

The mission: get in and get as much Polo as you can. Walk inside the store. Saks Fifth Avenue. Or Bloomingdale's. There's a security guard right there, so don't do nothing too crazy. Then it's go-time. Rush the racks. Grab as much Lo as you can—coats, rugbys, jeans, whatever. Push anybody aside. Smash a few windows if necessary. The merchandise is hot—you're holding a few hundred, maybe even a thousand dollars' worth. Good thing these stores don't have sophisticated surveillance. Okay, now let's get the fuck out of here.

The Lo Lifes terrorized high-end retail in New York City by boosting Polo Ralph Lauren. Unlike that of drug dealers, their hustle was the good old-fashioned five-finger discount or shoplifting (and reselling on the black market). Among their peers, they became synonymous with Polo and an integral part of its infusion into hip-hop. They were walking advertisements for the brand. "When we would come back to our neighborhoods wearing these clothes, you looked like somebody. You felt like somebody," said Thirstin Howl The 3rd in the 2019 Ralph Lauren documentary *Very Ralph*. The Lo Lifes began when two disparate boosting crews in Brooklyn—Ralphie's Kids from Crown Heights and Polo U.S.A. (United Shoplifters Association) from Brownsville—joined forces in 1988. Thirstin Howl The 3rd (aka Big Vic Lo) and Rack-Lo were widely credited as founders of the new supergroup (although the former told me that there were "many founders"). The name "Lo" was shorthand for Polo Ralph Lauren, hip-hop's favorite line of American luxury. "I was born when hip-hop was born, so I was able to see everything as it developed and as it evolved. I always evolved with the styles and the fashion within hip-hop," Thirstin said in the 2017 retrospective *Bury Me with the Lo On* (released in connection with his book of the same name). He was a break-dancer and graffiti artist and later embarked on a rap career. "I'm a hip-hop fiend. I study all the music like a fiend, not a fan. It's a drug for me." He started his shoplifting career with affordable entry-level brands like Pro-Keds, and then elevated to price tags with more zeroes. As he explained to me: "We didn't start off with Polo Ralph Lauren. There were many other brands before that. We were wearing Adidas, Puma, Guess, Lee, Benetton, Izod. There were so many brands we were touching before we really got into Polo like that. It was an evolution." Polo had a range of different designs, from Ivy League sweaters to sportswear, and it was exciting chasing the latest release. Said Thirstin: "When we got to Polo Ralph Lauren, it was the only brand that we were seeing that was seasonal. It had a variety of logos, sizes of the logos, colors. That's what really brought us to Ralph Lauren and made us stick to it."

Shoplifting might have appeared on the surface as a victimless crime, but the stakes were high for the Lo Lifes. "As far as attending boosting sprees with us, it wasn't for the weak," Rack-Lo said. "You had to have heart. The consequences were so stiff. At any time, at any moment, on any day, you could've been facing some real heavy consequences." Jail time was realistic, especially for someone with an existing criminal record. As Rack-Lo explained: "You could have gone to jail for what, the time varied. It could've been a week, a month, two years, five years depending on the offense. You could've been hitting Rikers Island. You could've been on your way to spending your time in the state penitentiary because the offenses and charges were so serious. You could have put yourself in the situation where you wasn't coming home."

The Lo Lifes reigned when Brownsville was known as one of the most dangerous areas in Brooklyn. The contrast between their preppy fashion and their surroundings was not coincidental. The neighborhood had a reputation for being tough. Initially a settlement for factory workers, Brownsville was predominantly Jewish from the 1880s until the 1950s. "When I was a child, I thought we lived at the end of the world," wrote literary critic Alfred Kazin in his 1951 memoir *A Walker in the City*. "We were the end of the line. We were the children of immigrants who had camped at the city's back door, in New York's rawest, remotest, cheapest ghetto." In the 1940s and the decade after, an influx of African American residents moved to Brooklyn for employment opportunities in the growing industrial sector, and by 1950, the Black population in Brownsville had almost doubled to 14,209. The neighborhood became an epicenter for public housing—Brownsville has the highest concentration of public housing in the nation—and white flight ensued in the 1960s and '70s, leaving behind crime, declining public services, and urban decay. The *New York Times* described Brownsville as a bleak wasteland ravaged by crack vials and gun violence in 1990, where it wasn't uncommon for a thirteen-year-old to witness murder in broad daylight. "We supported each other through some of the harshest times in Brooklyn's history—crack was raging and guns went off daily," Lo Lifes member Big Haz Uno said. Against this backdrop, there wasn't any particular moral judgment around their ill-gotten gains. "My family condoned it," Thirstin said. "I witnessed it at home. My mother shoplifted meat from the supermarket. I was always a poor kid. If I wanted a soda or sunflower seeds and potato chips, I had to go to the store and steal it."

The Lo Lifes wanted better for themselves, and clothing was the means. "How I felt having them on and how everybody else looked at me. These were items of respect and gave you social status in your neighborhood," Thirstin said. There was a resonance in nice things. The feeling of worth from a high price tag was the same emotional trigger that luxury brands used to attract consumers since time immemorial. And the fact that they were wearing Polo out in the open—and not getting it stolen off their backs—was an added badge of honor and status. Thirstin reflected: "To actually come back with some high-end stuff from Fifth Avenue and wear it in the projects, it made you somebody."

———————————

Ralph Lauren realized the power in his name when he changed his at sixteen. Born Ralph Lifshitz in the Bronx, New York City, on October 14, 1939, he experienced early that having an ethnic last name made him a target of bullies. He explained to Oprah Winfrey: "My given name has the word *shit* in it. When I was a kid, the other kids would make a lot of fun of me. It was a tough name. That's why I decided to change it." He picked "Lauren" after his cousins in California had changed theirs to "Lawrence." It was easy to pronounce, a nice vanilla name without any ethnic baggage. As Winfrey pointed out, "Yes—Lifshitz is a hard one. I don't know if I'd want to buy the Lifshitz towels." His parents, Frieda and Frank, were Ashkenazi Jewish immigrants who had fled Belarus. He grew up one of four siblings during an idyllic time when his childhood heroes were baseball greats Joe DiMaggio and Mickey Mantle, and it was safe to ride bikes around the neighborhood or go roller skating at night. "The world was a little simpler. A little more magical. There were more heroes," he said on *Charlie Rose*. Style was inherent even though he wasn't conscious of it. "I was the cool guy. I never thought of style. I did what I did and wore what I wore."

Lauren dismissed the idea that he Anglicized his surname in order to assimilate. However, as he embarked into fashion as a career, his chosen moniker would be a target for xenophobia and anti-Semitism. "Then people said, 'Did you change your name because you don't want to be Jewish?' I said, 'Absolutely not. That's not what it's about,'" he said. "There were also people who thought that because I was Jewish, I had no right to create these preppy clothes."

Lauren dropped out of Baruch College, where he studied business, and enlisted in the U.S. Army from 1962 to 1964. He briefly took a job at Brooks Brothers as a sales assistant before joining tie manufacturer Beau Brummell. His time at Brooks Brothers was especially formative. He saw how the retailer sold to men in the Ivy League—Harvard, Princeton, Yale—and thus created an air of exclusivity; it was a special members-only club that appealed to the wearer regardless of whether he matriculated or not. At twenty-eight years old, Lauren decided to try his hand at designing—with the support of Beau Brummell—and launched his namesake line originally focusing on ties. "I didn't know how to make a tie. I didn't know fabric. I didn't know measurements. What I did know? That I was a salesman. That I was honest. And that all I wanted was quality." The Ralph Lauren Corporation was founded in 1967 and focused on handmade ties made from high-quality materials. He and his brother brainstormed several names for the line that invoked wealth and class, including: "Cricket," "Players," and "Polo," maybe inspired by attending his first polo match with childhood friend Warren Helstein. "We were exposed to fabulous things. Silver, leather, the horses. The tall, slinky blondes. Big hats," Helstein said. "High society, [which] we weren't really knowledgeable of but certainly it didn't take us a moment to appreciate it."

One of the first indicators of Polo's success came from its wide-lapel ties, which went against tie conventions of the time. Bloomingdale's was interested but wanted to nix his logo for its own. Ralph Lauren refused to relinquish his name. "He closed his sample case and said, 'I will not accept the order without my name,'" remembered Marvin S. Traub, the CEO of Bloomingdale's at the time. Lauren walked and the retailer came calling back several months later. "I thought the ties were terrific. If he wanted his name on it, that was fine." Other high-end retailers like Neiman Marcus and Paul Stuart also wanted in, and according to *Bloomberg*, Ralph Lauren had sold $500,000 worth of ties within a year. It was proof the designer needed to always believe in his gut. "Had I changed that tie, I would not be here today."

When the designer launched a full menswear line, he looked to Hollywood icons like Cary Grant and Fred Astaire as sophisticated, masculine muses—something he felt was missing in the market. The first collection featured a white flannel suit and dress shirts in sport shirt fabric. The brand's success led to Ralph Lauren's shop inside Bloomingdale's in 1970, the first of its kind. The designer was meticulous in the retail experience, overseeing every aesthetic detail, down to the wood paneling. "The business grew very rapidly," said Traub. "He knew what he wanted in the shop. It really created a Ralph Lauren environment."

Ralph Lauren opened its first stand-alone store on Rodeo Drive in Beverly Hills in 1971, followed by locations in Houston, Palm Beach, Atlanta, and more by the end of the decade. The next year, the designer introduced his most iconic piece: the Polo shirt. The collared shirt, available in a panoply of colors, featured the insignia of a polo player riding a horse on the front of the shirt. The Polo shirt and logo became synonymous with the house. "The Polo shirt is to Ralph Lauren what the Swoosh is to Nike, what Mickey Mouse is to Disney, or what the Empire State Building is to New York," the brand proclaimed in its book devoted to the Polo shirt. Said Lauren, "It's honest and from the heart and hopefully that is what touches the diversity of all who wear it. It was never about a shirt, but a way of living." The branding made the shirt special and allowed Ralph Lauren to elevate a casual garment into something more versatile—taking a generic lowercase "polo" shirt and making it the luxury "Polo."

Ralph Lauren expanded its brand over the years to include multiple collections: Ralph Lauren Collection, Ralph Lauren Purple Label, Polo Ralph Lauren, Double RL, Lauren Ralph Lauren, Polo Ralph Lauren

Children, and Chaps. Ralph Lauren Purple Label (established 1994) was the prestige line of timeless classics, while Chaps (established 1978) would be sold at big-box retailers like Walmart, Meijer, and Boscov's—covering the entire price gamut. He launched a women's collection (established 1972), and actress Diane Keaton popularized the notion of women borrowing from his menswear with her famous *Annie Hall* look—khakis, vest, and tie—in 1977.

"He came from the trenches, he came from the Bronx," said rapper A$AP Ferg about Ralph Lauren. "He came from the dirt, just like me." Dapper Dan echoed the sentiment: "Here comes this Jewish guy . . . He's not a designer. He can't sketch. He can't do none of those things. And he completely revolutionized the fashion industry through marketing." As outsiders, Ralph Lauren and hip-hop shared an inexorable desire for success and entrance into traditionally unwelcoming spaces. Producer Just Blaze, an avid collector, likened Polo Ralph Lauren to other symbols of accomplishment. "It was a status symbol in the hood, the same way you might drive a BMW. Those kind of things meant you made it." A parka or shirt was far more affordable than other status symbols. From a design perspective, the pieces were sporty and wearable on the average male physique (unlike avant-garde silhouettes seen walking down high fashion runways) and could be paired with staples like denim, Timberland boots, and sneakers. The sizing was more inclusive (with Big & Tall offerings), and the big logos and details such as patches and flags were visible status signals.

Raekwon grew up in the streets of Staten Island—what he and the Wu-Tang Clan called "Shaolin"—but he might as well have been from Aspen with his Polo Ralph Lauren Snow Beach jacket. The rapper remembered clear as day walking into the Abraham & Straus (A&S) store in Brooklyn and being immediately drawn to the yellow, red, and navy pullover. "When I seen that jacket, the first thing I thought about was, 'Yo this ain't something I seen before,'" Raekwon said. "I was always a fan of Polo, but when I seen that, I felt like I was the only one who had it." Previously, Raekwon had memorably shouted out his "'Lo sweater" on Wu-Tang Clan's 1993 classic "C.R.E.A.M." The limited-edition Snow Beach became coveted, with its bold colors and large lettering. "As far as clothing grails go, this jacket easily cracks the top ten," GQ declared. And at around $300, the then up-and-comer could afford it. Raekwon gave the Snow Beach his hip-hop flair by pairing it with baggy jeans, white Air Force 1s, and a baseball cap flipped to the back for his appearance in Wu-Tang Clan's "Can It All Be So Simple" music video in 1994. "I wanted to wear something that I felt could relate to my culture," he said. "Next thing you know, the jacket became famous." The jacket stood out in the grimy, urban milieu of the visual. Just Blaze remembered seeing the jacket in the music video and being compelled to get one. "Every kid was like 'What IS that? I want that!' And I remember—I ended up getting that at Macy's. I started working at the mall shortly after that video came out and that was one of the first things I bought," he said. The jacket continued to be a coveted piece for Lo heads for decades to come.

Ralph Lauren's world was America. Or, an immigrant's simulacrum of it: attractive, carefree people doing quintessentially blue-blooded things. All play, no work. Every photoshoot, advertisement, and in-store display showcased the one percent in situ: a handsome WASP lounging in seersucker. Horseback riding in a chambray button-down. Cozy co-eds in cashmere knits with the American flag. The aesthetic was the lifestyles of the rich and preppy—from Martha's Vineyard and the Hamptons to the fraternities of Cambridge and New Haven—and all that was missing was the apple pie. Forget Norman Rockwell. Wearing Ralph Lauren was an invitation, even if only symbolic, to participate in the American Dream.

Most of the vision was, unsurprisingly, told through a predominantly white narrative. "All-American" has long been coded language in the fashion industry for those with blond hair, blue eyes, and Nordic features. In March 1978, Time magazine ran a cover story called "The

All-American Model" featuring supermodel Cheryl Tiegs, who fit the bill: tanned, blond, and toned, with girl-next-door innocence. This was visual shorthand for the head cheerleader, the homecoming queen. That archetype—and its equally unattainable buff and handsome male counterpart—became Ralph Lauren's staple, with models like Elaine Irwin, Cindy Crawford, Burton "Buzzy" Kerbox, Tim Easton, and Argentine polo player Ignacio "Nacho" Figueras.

That was, until Tyson Beckford—the fashion industry's first hip-hop model—came to Ralph Lauren. The Bronx native was discovered hanging out in Washington Square Park by *The Source*'s art director, Erik Council. *The Source* was the definitive rap magazine, and its fashion editors, Julia Chance and Sonya Magett, recognized his streetwise appeal and put him in a three-page spread. "They were the first publication who ever gave me a job as a model," Beckford said. "Things just started happening. People started seeing it. It was a big publication in New York . . . I got a lot of calls for different jobs all over."

At twenty-three, Beckford appeared in a Polo Sport advertisement in 1993, shot by renowned photographer Bruce Weber, wearing a bright red sweatshirt with "USA" written across it. He was stunning: six feet tall, with the body of a Michelangelo marble statue. And he was undoubtedly masculine, with a shaved head, sinewy physique, and velvety brown skin. His prominent almond-shaped eyes were inherited from his multiethnic Jamaican Chinese background—he was teased and called "Mr. Chin" as a kid—and his gaze smoldered off the page.

As a young Black man immersed in hip-hop culture, Beckford brought a rare street cred to high fashion. He could break-dance and rap (under the name "Ty-Ski"). He was scrappy when he had to be. He knew the Lo Lifes from hanging out in Brooklyn (although he didn't realize *how* they got their Polo gear initially). He hustled in the streets while going to early casting calls and earned the nickname "Two Guns" because he always carried a weapon in his backpack. "Back then, it was survival of the fittest," he said. "You know how New York City was in the '80s and '90s. Hip-hop was just coming up. Dudes was getting robbed and killed in the street. I got robbed on the train before and I never liked that feeling of being vulnerable. It was a different lifestyle."

Bethann Hardison, a noted Black high fashion model in her own right, began managing the neophyte in the early '90s and sent him to Bruce Weber to get photos for his model book. Weber was the man for the job. He had made a name for himself as the master of male navel-gazing, literally. "Over the years, Weber has become synonymous with erotically charged depictions of good-looking young men," the *New York Times* heralded. He was famous for shooting titillating images for Ralph Lauren, Versace, and Calvin Klein, including the latter's barely there underwear advertisements. His images were voyeuristic, with messages of power, desire, and sexuality. "It changed my whole life. It was his idea to send me to Ralph Lauren for castings," said Beckford. He went in for suits, but upon seeing his muscular build, the casting associates wanted him for the more active Polo Sport line. He remembered Ralph Lauren seeing his Polaroid and connecting with their shared heritage, vis-à-vis being from the Bronx and children of immigrants. He was booked immediately.

Tyson Beckford's ascent to supermodel came fast. In 1994, the *New York Times* ran a profile commemorating his arrival: "Black, Male and, Yes, a Supermodel." Beckford was by no means the first Black male model, but his look and attitude as a streetwise child of hip-hop were special. His dark complexion and multicultural features challenged the prevailing paradigm of beauty, which historically skewed very Anglocentric, even for people of color. "Tyson is not, of course, your traditional Black male model," said Stefan Campbell, the former fashion editor of *Vibe*. "Other successful Black models weren't as dark, and they had straight noses and thin lips and curly or processed hair. He represents a beauty that people weren't willing to acknowledge before." Beckford was the new, modern definition of "all-American."

Beckford signed an exclusive contract with Ralph Lauren and

was the first Black male model to land such a deal. His visage graced Polo Sport, Ralph Lauren, and eventually non-fashion categories like housewares. "He's the great-looking guy from around the way," wrote Robin Givhan in the *Washington Post* in 1996. "He was the first model whose Blackness seemed to be a selling point. Beckford also exudes a toughness. And so does hip-hop." The rare combination of being handsome and tough was appealing to rappers. The supermodel was friends with The Notorious B.I.G. and was asked by him to make a cameo in the "One More Chance" music video—an all-star visual that included Sean "Puffy" Combs, Heavy D, Queen Latifah, Mary J. Blige, and Aaliyah—in 1995.

Tyson Beckford was the face of Polo, but he didn't forget where he came from. He gave props where they were due. "He always extended his hand and showed love to Lo Lifes," said Thirstin Howl The 3rd. "We always saluted him properly, like one of our own." At heart, they were one and the same. Like anybody wearing the Lo, they were just chasing the American dream.

Chapter Five

1991

Chanel's Fall/Winter ready-to-wear show was set in Paris in March 1991, but its soul was right off the streets of New York City. Supermodel Linda Evangelista paused on the runway. She angled her head slightly, showing off exquisite bone structure—a razor-sharp jawline that could slice through glass—and catlike eyes. She wore a gold baseball cap, tilted to the back with attitude. Her famous athletic physique was draped in a royal-blue jacket, but it was the extravagant accessories that took center stage: a cascade of gold chains adorned her neck, including a large nameplate emblazoned with the word "CHANEL." A remix of Nancy Sinatra's "These Boots Are Made for Walkin'" and "deafening rock and roll rhythms by Madonna" blared overhead as one thousand or so spectators, like *Rocky* actors Sylvester Stallone and Dolph Lundgren, gazed at leggy models jaunting down the runway in bold and provocative silhouettes: Karen Mulder in a black leather trench, her waist circled by layers of gold rope chains that created a shimmying hula skirt, Helena Christensen in a see-through black mesh bodysuit, her décolletage perfectly accented by long Cuban links.

Streetwear, kitsch, and glitz collided in a smorgasbord of delicious excess on the runway during Chanel's Fall 1991 show. The 'round-the-way girls from the streets and the bougie, or posh upper-class, girls intersected. There were leather baseball caps worn backward, jackets with "Chanel" scripted across the back in pearls, distressed and ripped denim, and quilted jackets that would be as at home on 125th Street in Harlem as on the Champs-Élysées. Chanel also showed appreciation for Madonna with tulle skirts and layered jewelry à la the singer's 1984 breakout "Like a Virgin." Jeans added a youthful edge, while risqué catsuits and nipple covers, made from the House's Camellia roses, kept things a little bit naughty. Silhouettes traditionally associated with Chanel's aristocratic lineage, like the iconic tweed jacket and chiffon dresses, were updated and offset by hip-hop-inspired *bling*—chains, medallions, earrings, and bracelets—piled high atop each other.

"It's the 'nouveau' rapper look," said Karl Lagerfeld of his vision. The designer became Chanel's creative director in 1983 and held the role until he died in 2019. His tenure was that of a consummate chameleon, evolving and giving zero fucks in the process. An avid student of the zeitgeist, he leaned on diverse source material in creating his visions. "I think what Lagerfeld has always done amazingly well is completely capturing the mood of the moment," said Tim Blanks, editor-at-large at *Style*, in a 2014 retrospective of the nouveau rapper show. "He listens to everything, reads everything, sees everything, and then distills it into these potent fashion images. In this collection, you get the sense that he was probably listening to rap music."

What would become known colloquially as Chanel's "hip-hop collection" was a watershed moment, the pinnacle of French prêt-à-porter (ready-to-wear) welcoming hip-hop into its sanctum. "Lagerfeld is deliberately provocative," observed *Vogue*, "taking his Chanel show to the edge of an abyss of kitsch and funk." "It's young, colorful, taken right from the street fashion scene," gushed Rose Marie Bravo, chief executive at the historic I. Magnin & Co. department store at the time.

There was also sampling, albeit unspoken, of the cultural tour de force of *In Living Color* (Fox's hit sketch comedy show that aired from April 15, 1990, to May 19, 1994) and its popular hip-hop dance quintet the "Fly Girls." The dancers in season three—Lisa Marie Todd, Carrie Ann Inaba, Cari French, a then-unknown Jennifer Lopez, and Deidre Lang—choreographer Rosie Perez, and stylist Michelle Cole combined feminine elegance with masculine street. It was described as "a little bit of girl and a little bit of boy"—ready for any hip-hop club or house party. High- and low-budget items were thrown together (called high/low), like spandex jumpsuits and biker jackets or pearls and combat boots, something a young woman could feasibly put together by riffling through her closet or browsing a thrift shop or mass-market retailer. The clothes were sexy and fun, and allowed freedom to move and suggestively gyrate as the show dissolved into commercials.

Not everyone was a fan of Chanel remixing its classic French heritage with the now. The core clientele invested in Chanel because they knew they were getting timeless classics and staple pieces. "How many women are going to wear a silver catsuit?" complained a retailer during a preview of the collection.

The House of Chanel was founded several generations before the birth of hip-hop, but the origin story of founder Gabrielle "Coco" Chanel was on par with any rags-to-riches rap lore. Coco was born on August 19, 1883, in Saumur, France. Her mother died of tuberculosis and she was abandoned by a deadbeat father. As an orphan, she was banished to live at Aubazine Abbey, or Abbaye d'Aubazine, in Corrèze at the age of eleven with her sisters, Julia and Antoinette. The Cistercian monastery set against lush green hilltops was founded by pious St. Stephen of Obazine in the twelfth century. Little Coco made the best of her hard-knock life. She learned how to sew, and the abbey's austerity and aesthetic were believed to have inspired Chanel's brand bible: the house's logo was made up of the interlocking double-C patterns in stained glass windows and the black-and-white palette was lifted from the nuns' habits.

As an adult, Coco envisioned her name in lights. She had a brief fling as a singer—not a very good one—and performed in seedy cabaret clubs in Vichy and Moulins. She realized early on the power of economic mobility, especially for women, and believed: "Without money, you are nothing, that with money you can do anything. Or else, you had to depend on a husband . . . Money is the key to freedom." She was romantically involved with wealthy and powerful men, which didn't hurt in subsidizing (and galvanizing) her professional aspirations—the City Girls of the future would be proud—including, notably, Arthur "Boy" Capel. The handsome British polo player took her to the sea at Deauville, France, where she saw (and balked at) how wealthy women dressed. Womenswear in the early twentieth century was often synonymous with restrictiveness, tight-fitting, with elaborate layers of fabric and complex networks of snaps, gussets, and corsets. Coco wanted a more streamlined silhouette—in just a few colors—that would emancipate women from the shackles of discomfort.

She opened her first shop, Chanel Modes, on 21 rue Cambon in the center of Paris in 1920 and sold hats. As business grew, she expanded and acquired the entire building at 31 rue Cambon. Coco's big break came from one of the most basic pieces in a woman's closet to this day: the little black dress. Coco wanted something warm to wear and repurposed one of Boy's jersey sweaters by cutting it down the front, adding a collar and a knot, and finishing the edges with ribbon. Women began requesting the flattering dress when she would step out. "My fortune is built on that old jersey," she said. "By inventing the jersey, I liberated the body, I discarded the waist, I created a new shape; in order to conform to it, all my customers, with the help of the war, became slim. Women came to me to buy their slim figures."

In 1916, *Harper's Bazar* (the second *a* was added later) heralded Coco as "a canny little French woman and very exclusive," and included an illustration of her "charming chemise dress of gray silk jersey" in its pages. The frills-free design resonated with the austerity of World War I, and Coco proved that fashion didn't require the most fussy or expensive fabrics. She was a huge success by 1919 at the age of thirty-six (there is discrepancy with her date of birth, and she was known to lie about her age). In October 1920, her couture collection received even more coverage, including an image of Cécile Sorel, a noted French actress of the time, wearing a black satin and lace evening gown over trousers (shockingly, without a corset).

Her clients were starlets, well-heeled women, and European royalty, but Coco herself was a woman about town. She partied with the glitterati and artists. She cavorted with the likes of wealthy textile heir Étienne Balsan (who helped her open her first boutique when she was his mistress) and artist Pablo Picasso and socialized with British prime minister Winston Churchill. Her bitter rivalries—sadly, too early to be splashed all over social media—were fabulous, especially her feud with experimental Italian designer Elsa Schiaparelli. One time, Coco allegedly steered Schiaparelli, whose colorful, eccentric work was the polar opposite to her own, into a chandelier during a costume party and set her on fire. Luckily, the flames were put out and Schiaparelli was saved by "delighted guests squirting her with soda water."

Christian Dior was another target on Coco's hit list. In 1947, the French designer's "New Look" debuted to fanfare, with its cinched waists, glamourous full skirts, lifted busts, and rounded shoulders. Dior silhouettes were unabashedly opulent and ultrafeminine despite the utilitarianism in the years surrounding World War II. Forget pragmatism and rationing fabric! A single Dior gown was a masterpiece in architecture and design, complete with multiple layers, underpinnings, and a bustier that could include several yards of satin, silk, and tulle—some weighing even thirty-five pounds. Coco saw Dior's eponymous line as a travesty, a Svengali puppeteering his vision of femininity while disregarding the actual woman. "Look how ridiculous these women are," she scoffed, "wearing clothes by a man who doesn't know women, never had one, and dreams of being one."

Meanwhile, Coco branded herself as the real modern woman. Before Lil' Kim and Foxy Brown preached the prosperity gospel in the '90s or Megan Thee Stallion rallied Gen Z "hotties" with body positivity rap, Coco lived the life of an independent woman. She purchased a villa in the south of France and was driven around in a Rolls-Royce limo. A predecessor to "girl boss," she was her own muse and ambassador, and exuded the lifestyle of a true bon vivant. "I didn't go out because I needed to design dresses, I designed dresses precisely because I went out, because I have lived the life of the century, and was the first to do so," she said. "I lived a modern life; I shared the habits, the tastes and the needs of whom I dressed." Being both designer and consumer was powerful. "The ability to wear her own clothes, to set an example through her own personal style," Lagerfeld said of his forebear in 1989, "that was what set Chanel apart from other designers of her time."

The modern woman deserved nice things. Explained Coco: "Luxury is a necessity that begins where necessity ends." Chanel established itself as a luxury powerhouse with releases like Chanel N°5 perfume, launched with perfumer Ernest Beaux in 1921 and believed to incorporate over eighty ingredients; the Chanel 2.55 handbag, named after its launch date in February 1955; and notably, the classic tweed bouclé jacket.

The Chanel tweed jacket debuted on February 5, 1954. Derived from the French word for "curled" or "ringed," bouclé refers to yarn made from a series of looped fibers or the fabric made from it. The jacket, designed in various iterations over the years, has been seen on prominent and diverse shoulders throughout fashion history, from Princess Diana and Audrey Hepburn to Cardi B, Rihanna, and Jennifer Lopez. Jacqueline Kennedy Onassis memorably wore a raspberry-pink bouclé suit, along with a matching pillbox hat and white gloves, when her husband, President John F. Kennedy, was assassinated on November 22,

1963, in Dallas. The grieving widow wore the blood-spattered suit to the swearing in of successor Lyndon B. Johnson, despite being encouraged to change, to send a message to her husband's killers: "I want them to see what they have done to Jack." The suit was forever attached to the former First Lady's legacy as a fashion icon and imprinted onto the American psyche.

Whether the suit was actually a Chanel or a designer dupe has been contested by fashion historians. The design came from Chanel's 1961 Fall/Winter collection. But some say that the First Lady was pressured to dress patriotic publicly and wear an American designer, so she had New York shop Chez Ninon create a line-for-line copy.

Interestingly, the inspiration for the female power suit came from menswear. In the 1920s, Coco saw tweed fishing and hunting jackets worn by men in Scotland, when she was there with her wealthy lover, the Duke of Westminster. Decades later, she reimagined the fabric into a feminine and wearable silhouette. "It enables women to move with ease, to not feel like they're in a costume. I'm not changing the attitude of mannerism. This time it's very different because the human body is always on the move," she said. She rejected froufrou jacket conventions like shoulder pads and collars and embraced minimalism and straight cuts. Her inner lining featured a chain to ensure the jacket fell in a flattering way, and four pockets held essentials for women like lipstick, coins, and cigarettes. Branding was key with stamped buttons embossed with the Chanel logo. "The Chanel jacket . . . has definitely come to symbolize a certain nonchalant feminine elegance that is timeless, and for all times," said Lagerfeld.

Despite his reverence for the house of the double Cs, Lagerfeld was his own visionary. "The idea that Chanel should be respected and never touched again is a joke," he said. "I have no respect for anything. In fashion, you have to be rough and tough. In every decade, there is a way to put Chanel back on the fashion map." His vigor kept the brand relevant. The iconic Chanel jacket was a runway staple under Lagerfeld's stewardship but updated throughout the years by pairing it with jeans or mismatched skirts, embroidered versions, adding pops of vibrant color. "There are things in fashion that never go out of style—jeans, white shirt, and a Chanel jacket," he said.

Lagerfeld took Chanel's staple 2.55 handbag—a quilted, rectangular bag with a metallic link shoulder strap that was released in February 1955—and reinterpreted it into the 11.12 (or Classic Flap) bag in the 1980s. Lagerfeld's version became the house's signature handbag, with a leather woven chain and interlocking Cs for the turn-lock closure. "It's called the classic for a reason. It's a simple statement in everyone's closets," wrote *Who What Wear*. "When you think of a Chanel bag or see one on the arm of a celeb, there's a good chance it's an 11.12." The bag got a flashy, hip-hop reissue during the 1991 runway show. In one look, a model carried a metallic silver version to match her quilted silver baseball cap. Another iteration of the handbag was in gold lambskin, which coupled with the gold hardware made the bag look like a gleaming piece of statement jewelry.

It's challenging to step into an established, eponymous line, especially as the job of the creative director is nebulous at best. Based on whom you ask, the creative director is the all-encompassing leader; someone responsible for design and aesthetic decisions but also shrewd at engaging celebrities and customers. Over time, that role has evolved with more expectations like social media expertise. Lagerfeld was the consummate multihyphenate. He was the personification of the brand but also utilized his creative skills as a photographer and started shooting the house's fashion ads in 1987. This would be no different than when rappers would begin to own clothing lines and were required to be the master of many functions: creative visionary, model, and evangelist.

———————

Born in Hamburg, Germany, on September 10, 1933, Karl Lagerfeld got the coveted job of assisting designer Pierre Balmain at seventeen and later designed for Jean Patou. He was the definition of a hustler—moving between France, Italy, England, and Germany and collecting checks with several brands (including his own eponymous line), shaping the idea of a fashion freelancer. Lagerfeld began working for Chloé in 1964 and became a consultant for Italian design house Fendi in 1965, a post he held until his death. "It's the longest collaboration in fashion," he bragged of his tenure. This was unusual, but his reputation allowed him to supersede corporate policy and retain multiple, competing gigs. Everyone wanted Karl Lagerfeld, even if just a little piece. He inspired future designers (or at least, those who could negotiate it) to leverage their power and to attain as many positions as possible.

Lagerfeld modernized Fendi and infused it with a youthful, playful energy. He created the double-F logo (which stands for "fun fur") that is still used and recognizable today and incorporated nonconventional designs like vibrant colors, pleating, and even twenty-four-karat-gold gilding into the fur. "We are not doing basic mink coats," he said in 2016. "We are a thousand miles away from that."

Fendi had brand presence in hip-hop culture since the beginning. When Mike Tyson made headlines for fighting Mitch Green outside of Dapper Dan's shop on August 24, 1988, he was wearing a custom $850 Fendi jacket that read: "Don't Believe the Hype." The jacket made it onto Fendi's radar and eventually led to the atelier being shuttered in 1992. Hip-hop loved Fendi's fine furs and instantly recognizable double-F logo. In 1990, when LL Cool J was looking for his ideal woman in "Around the Way Girl," his first top 10 single, he rapped that she would have "*a Fendi bag and a bad attitude.*" Lil' Kim responded to this on "Gettin' Money (Get Money Remix)" in 1996, with "*Who remains in Chanel frames and* (Haha) */ Animals of all kinds / Russian Fendi sables* (What?) */ With matching pool tables.*" Fendi became one of the most name-checked brands in hip-hop lyrics.

Lagerfeld never apologized for being a thousand miles ahead of everybody, even the namesake of Chanel. "What I do, Coco would have hated. The label has an image and it's up to me to update it. I do what she never did," he said. He revealed that he had total autonomy in his role, something uncommon in the industry, when he was tasked with resuscitating the heritage brand struggling both financially and for relevancy. "I had to go from what it was, what it could be, what it should be, to something else." Bravado paid off. Lagerfeld redefined Chanel into a modern luxury house and positioned it as an industry leader with success in ready-to-wear, cosmetics, jewelry, and fragrance. According to *Bloomberg*, Chanel grew to become a "$10 billion global fashion machine" under the auspices of King Karl, the man who bragged, "I can Chanel-ize anything!"

Lagerfeld not only stepped into Coco's famous two-tone shoes but became a celebrity in his own right. With stark white hair always pulled back into a ponytail, black sunglasses, and fingerless gloves, he was one of fashion's most recognizable and dramatic figures, leaving a trail of air kisses wherever he went. He wasn't a celebrity designer; *he was a celebrity.* "I think it's flattering. I don't sing. I'm not an actor. I have no scandals," he mused. A walking quotable, his adages could be acerbic and blunt. This devil-may-care attitude made him even more intriguing. There was no modern fashion maestro quite like him.

Lil' Kim loved Chanel since the inception of her career in 1994. "What I loved about Chanel was the edge. It was edgy but feminine— like powerful femininity," said Lil' Kim's stylist, Misa Hylton. In the early years of the rapper's career, they had no direct plug, or access, to the luxury house, so they bought off the rack using their own money. "We would buy our own pieces," Hylton said. "They were statement pieces. And, then again, you can't leave out the fact that it says 'luxury.'"

Karl Lagerfeld always had a keen eye for rising talent and female muses. Parisienne Inès de la Fressange was one of Lagerfeld's earliest inspirations as the first model to sign an exclusive modeling contract with Chanel in 1984. Baby Phat founder Kimora Lee Simmons was discovered when Lagerfeld called her "the face of the twenty-first century." He deserved credit for putting the thirteen-year-old biracial model on the Chanel runway in 1988, before inclusivity was considered in fashion. "Karl transformed me. He made me who I am today," said Kimora, who is of Black and Asian descent. "As a young teenager he pulled me out of a small town in the Midwest and gave me wings to fly. Every other casting agent told me I was ugly and that I didn't have what it took to succeed in modeling. Karl saw things in a radically different way than other designers who weren't willing to risk putting a multiethnic girl on the Parisian runway." Kimora would pay it forward when she became the head of Baby Phat, by casting multiethnic models for her runway.

Lagerfeld's legacy was a blueprint for creative directors at luxury houses. Creative directors after him strived to become as recognizable as their employers—Tom Ford at Gucci in 1991, Alber Elbaz at Lanvin in 2001, Oliver Rousteing at Balmain in 2011, Hedi Slimane at Yves Saint Laurent in 2012, Demna (formerly known as Demna Gvasalia) at Balenciaga in 2015, Virgil Abloh at Louis Vuitton in 2018—thanks to him. "I was in design school at Parsons in Paris when Karl went to Chanel and I just remember it was incredible," said designer Tom Ford. "He was the first—way before me reviving Gucci, and Nicolas [Ghesquière at Balenciaga] and Marc [Jacobs] at Vuitton and Phoebe [Philo at Chloé]. Karl was the first. And he survived longer than all of us. Karl is still there. It is remarkable."

Chanel was the ultimate European luxury cosign, but innovative designers on both sides of the pond were taking notice of hip-hop in the early '90s: In April 1991, *Women's Wear Daily* featured a cover celebrating the "Rap Attack" with American designers Isaac Mizrahi, Charlotte Neuville, Adrienne Vittadini, Randolph Duke, and Norma Kamali. *W* magazine and *Newsweek* followed suit, running features and using racially coded terms like "homeboys" and "homegirls" to describe the trend. Brits

Katharine Hamnett and Rifat Ozbek showed collections with sneakers and tracksuits à la LL Cool J, oversized hoodies, and Afro-centric prints similar to Queen Latifah or A Tribe Called Quest. Donna Karan, who launched her more affordable, youth-centric DKNY line in 1989, showed gold bodysuits and zippered accents.

"The most stylish people are the homegirls and homeboys," said American designer Isaac Mizrahi, who was inspired by his elevator operator Arthur Hubbert to add oversized Star of David medallions, wrap skirts, and bodysuits into his Fall 1991 collection. In a black-and-white archival photo (shot by Richard Bowditch) for *Women's Wear Daily*, Mizrahi is holding an armful of chains with humongous pendants and dressing Hubbert—wearing a camouflage jacket, beanie hat, and high-top sneakers—like a Christmas tree.

It's unclear whether Mizrahi and the like appreciated hip-hop or saw it as a grab for cache and cash. "Every era and every time has something of an undercurrent of some ethnic culture that influences it and gives it movement and currency," Mizrahi said at the time. The image of the white Jewish designer fussing over Hubbert, a blue-collar Black man, was tone-deaf and exploitative when analyzed through a modern lens. The designer's fall show in New York City with comedian Sandra Bernhard "rapping" in what she thought was hip-hop slang was also cringeworthy: "*So girl you know it's fresh and new / He's got the look that's unky-fey / Big gold jewelry you're proud to be seen in / Homegirl look is the only way.*" Mizrahi admitted that he sampled Black culture for his collection and seemed happily naive that this cherry-picking could be seen as parasitic. Culture was a holistic concept and parsing it into its "cool" elements without regard for the Black and brown people that made it was all too convenient. "We had to look to the Black cultures to give us some clues about style," said Mizrahi. "We take these styles, refine them, give the customers as much a dose as they can deal with and bring a little funk into their lives."

As much a dose as they can deal with. The ladies who lunch were high fashion's core audience, and hip-hop had to be taken in microdoses. "There's a fine line between down and dirty and chic rap," said Kalman Ruttenstein, senior vice president for fashion at Bloomingdale's, in 1991. "The rap message simply means it's okay to say 'Look at me.'" American designer Charlotte Neuville, a white woman in her forties, showed a rap-themed collection in New York City that season. "The fun is to push that rap influence as far as it will go without getting trashy," she said at the time. These designers wanted the positive and fun attributes of hip-hop without having to commit to the culture and assume any of the stereotypes that came with it.

Thirty years later, Charlotte Neuville was in a completely different chapter in her life. She owned and operated custom bakery Charlotte Neuville Cakes and Confections. She told me that she took inspiration from the streets for her 1991 fall collection but did so without ill intentions. "It was really something that was much more urban and on the subways and out when I was walking around. Manhattan is just incredible, just such an inspiring city," she said in 2021. The line included faux fur jackets (described in the press as "homeboy jackets"), star medallions, gold-quilted trenches, and metallic baseball jackets.

For consumers, this fashion was cultural tourism and a way to experience hip-hop culture without going above 96th Street. There was understandable hesitancy from hip-hop and Black fashion critics on whether the trend was celebratory or parasitic. "The designers are way off the mark," said Fab 5 Freddy, host of *Yo! MTV Raps*, in 1991. "These styles don't reflect what's on the street anymore." In his mind, these designs were *played out*, caricatures, and nobody who actually was a part of hip-hop would wear them. If history proved anything, once the powers that be sucked up counterculture and regurgitated it to the masses, it immediately lost any semblance of cool. The conversation around cultural appropriation—decades before that term made it into the general lexicon—was happening. "When Black kids were wearing a lot of gold chains, they were condemned by society," said Denise

Burrows, a buyer for Ebony Fashion Fair, the historic traveling runway show featuring iconic African American models like Pat Cleveland and Dorothy "Terri" Springer that began in 1958. "But then Lagerfeld does the same thing for rich women, and he is applauded. There is a double standard here."

The *Los Angeles Times* harangued Neuville's collection for being a yuppie take on fly: "At heart, her style is closer to the Connecticut suburbs than the South Bronx. Trying to disguise it with jewelry fit for 'New Jack City' was a reach, to say the least." She admitted that her collection was a departure from her usual brand ethos of sportswear-inspired boyfriend blazers, blouses, and trousers for career women. "It was a really big visual departure from my look, from my brand. It taught me a lot. I really loved challenging myself and expressing myself in a way I think is new and fresh—and my customers expect that from me," Neuville said to me. Still, the critique that she was exploitative didn't sit well with her. "If somebody doesn't get it, you do have to wonder, 'Did I not express it?' You look at it, was it too much too soon? Is it just sour grapes? Is it racist? All of the things that go through your mind that never, in a million years, you would consider when you were designing it."

The *New York Times* was brutal to the 1991 shows in New York City: "Rap street style, with its jumble of jewelry and tongue-in-cheek references to high fashion—for example, street-peddler Gucci and Louis Vuitton shirts, caps, and belt packs—is already a form of fashion self-mockery. On the runway, it's a joke on top of a joke." There was a bias, implicit or otherwise. The establishment of predominantly older and white critics viewed hip-hop as *gauche*, a caricature, beneath their high standards. Rappers were in costumes and not fashion.

"It doesn't have to be overt to be racist," Neuville said. "At the time, we hadn't seen the incredible fashion icons of color. There's so much richness out there, and I don't remember any collections before what we did—white people inspired by other cultures." In hindsight, she understands how her collection could be polarizing. "Some people really understood it and other people really rejected it," she told me, reflecting back. "It didn't matter if it was me or Karl Lagerfeld. People had a hard time understanding it. I think if we had done it today, it would have been totally understood. Sometimes you can be too early."

Bad timing or not, hip-hop style was officially gentrified. This tension, the constant push and pull of the old guard playing on a new block, was only just beginning. And just like any neighborhood undergoing a transition, the originators would collide with the transplants. The turf wars had just started.

Chapter Six

BROOKLYN'S FINEST

So recognize the dick size in these Karl Kani jeans / I wear thirteens, know what I mean?
—The Notorious B.I.G., "One More Chance"

K arl Kani's story began in Brooklyn by way of an immigrant journey. He was born in Costa Rica to a Panamanian father and a Costa Rican mother and moved to the United States in 1971, when he was three years old. For generations, Brooklyn had been a haven for new arrivals seeking a better life. The first wave of Irish immigrants came at the turn of the eighteenth century and settled along the waterfront in an area known as Vinegar Hill or "Irishtown." By 1860, a second wave of Eastern Europeans, including Russian Jews, Italians, and Polish people, grew the borough into the third-largest city in the United States. The opening of the Brooklyn Bridge in 1883 enabled easy access to Manhattan and made Brooklyn an attractive destination for those seeking affordable housing and better living conditions than the city. The next great wave included African Americans from the South and those leaving Harlem seeking middle-class housing or ship-building jobs during World War I. By 1930, more than 60 percent of the African American population in Brooklyn was born outside of the borough. The passing of the Immigration and Nationality Act of 1965 (also known as the Hart-Celler Act) repealed immigration limits based on race and ethnicity and encouraged new arrivals from the West Indies. And by 1983, 62 percent of Brooklyn's immigrants originated from the Caribbean with neighborhoods like Flatbush, Canarsie, and Crown Heights becoming favored enclaves for those from Jamaica, Trinidad and Tobago, and Haiti. The influx of immigrants brought with them their own distinct slang, food, music, and style.

Many of Brooklyn's prominent rappers have Caribbean roots. The Notorious B.I.G. was born to Jamaican immigrant parents. Foxy Brown had Trinidadian heritage, while Shyne was born in Belize. Lil' Kim showed off a myriad of wigs in the music video for "Crush on You" in 1996—including a neon-green bob, cascade of yellow Marie Antoinette curls, and electric-blue blunt bang—and she was likely inspired by Caribbean women in her borough who had long been rocking similar styles. The rapper dipped into her lineage for several songs, including throwing patois into her verses.

Karl Kani was taught the American Dream from day one. His father wanted the family to assimilate, so he changed their surname from Casanova to "Williams." "My dad had vision: We're going to America. We're going to make it there. We're going to speak English. That was his whole philosophy of what it would take to make it here." His mother was a registered nurse who worked the early shift, and his father owned a typesetting company. They moved to a middle-class neighborhood in Flatbush and lived among transplants from Trinidad, Jamaica, and Haiti.

But after his parents divorced, he moved to the projects, where he learned about luxury labels from his friend Az, who worked in the stock-room of the Ralph Lauren store on Madison Avenue. "He was the first one that introduced us to Polo in the hood," Kani told me. "That was one of the first expensive brands that everyone aspired to wear, and we couldn't afford it. So we started hustling so we could be cool and rock expensive clothing." Az was a niche influencer before being an influencer became a veritable career decades later. "Back in 1985, he had a Louis Vuitton bag and a Polo shirt at sixteen years old. He just introduced us to more expensive fashion. I realized the secret to be cool in the hood is all about what you're wearing. If you don't got cool clothes on, you're done."

Kani learned the art of tailoring from his culture. "My dad was Panamanian. He wanted his clothes a certain way; he wanted his pants to be kind of fitted on top and flared at the bottom, and he couldn't find it in the stores. So he used to go to Delancey Street in Manhattan and buy fabric. And then, he had his tailor custom-make his clothes for him." These father-son excursions were a mental trip. "As a kid, I would go with him to buy his fabric. I saw him buy fabric and then all of a sudden, he had fresh clothes on. I was blown away how easy it is to make clothing. That's what really inspired me in the beginning to make clothing. My dad didn't know how to sew, he just had ideas and would hook up with a tailor. So I understood the philosophy of surrounding yourself with people who had talent that you don't have, to achieve a goal."

New York City was the hub of all aspects of textile design, manufacturing, and production. In the early 1800s, hundreds of thousands of immigrant garment workers were pushed into the Garment District (also known as the Fashion District) of Manhattan and created a localized headquarters for the garment industry. Clothing was made by hand before the advent of the sewing machine in 1846. After mass production became the norm, discerning clientele preferred the personalized design and fit of custom clothing.

"Back then, you gotta think, the choices of fashion was limited in terms of design. Even the fit of clothing that *we* wanted; no designers were making clothes that we truly wanted. Custom tailoring was your only last resort," said Kani. "Either you're going to buy what's there for you or dictate and create your own style. That's what really inspired all of us. You could be an individual and stand out." For certain pieces, it was more cost-effective to purchase fabric and head to the tailor instead of paying a premium for brand names. And many immigrants were accustomed to bespoke clothing from back home. When Dapper

Dan visited Liberia in 1974, he was shocked by the craftsmanship and skills of a tailor named Ahmed. Together, they altered the cut on pants, changed the color on a blazer, and added lapels and flares to "resonate with the trends back on the streets." Dap remembered: "I'd never met a Black person who could do what Ahmed did," he said. "No one in Harlem had ever seen the designs and materials I was about to have . . . Those clothes I collaborated on with Ahmed were my very first Dapper Dan original fashion designs." I remember visiting India with my family in the early '90s with suitcases of fabric—gingham, Madras cotton—and coming back with frilly frocks and dresses, at prices (and quality) OshKosh couldn't compete with.

———————

Big Daddy Kane's tailor was his secret weapon, or in his case, *weapons*, plural. "I actually had several tailors," he said to me. "I had Dapper Dan and another brother named Rashad, both of them in Harlem. And then I had a woman in LA named Linda Stokes." The Bed-Stuy rapper was one of hip-hop's first sex symbols. His song "Smooth Operator" didn't lie; he was a mean combination of vicious bars, bedroom eyes, and sophistication. Kane pointed to his father, Clay Bradley, as his style inspiration. As a kid, he watched the truck driver treat his off-duty fashion like a job, meticulously lining up accessories and paying attention to every detail. "You know, he was the type of guy that wore three- or four-piece suits and Gators [alligator] or snakeskin shoes. Fur coats. Big brim hats. He just liked being fly."

Big Daddy Kane is indisputably one of the greatest rappers of all time, and his style is as much a part of his legacy as his music. The Smithsonian National Museum of African American History and Culture has archived a photograph of the rapper getting a shape up in 1989 (shot by photographer Al Pereira) and his purple leather chevron jacket and pants (designed by Dapper Dan) from the "Nuff' Respect" music video in 1992.

Kane started his career as a battle rapper and member of the famed
Juice Crew in 1986 and became a solo force with his breakout "Ain't No
Half Steppin'" in 1988. As his popularity grew, so did his wardrobe. He
wore everything—tailored suits, leisure jackets, velour tracksuits, and
gold rope chains—with class. His signature high-top fade, which he
first saw on Larry Blackmon of R&B group Cameo, was regal. "I thought
that it looked so royal. It gave off the essence of Nefertiti, and the look
of like, an Egyptian god." Even Kane's birthday suit, which appeared
alongside supermodel Naomi Campbell and Madonna for the latter's
photo book *Sex*, was hot. It was risqué for a masculine emcee to strip
down for a sex-positive, NSFW shoot. Looking back, he has no qualms
about baring it all. "When I met Madonna, she was so down-to-earth and
friendly. And when she asked me to be in the book, I was like, happy."

Initially, the rapper shopped at a store in Albee Square in Brooklyn
for his performance clothes. "Me and my two dancers would get silk leisure suits that we'd wear onstage." But he started noticing other people
copying the same looks. That was when a singer—he can't remember
who—gave him the insider tip: buying off the rack was for suckers.
Real stars didn't do that shit. "You never want to be onstage and look
down on the crowd and see someone else wearing the *same thing* you
are," explained Kane. "That's the reason why I always used tailors as
opposed to rack shopping."

So the cheat code was to have clothes nobody else had. When Karl
Kani was sixteen years old, he took five yards of linen to his dad's tailor,
a Haitian guy named Jack from Flatbush, and asked him to create a
jacket and a pair of pants. The fit had to reflect what he, as a young,
Black teenager, wanted to wear: "I want you to make the pants baggier
because we can't find any loose-cut pants in the stores." The outfit was
a hit. "Everyone's like, 'Oh man! Where'd you get that from? Where'd
you get that from? That's so cool.'" Kani didn't want to give up his tailor
plug, so instead, he offered to make his friends clothes. A designer was
born. "Literally, that's how it started. I started making clothing for my

friends in the hood and my name started to get out there a little bit. I had dudes come up to me with wads of cash and asking for things. That's how the game got started."

At nineteen, he learned the value of branding himself. "I'm bragging to these girls in the park one day. I was like, I made these outfits for this guy walking by, a big-time drug dealer. They didn't believe me. A girl, Casey, asks to see the jacket. She takes the jacket and looks at it up and down and says, 'Yeah, if Karl made the jacket why his name ain't on it then?!'" Burn. She had a point. "That's when it hit me. I was just making custom-made clothing with no label, no logo, nothing." He went home that night, thinking about the eponymous luxury brands he looked up to: Ralph Lauren, Tommy Hilfiger, Calvin Klein, Donna Karan, Giorgio Armani. All signature lines. "I wanted to do like them. I'm going to name the brand after myself." His government name, Karl Williams, didn't sound right. As Phil Collins's "In the Air Tonight" played, a favorite pop song among hip-hop fans, he'd be in his bedroom contemplating his line. One thought kept running through his mind: "Can I build a brand?" Can I? Eventually that question became his answer: *Can I → Kani*.

April Walker was a hip-hop head since way back. Of Black and Mexican descent, she grew up in the Bedford-Stuyvesant (or Bed-Stuy) and Clinton Hill neighborhoods of Brooklyn surrounded by legends. In Clinton Hill, her neighbors were Guru from Gang Starr (back when he was known as "Keith") and producer Easy Mo Bee, who helmed The Notorious B.I.G.'s masterpiece *Ready to Die*. Actress Rosie Perez lived one block over and her *Do the Right Thing* director, Spike Lee, wasn't too far either. At one point, Walker's father managed a fledgling rapper from Marcy Projects named Jay-Z. "The neighborhood was very creative," Walker told me. "It was a special time."

She had the best of both worlds as a burgeoning creative. Her father had a home studio. Her mother made sure she went to Catholic school. "I think I inherited a little bit of both of their DNAs; wanting to be somewhat grounded but still having the heartbeat of a free spirit." She loved Black designers like Willi Smith, the brilliant mind behind streetwear line WilliWear, and Patrick Robinson, a fashion veteran with stints at Giorgio Armani, Perry Ellis, and Paco Rabanne.

Walker was in the building when Run-D.M.C. tore up Madison Square Garden holding up their Adidas sneakers in 1986. "Hip-hop was our rock and roll. It defied everything I've been taught . . . and latched on to my rebellious teen spirit," she said. "I felt it. I breathed it."

One of those trips Uptown ended at Dapper Dan's atelier, store by day, afterparty by night in the mid-1980s. "There was *a lot* going on," she said on the *Drink Champs* podcast, as host/rapper Noreaga underscored the cocaine deals transpiring outside. Walker remembered seeing the Dap machine at work: "We walked in, fabric everywhere. He's hustling. He's out there. His cheapest velour sweatsuit was $300 in the '80s! Without logos. Plain velour sweatsuit." It was there that Walker realized that her style could be distilled into a business. "In school, I was always that fashion person. But the lightbulb never went off until I went to Dap's." There was opportunity in an underserved market. "He was making mink coats, reversible, Gucci. Everything. He was doing it better than they were at that time," she said. "We have nothing like this in Brooklyn, *for us*. I was like, okay, like, I can do this. I didn't go to school for fashion, but I knew that I could just figure it out."

In a city divided by expansive blocks and serpentine subway lines, every borough in New York City had its own pin on the fashion map: Jamaica Colosseum Mall in Queens, Dapper Dan in Harlem, Albee Square in Brooklyn, Canal Street and the Diamond Exchange in Manhattan. The shopping hot spots varied by personal preference and budget but included: DrJays, A.J. Lester's, and Belle in Harlem; Karl Kani in Brooklyn; Macy's in Midtown; Jew Man's sneaker seller in the

Bronx; and Shirt Kings in Queens. The title of best-dressed borough is perpetually debated to this day: Harlem had money and was the flyest and flashiest. Brooklyn was the street hustler; low-key and paid. Queens was fun. The Bronx was straight grimy with a touch of B-boy. Explained Walker: "Brooklyn was very different from Harlem. Harlem was very different from Queens. Boroughs were everything." Borough pride was real.

April Walker began her business out of her home in 1986. Six months later, she opened the brick-and-mortar Fashion in Effect in Clinton Hill (on 212 Greene Avenue between Grand and Cambridge in Brooklyn), funded by a small business loan and savings from working at American Express. She followed Dapper Dan—proverbially and literally—and hired some of his tailors to create designer knockoffs, ready-to-wear, and original designs. "We bought the fabrics. We were the creative directors and designers. We bought the machines. And we got busy." Inspired by the hip-hop lifestyle, Walker designed sweatsuits, denim suits, and leathers. There were colorful fabrics—sometimes mixed with kente cloth or terry cloth—and airbrushed images of pop culture figures. She prided herself in being able to create anything from a sweatsuit to a tuxedo. "There was no blueprint. I had no mentor. No one had a line. We were all making one-of-a-kind pieces at the time and figuring it out. It was really feeling your way and trusting your instincts." It was rough in the beginning, and the first year was filled with growing pains: Walker broke her leg and couldn't come in for months as the bills piled up. One time, the electricity got shut off and a customer anonymously paid the balance.

Through word of mouth, business increased. The store and Walker's styling services, which began when she made custom looks for Audio Two's "I Don't Care" music video in 1988, became a magnet for everyday people working nine-to-fives and local Brooklyn rappers including a "little round kid" who would go on to become The Notorious B.I.G. Biggie came into the store after seeing an airbrushed shirt of Eric B. and Rakim in the window. "This airbrushed shirt [at the store] stopped him and he came in," she remembered of a teenage Biggie, just getting started in rap. "He was real cool. That's how we built those relationships."

Customization was a core service. "We had three customers," said Walker. "We had a customer that wanted something special and they didn't know what they wanted. We had a customer that had an *idea* of what they wanted and they wanted us to co-create with them. They became involved with the design process. And then we had a customer that wanted ready-to-wear."

In 1991, she launched Walker Wear with the specific focus to "create fashion that wasn't out there." Bringing together her talents for customization and styling, she designed with her demographic in mind. Her customers were young Black and brown men who wanted clothes that would traverse the concrete jungle. They didn't fit standard sizing. They wanted accouterments not found at other labels: larger pockets, bigger sizes, longer crotch areas. Customers loved pairing their Walker Wear with Timberlands, the perennial year-round boots of New York City, so her colorways were often muted and neutral to match the footwear. Her signature Rough and Rugged suit elevated the button-down and jeans combo men wore. It was upscale enough to satisfy the nightclub dress code without sacrificing comfort. The suit was flattering on all body types. Everyone from muscular Treach of Naughty by Nature to tall and slim Snoop Dogg and heavyset The Notorious B.I.G. wore it and looked good.

In 1992, Walker linked up with Tupac Shakur when she went to audition for the movie *Juice*, which the rapper was in. "I wanted to get my clothes out there, any way that I could. I wore a custom velour sweatsuit, that was crazy, with the bucket hat. I remember [Tupac] stopping me like, 'Yo! Where you get that?'" So she gave him her business card. Shakur's rebellious spirit and silver screen looks were a perfect match for her label. The rapper was a unicorn: the son of Black Panthers, he was a streetwise intellectual who wrote poetry and studied performing arts. His boyishness and thousand-kilowatt smile offset the "Thug Life" tattooed across his torso. Shakur was a walking contradiction—both incendiary and sensitive—and straddled that coveted dichotomy: men wanted to be him and women wanted to be with him. Said Walker: "He would be in the press a lot and he would always be photographed in a bandana or his hockey jersey. He became this iconic figure that fashion designers lined up and wanted to be a part of."

Walker Wear outfitted every bold-faced name from rappers to those in the hip-hop zeitgeist. Check the credits: The Notorious B.I.G. and Run-D.M.C.'s Jam Master Jay in Rough and Rugged suits in 1993. Tupac Shakur in a yellow Walker Wear vest in the film *Above the Rim* in 1994, a look that was resurrected in his biopic *All Eyez on Me* in 2017. A baby-faced Usher color-coordinated his Walker Wear sweatshirt with his wheat-colored Timbs. Boxer Mike Tyson flexed his bulging muscles in a black Walker Wear shirt in the ring at the MGM Las Vegas in 1996. And though the brand was technically menswear, gender-bending trendsetter Aaliyah rocked a one-of-one custom Walker Wear rain suit for a promotional photoshoot in the '90s. Aaliyah, like Shakur, would prove an important style cosign for a few lucky brands over the course of her career, including Tommy Hilfiger, Baby Phat, and Rocawear.

When it came to distributing Walker Wear, the designer leaned on grassroots marketing common in hip-hop and leveraged young people into a promotional street team. "I'd pick five stores in five cities and we made sure before [the product] got there, we had kids calling every day before the delivery." She sold to local retailers like DrJays and national chains Merry-Go-Round and Macy's. Her first trade show took place in an off-site hotel suite in Midtown Manhattan during the National Association of Men's Sportswear Buyers (NAMSB), and she remembered generating about $300,000 in sales. With success under her belt, she went to MAGIC, the biannual fashion trade show in Las Vegas. The trade show—formerly an acronym for Men's Apparel

Guild in California—was the largest apparel show in America and brought together brands and retail buyers at the Las Vegas Convention Center. Streetwear wasn't getting a prime spot on the floor, so she and fellow early adopters Karl Kani and Cross Colours took over a conference room and turned it into a makeshift jail cell. They enticed buyers with cheeky invites to "Come serve your sentence"—and pulled in $2 million. It was fun, lucrative, and a fresh breath of diversity and youthful energy at a typically stodgy trade show.

Karl Kani opened his first store in South Central, Los Angeles, in 1989. Crenshaw Boulevard might as well have been the boulevard of broken dreams. "We sold *nothing*. We made $0. We were starving. We had great ideas, and these guys weren't buying nothing," he said. Angelenos had their own style, including khakis, Dickies, and strict rules about gang colors. "We thought we were gonna be paid in full. We saw all the palm trees and nothing. Zero. Nada. We couldn't even afford a McDonald's breakfast. We were living in the store, starving."

He headed back to New York City to fundraise for his fledgling empire. In his absence, the store was robbed at gunpoint and everything was cleaned out. He had to face reality: How was this brand nobody had ever heard of supposed to become known without breaking the bank? In a brilliant move, the designer targeted consumers by taking out ads in *Right On!* and *Word Up!* magazines for $1,000 apiece. These magazines were popular among young fans through the '90s, with glossy covers and colorful pull-out spreads. My childhood bedroom was plastered with photos of Ma$e, Silkk the Shocker, and other rapper crushes ripped out of those pages. The ads enabled the designer to employ guerilla promotion. Explained Kani: "We did some really grassroots marketing. We had an 800 number in the ad: 1-800-221-K-A-N-I. So kids used to call the number and ask about our clothes. We would ask them where they were from and what were the top stores they were shopping at."

Kani would encourage the kids to call local retailers, like Up Against the Wall in DC, and request the clothes. Retailers were flooded and had no choice but to stock Karl Kani.

Tuma Basa, Director, Black Music & Culture at YouTube, remembered reading those magazines from cover to cover to get his fix of hip-hop culture a continent away in Zimbabwe. Magazines were powerful passports. They were cheap, easy to bring to Africa when somebody visited overseas, and each issue satisfied the craving for American pop culture. "Magazines were my reference. They would go through a hundred hands," he said. Magazines transported a kid in Zimbabwe to New York City. It was in these pages that the music industry veteran developed a lifelong affection for Karl Kani. He still has a Karl Kani flannel that he bought in 1996. "That tells you something about the quality of the shirt!" He laughed.

Kani was meticulous at marketing even at the most granular level. Veteran retailer Antonio Gray, of Merry-Go-Round (which did $3 million worth of business for Kani at one point) noted how impactful even the hang tags on the jeans were. The tags featured an image of Kani and resonated with young Black and brown consumers. Said Gray: "There was this image of a young Black man with his name on the back pocket of the jeans. That was really revolutionary at the time."

The designer struck the lottery when it came to working with celebrities. In 1991, he didn't have the budget to afford a big name to model his clothes, so he hired a young upstart by the name of Sean "Puffy" Combs. "Puffy was the first business mogul to wear my clothing for an advertising campaign. It was for my debut in *The Source* magazine," Kani said. Back then, Combs was still largely unknown outside of the hip-hop industry. He wasn't the indefatigable impresario with the "can't stop, won't stop" hustle. But like with everything he would go on to do in music and fashion, Puffy modeled with utmost swagger. In one pose for the ad, he bared his taut chest in a crisp, white-on-white look that's accented with orange boxers emblazoned with the brand name.

It was hip-hop through and through. He had on a gold chain, his jeans were baggy and sagged below his navel, and his Timberland boots were loosely untied—how anyone with a hip-hop bone in their body knew they were *supposed* to be worn. Only squares choked their ankles by lacing up their Timbs. His arms were outstretched, beckoning almost messiah-like. "The imagery was iconic and helped to catapult the brand," said Kani. "He really believed in the idea of a Black-owned business. He was the first one to step out into the mainstream wearing the brand, and it worked out to be a success for both of us."

Around this time, Kani connected with Carl Jones and Thomas "TJ" Walker of Cross Colours, the popular socio-conscious streetwear line known for its red, black, and green palette (colors of the Black American flag) and the feel-good slogan "Clothing Without Prejudice." Cross Colours was a giant in the market and saw its sales explode from $15 million in 1991 to $89 million in 1992. "Anything associated with Cross Colours, at its height, came in the limelight," said Deirdre Dube, West Coast senior editor of *Sportswear International*. Cross Colours' parent company, Threads 4 Life, became Kani's majority owner. It was a decision that proved fateful in the future.

———

Tupac Shakur typed furiously on the computer at the Hotel Nikko (now the SLS Hotel) in Beverly Hills. Given the time, it was probably a clunky PC running on Microsoft Windows 3.1. He stopped to take a puff from his blunt. Karl Kani remembered that the rapper was working on a script. For what? He didn't know. The rapper would be a prolific film and TV actor by the time his life was tragically cut short in 1996. This was their first meeting. Kani had previously met Pac's collaborators Tha Dogg Pound and Snoop Doggy Dogg (who did ads for Cross Colours), and the rapper was already an appreciator of the brand. He wore an orange-and-white-striped Karl Kani T-shirt in the music video for his ode to women "Keep Ya Head Up" in 1993, as well as in MC Breed's "Gotta Get Mine" music video that same year. "Tupac used to wear my clothes all the time," said Kani. Although both young creatives and Geminis, they weren't really clicking. "Tupac never looked at me. He never looked at me! Never ever. I was like okay, this guy is *different*," Kani remembered. Room service arrived and the designer saw this as his shot to ask the rapper the one, burning question he came with. "I was like, 'Yo! Pac. How much would you charge to do an ad?'" The rapper got quiet. *Fuck.* Maybe Kani had jumped the gun asking for the favor? It was all love. He remembered what Tupac said vividly: "He looks at me and says, 'Yo. You're Black. I don't charge my people for nothing.'"

The photogenic rapper not only became the face of Karl Kani but he was also the ad hoc creative director for the 1993 campaign. He conceptualized being shirtless in baggy Karl Kani jeans and sitting atop a basketball rim in Harlem. A nod perhaps to his role in the basketball film *Above the Rim* the following year. "It was the most iconic campaign I've ever done," said Kani. Decades later, that image is still associated with the brand. Shakur was an invaluable ambassador for early hip-hop streetwear—and remarkably, never charged a dollar. Kani remembered: "He just wanted to support. He told me, 'Yo. I'm gonna blow your line up. Everyone needs to know who you are.'"

The prophecy came true. Karl Kani was name-checked by everyone. The Notorious B.I.G. shouted him out on 1994's "One More Chance" (probably not coincidentally produced by Sean "Puffy" Combs). Aaliyah gave him girl-next-door appeal when she wore his hoodie on the cover of her debut album, *Age Ain't Nothing but a Number*, that same year. As an early adopter, he was able to work with several future superstars.

Kani, however, learned the capricious nature of the fashion industry. In 1992, he closed a $6 million order from Merry-Go-Round, Cross Colours' biggest retailer. Two years later, Merry-Go-Round filed for Chapter 11 bankruptcy protection, and Cross Colours subsequently went out of business. "Our biggest retail partner at the time, Merry-Go-Round, announced that they would be filing for bankruptcy. And with that bankruptcy went millions of dollars in products that we could neither receive payment for nor get back to sell on our own or through another retailer," said Thomas "TJ" Walker, co-founder of Cross Colours.

Karl Kani needed a new home. He went to LA Gear and Skechers founder Robert Greenberg (whom he had previously licensed his footwear business with) as his new partner. However, in 1996, Skechers sold 1.4 million common shares of Karl Kani in an initial public offering (IPO). As part of that deal, Kani would be required to relinquish ownership of his name to Greenberg. "They thought I was going to go along with the deal, but I wouldn't sign it," he said. "This is my name. It's who I am." The designer went on the offensive. "I went out and looked at who Ralph Lauren's attorneys were, and I hired them. I figured, let me get some high-powered attorneys. That was the end of the road . . . They stopped talking to me."

The fashion business was a shrewd game. Negotiations stretched out and stalled Kani's ability to put out new products and remain visible in the marketplace. Eventually, they came to an agreement in which Kani would get his name back by paying more than $10 million, in installments. Over the next decade, he paid every penny of it.

In New York City, April Walker was going through her own business issues. A collaboration with Cross Colours didn't happen as expected. She went on to work with other partners including USA Classics—which she said declared bankruptcy the day after she signed with them—AND1, the footwear and clothing company specializing in basketball; and Mike Tyson.

By the late '90s she felt jaded, like she was chasing the check over creativity. "It was very heavy. It was all about the business. Everyone was congratulating me, and I felt like shit. I had a New York showroom, an LA, and a Vegas showroom. I'm traveling all the time. I was all over the place. I wasn't being creative." The playing field was becoming oversaturated. As a solo entrepreneur who owned 100 percent of her equity, it was isolating to go through it alone. "Being an independent company for so many years, and being the only woman in a male-dominated industry, took a toll on me and I just needed a break."

Chapter Seven

RED, WHITE, AND BLUES

"Yo, Andy. It's Snoop. I want to come check you out." Andy Hilfiger stared at his answering machine in bewilderment. Just yesterday, he was telling his brother Tommy about Snoop Doggy Dogg. The breakout rapper had made his arrival with Dr. Dre on 1992's "Deep Cover," and "Nuthin' but a 'G' Thang" the following year was a platinum hit. *Doggystyle*, Snoop's solo debut, wasn't out yet, but there was anticipation for the neophyte with the laid-back flow and penchant for pups. "Tommy, he's the hottest rapper in LA right now," Andy said, pointing to Snoop at a Grammy Awards after party. They introduced themselves and the rapper gave them the pleasant but perfunctory industry response: "Oh cool, cool. Yeah, I've heard of your stuff. I've seen it."

Nonetheless, Andy had to seize the opportunity. "Look, if you guys want to come up, I've got great stuff. I've got great suits, I've got rugbys, I've got great gear." Then he dropped his number. Hours after hearing the message, Andy gave Snoop a personal tour of their New York City showroom. A basketball hoop entertained the rapper in the CEO's office and he and Tha Dogg Pound crew picked out thousands of dollars' worth of clothing. This connection to Snoop would pay off beyond the brothers' wildest dreams.

Tommy Hilfiger started his fashion empire as a high school student. In 1969, he opened his first store, People's Place, in his hometown of Elmira, New York. "It was by mistake in a way because I had no idea I would ever go into the fashion business," he said. "I was too small to play on the basketball team at school. Too small and frail to play on the football team." He loved fashion and music of the '60s and '70s: the Beatles, the Rolling Stones, the Who, Led Zeppelin, and Jimi Hendrix. "Music was my first love. It's what first got me into fashion, because I wanted to dress like my favorite rock stars," he told me. If he couldn't play an instrument, then he could at least *look* the part. At twenty-five, he filed for Chapter 11 bankruptcy protection and moved to New York City. It was difficult to get a job without credentials from a design school. He decided to freelance for some denim lines, including Jordache, before heading to Mumbai, India, to design his first collection under the name Tommy Hil. He met Indian businessman Mohan Murjani, who oversaw the Gloria Vanderbilt brand, and realized "a certain something" in the upstart and partnered with him to set up an eponymous label in 1985.

From the onset, the designer was confident of his place in fashion. He launched a ballsy ad campaign in the first year of business. The hangman-style billboard in New York City let luxury designers know in no uncertain terms that he was coming for their necks:

The 4 Great American Designers for Men Are
R_ _ _ _ L_ _ _ _ _
P_ _ _ _ E_ _ _ _
C_ _ _ _ _ K_ _ _ _
T_ _ _ _ H_ _ _ _ _ _ _

Tommy Hilfiger had appointed himself on the Mt. Rushmore of American menswear alongside Ralph Lauren, Perry Ellis, and Calvin

Klein. The unknown with the unpronounceable last name had the industry talking with his boldness and $200,000 ad. "My opening ad challenged the reader with an audacious claim. Overnight, the burning question in town became 'Who the hell is T_ _ _ _ H_ _ _ _ _ _ _?'" explained art director George Lois. "Tommy Hilfiger became instantly famous and set off an avalanche of national publicity within days." Three more spreads positioned Hilfiger as the next wave of great menswear designers—after Geoffrey Beene, Bill Blass, and Stanley Blacker. As Lois remembered, "Tommy's impish face pissing off every inhabitant of the Seventh Avenue schmatte business."

The Tommy Hilfiger brand was preppy and classically American with its red, white, and blue logo. It was sportswear and casual wear with a youthful vigor and spirit of independence. "My vision was always to reimagine classics—to take something that was classic and iconic and give it a fun, youthful twist. I wanted to create new American staples, and drew inspiration from the culture, art, and music at the time," the designer explained. The first Hilfiger store opened in New York City in August 1985, on Columbus Avenue near 73rd Street. Murjani shared that the store did $1 million in sales in the first twelve months. By the end of 1986, there were five Hilfiger stand-alone stores and eighty-five department stores that carried the label. Hilfiger had an internal checklist—fit, quality, colors, and price—that he adhered to. "You have to have a great fit. You have to have excellent quality. You have to have the right colors. You have to have a style that is wearable and affordable," he said. "You could have the greatest item, but you won't sell it if it doesn't fit. You could also have something great-looking, but if the quality isn't good, you won't sell. You could also have something incredibly stylish and cool and relevant, but if it's too expensive, you might sell one or two pieces." This philosophy would be one of the reasons that hip-hop was attracted to Tommy Hilfiger. He designed sportswear and casual wear that was instantly recognizable with large, visible logos and bright colors. The fit matched hip-hop brands, focusing on baggy silhouettes, and the prices were relatively affordable for luxury, especially compared to the European houses. A Tommy Hilfiger T-shirt was around $60 and a pair of boxers was only $20.

The Tommy Hilfiger brand began as a family affair. Sister Ginny was head designer. Andy oversaw publicity, marketing, and styling and was instrumental in nurturing celebrity relationships, including overseeing photoshoots, seeding products, and event sponsorships. In 1994, Andre Harrell introduced Andy to It girl Kidada Jones, who was immediately hired as a creative stylist with her pulse on what was happening and a vast network of cool friends. The symbiotic relationship with celebrities was evident even with the first collection. Movie star Robin Williams wore the brand's $56 khaki trousers in the 1986 film *Club Paradise*. As the *New York Times* noted, "One pair of pants seems destined for stardom."

Tommy was clear in his vision from the beginning. "When I started, I was told by many, many people to take that logo off the clothes, because nobody wants to wear logos. And if I listened to the buyers, for instance, I wouldn't be in business today," he said. Buyers like Bloomingdale's thought that big logos were tacky and ostentatious. "When I blew the logos up and made them really big, buyers, retailers, and people inside my business said, 'This is ridiculous. Don't do it. People don't want to be a billboard. People don't want to wear big logos.'" Good thing he didn't listen. His large, recognizable logos were a huge reason why hip-hop became his biggest fan.

Aaliyah lazily pirouetted—a wink to her ballet training—showing off a 360-degree view of her red, white, and blue Tommy Hilfiger outfit. She wore a bandeau top with baggy jeans adorned with the brand's name down the leg and slung low, so that the waistband of her matching boxer shorts was visible. "My father has beautiful chestnut eyes,"

Aaliyah purred, peering directly into the lens. "I've got my voice from my mother." The fresh-faced singer was shooting a commercial for the brand in 1996. Aaliyah was the epitome of cool and androgynous chic, discernible in her R&B and hip-hop sensibility, in crop tops, low-rise jeans, oversized outerwear, and dark shades. There was a froideur about her that made her even more alluring. Aaliyah was the teenage dream fronting Tommy Hilfiger's Sports Tech Denim line with young Hollywood: Kidada Jones, actresses Kate Hudson and China Chow, MTV personality Simon Rex, and producer/DJ Mark Ronson.

"Kidada has an innate sense of taste—she knows exactly what's cool, and she knew that Aaliyah was someone we needed to work with," Tommy told me. "Aaliyah had this amazing, laid-back aura—she was effortlessly stylish, and she just radiated relaxed confidence. You couldn't help but be drawn to her." The timing was perfect. Aaliyah released her sophomore album, *One in a Million*, in August 1996. The breakout release featured laid-back grooves and futuristic sounds, launching producers Missy Elliott and Timbaland as multiplatinum forces, and positioned Aaliyah as the leader of innovative R&B. "I'm not gonna take the credit for that aesthetic because that came from Aaliyah and Kidada. Their swagger, how they put it together," echoed Andy. Aaliyah's personal style was tomboy; she would take menswear and add feminine touches that made it sexy. "We didn't have Tommy Girl yet. They took men's jeans with basketball shorts and the Tommy underwear waistband. And then we took men's shirts and cut 'em up into bandeau tops. One of the tops is men's underwear where we cut the crotch out and made a bandeau for Aaliyah. We mixed in men's outerwear. It was sexy tomboy."

"Brands had beautiful advertising campaigns with great-looking models, but I really wanted musicians and cool people to wear my brand," Tommy Hilfiger said. Of every genre, hip-hop was the first to embrace the brand at critical mass. "And what happened is the rappers started rapping about Tommy Hil." 1992 was the first milestone, when Grand Puba gave the brand a shoutout on "360° (What Goes Around)" with the line: *"Girbauds hangin' baggy / Hilfiger on the top."* The approval resonated because of its unlikely messenger. "The craziest thing about the Grand Puba co-sign? This guy was in a group called Brand Nubian, which was all about being antiestablishment," said Datwon Thomas, editor in chief of *Vibe*. "It was about us being on par, or better, than the white man. These were basically five-percenters, and for him to be talking knowledge of self while rocking such an American brand was cool, because he's not on that bull. He's a man of intelligence and integrity. That line solidified both the look for the '90s and Hilfiger's standing in the hood."

At the time, Ralph Lauren and Polo had a stranglehold on the block. But not everyone wanted to fantasize about sailing and après-ski. Tommy Hilfiger's designs—his overt logo versus Lauren's subdued horse—were appealing, as was a fit that encouraged pants to hang low (and show off the top waistband of boxers). And the price was right. Said Thomas: "I had a bunch of friends who were Lo heads, but personally, I didn't have the necessary Polo money. However, I could get Hilfiger for $40 to $60, compared to Polo, which was starting at like $100." "I would say between '84 and '89—Polo was king," said rapper Raekwon. "But Polo wasn't making the kind of stuff we felt was next level. So a lot of people stopped buying Polo at the time. We started seeing this line called Tommy Hilfiger."

———————

"Hey. I'm back in town. We need some more gear." It was Snoop Doggy Dogg. It was 1994 and the rapper was in New York City to be the musical guest on *Saturday Night Live*. The episode featured actress Helen Hunt hosting and Snoop performing. The rapper summoned Andy Hilfiger because he needed something to wear. Andy only had a few hours to figure out what to bring. At midnight, he headed over to the Hotel Macklowe in Midtown with a bag full of clothes. Snoop

wasn't there yet, but the entourage started rummaging. They needed more clothes. Andy ran back to the showroom and furiously undressed the mannequins. "I gave Snoop some special stuff that hadn't even been produced. It was just samples."

Tommy Hilfiger was adept at recognizing hip-hop culture and, more important, supporting the people behind it. Meanwhile, a brand like Timberland was grappling with its hip-hop popularity around this time. "We are cutting back the number of doors we do business in," said Jeffrey Swartz, executive vice president of Timberland and grandson of the company's founder, in November 1993. "So if you want to buy us and you are not our target customer, we don't have a point of distribution that speaks to your lifestyle. We are making hip-hop come to our distribution." It cost a brand next to nothing to gift a rapper some clothes. Building authentic relationships and product seeding had the potential for infinite returns.

On March 19, 1994, Snoop took the venerated stage at Studio 8H in a striped Tommy Hilfiger Rugby. "Andy! Turn on *Saturday Night Live*. Snoop's wearing my clothes," the designer excitedly called his brother during the airing. In all the chaos, Andy had forgotten to tell Tommy about what was going on. The happy surprise gave the brand coast-to-coast coverage and gangsta cachet. "Having Snoop Dogg wearing my clothes on TV was such a defining moment—it was the culmination of so many years of hard work," remembered Tommy. "I'll never forget his *SNL* appearance—overnight, we became a household name. A teenager living in Chicago named Kanye West thought so too. "Snoop wearing this Tommy Hilfiger Rugby was the most impactful marketing moment of my young life," the future fashion mogul, who was about sixteen years old at the time, said. "Other designers didn't get it. They didn't get into hip-hop," said Andy. "But Tommy and I? We knew. Wow, this is music and fashion at its finest."

———————————

You've got mail. The pleasant and comforting voice of Elwood Edwards marks a new incoming message on America Online. It's from an unknown address, but the subject line makes it impossible not to open.

> **To:** You
>
> **Subject:** Tommy Hilfiger on Oprah
>
> I'm sure many of you watched the recent taping of *The Oprah Winfrey Show* where her guest was Tommy Hilfiger. On the show, Oprah asked him if he had said, "If I had known African Americans, Hispanics, Jews and Asians would buy my clothes, I would not have made them so nice. I wish these people would not buy my clothes, as they are made for upper-class white people." His answer to Oprah was a simple yes when she asked him, and she then immediately asked him to leave her show.

This message, or some variation of it, was sent to countless people in 1997, forwarded chain letter–style. Everyone heard about it, creating a virtual game of telephone, and subsequent participants embellished what they heard. It made its way to Hillside Middle School, where my best friend, Sara L., had a meltdown. "I can't wear this jacket anymore." She pointed to her electric-blue Tommy Hilfiger puffer jacket. She had the most enviable Tommy Hilfiger wardrobe, and one of her favorite looks was wearing Tommy overalls so the waistband of her matching boxers peeked through. "What will people think?"

People thought that Tommy Hilfiger was racist. The goodwill the brand had generated within hip-hop dissipated. There were calls for boycott. Fans blasted the white designer for biting the hands that had fed him. It was the rumor that everybody heard but nobody really knew the origin of. News circulated fast on the information superhighway. Before cancel culture was invented, Tommy Hilfiger was canceled.

And it was completely false.

"Despite much investigation, we were never able to get to the source of the rumor," Tommy Hilfiger told me. "We know that it started as an email chain on the newly created internet and quickly spread through word of mouth." The rumor was pernicious and came in several iterations. In one version, daytime maven Oprah Winfrey was so offended that she threw the designer off her show. In another, he made racist statements against Asians on CNN's *Style with Elsa Klensch*. The rumor spread despite the fact that the designer had never appeared on either *The Oprah Winfrey Show* or *Style with Elsa Klensch*, which was confirmed by reps from both shows.

Some media outlets tried to dispel the myth. "Why are they saying all those mean things about Tommy Hilfiger?" asked *Slate* in 1997, noting that the rumor had been debunked by credible journalistic institutions like *Time*, *USA Today*, and the *Washington Post*, while it raged on race and conspiracy forums and message boards. That year, the designer sent out an email campaign underscoring that the rumors were false and that he wanted "people of all backgrounds" to enjoy his clothing. It continued to persist. In 1999, Pulitzer Prize–winning commentator Leonard Pitts Jr. criticized how unverified news and rumormongering could destroy someone's reputation in "Dissing Hilfiger" for the *Chicago Tribune*: "Yet some of us keep falling like rocks for these half-baked con jobs. The Tommy Hilfiger case demonstrates how easily a person's reputation and livelihood can be trashed, and how little he can do about it."

At this time, designers rarely spoke directly to consumers. Many consumers had no clue whether Tommy Hilfiger was a real person or a pseudonym. Even in its nascent stages, the internet was powerful in amplifying messages—whether they were true or false—and no number of press statements or op-eds could compete with the sheer speed and virality of misinformation on a hot-button issue. The influx of social media would be an equalizer, enabling brands to control their own messaging outside of traditional advertising and media. However, it would be a double-edged sword, as equal power would be given to the truth as to unverified sources and online trolls. Often, fake news would supersede facts in the algorithm.

Cultural appropriation is "the unacknowledged or inappropriate adoption of the practices, customs, or aesthetics of one social or ethnic group by members of another (typically dominant) community or society." The phrase was added to the *Oxford English Dictionary* in March 2018 but entered widespread usage in the 1980s. The dictionary's first citation comes from a 1945 essay by Arthur E. Christy in regards to "European cultural appropriation from the Orient." What constitutes appropriation is largely dependent on whether one side benefits disproportionately to the other.

In hip-hop, labels like "culture vulture" and "cultural tourist" invoked the same idea. It was a phrase attributed toward white executives and artists who benefited from hip-hop without offering mutual contribution. When larger issues around hip-hop and the Black community come into play, these voices were usually silent. Think of the white rapper who no longer wanted to be categorized as a "rapper" once he secured his first "crossover" hit, or the bubblegum singer who covets a rap guest verse to make their image more edgy or sexy.

In the context of fashion, sometimes cultural appropriation was overtly offensive, like a house promoting tone-deaf or historically harmful imagery like blackface. Appropriation could also be fetishization of specific racial traits but then not hiring models from that actual community. Other times, it was truly a loving pastiche. The distinctions between appropriation and appreciation were often vague. As Yuniya Kawamura, professor of sociology at the Fashion Institute of Technology and author of *Cultural Appropriation in Fashion and Entertainment*, concluded: "There are no easy answers because everyone has his/her own perspective and interpretation of a culture, which consists of multiple layers and dimensions."

Tommy Hilfiger wasn't the only white designer who faced inaccurate accusations about bigotry. A similar rumor about Liz Claiborne and her preference for white customers had circulated since the late '80s. The designer allegedly said problematic comments about not wanting Black women to wear her clothing on *The Oprah Winfrey Show* and she sized her line intentionally small to discriminate against larger women. The myth was circulated by word of mouth. Even noted director Spike Lee regurgitated the lie in a 1992 interview in *Esquire*. "It definitely happened. Get the tape. Every Black woman in America needs to go to their closet, throw that shit out, and never buy another stitch of clothes from Liz Claiborne," he said. Despite being corrected by the interviewer that the rumor was indeed false, the director refused to back down.

On July 11, 2001, the Anti-Defamation League (ADL) investigated the rumor about Tommy Hilfiger and found that it began circulating the internet via email and then continued to be shared "by means of chat rooms, bulletin boards, faxes, emails, and word-of-mouth in the United States and elsewhere." The organization shared its findings in a letter to the designer and stated: "ADL has investigated the matter in response to the requests of constituents and other community members. We have concluded after careful investigation that the malicious rumors circulating about you and your company are without merit and lack any basis in fact."

In 2007, Oprah Winfrey invited the designer to join her on *The Oprah Winfrey Show* to set the record straight. The talk show host confirmed that it was his first time on her show. He revealed that his investigators, including FBI agents, traced the origins of the email to a college campus, but that was as much as they could uncover. Oprah admonished her viewers for believing everything they heard. "The next time somebody sends you an email or somebody mentions this rumor to you, you know what you're supposed to say to them?" she said. "You're supposed to say, 'That's a big fat lie.'" Tommy Hilfiger continued to address the allegations in interviews into the following decade. Eventually it fell out of the public conversation. But for those who heard the rumor without bothering to understand the full story behind it, they continued to believe the lie.

Tommy Hilfiger would withstand the storm and become one of the most successful American houses, even eclipsing some of its peers on that first billboard. Despite the success, the man behind the name was affected personally by being accused of cultural appropriation. "It hurt my integrity, because at the end of the day, that's all you have. And if people are going to challenge my honesty and my integrity and what I am as a person, it hurts more than anything else," he said. "Forget the money that it has cost me."

The reputation of the designer was paramount as an eponymous brand. Tommy Hilfiger was the face of his company, and anything that he did or said—or was alleged to have done—affected his business. In the same manner that it was difficult (and sometimes impossible) to separate a rapper's discography from their personal life, a designer and their clothing were one and the same. Designers in hip-hop had to negotiate their reputation and cultural responsibility and continually make sure that their message was clear.

Chapter Eight

DON'T KILL MY VIBE

O ver my dead body," said Quincy Jones. The founder of *Vibe* glared at the cover of the June/July 1994 issue. Madonna looked back, smugly pushing out and exaggerating her chest and torso. Her milky skin looked paler against her jet-black hair and hot-pink minidress. Was it *technically* long enough to be called a dress? NBA player Dennis Rodman stood behind her and pursed his lips, with one arm extended midair like a Renaissance marble sculpture by Michelangelo. She popularized "Vogue," but he was striking a pose. The two would have a brief but fiery fling, and this was the precursor, the foreplay. "Talking Trash: Madonna Interviews Dennis Rodman," read the headline. It was one of two salacious *Vibe* covers—the other had the singer and the Chicago Bulls star looking postcoital, with his belt undone and her mouth mid-moan—that the public was never supposed to see.

By the time he started *Vibe*, Jones was already an acclaimed multi-hyphenate, spanning music, film, and television. His discography as a performer/songwriter/composer/producer was expansive; Dizzy Gillespie, Frank Sinatra, Ella Fitzgerald, Michael Jackson. He was no stranger to hip-hop and was the mind behind recruiting Will Smith for the lead in *The Fresh Prince of Bel-Air* in 1990. But his 1989 album *Back on the Block*, which featured intergenerational contributions from rappers like Big Daddy Kane and Kool Mo Dee, inspired Jones to create a magazine for hip-hop. As he remembered in *Q: The Autobiography of Quincy Jones*, *Vibe* was intended to be an "urban *Rolling Stone* for the '90s" or *The Source* with an "expanded reach."

The idea for *Vibe* ended up in Time Ventures, an incubator for testing and launching new titles like *Parenting* and *Southern Living*. "As I remember, no one knew where to put it because Time, Inc. was very conservative. This idea of a hip-hop magazine was anything but," Carol Smith, SVP, Group Publishing Director at *ELLE* (who was at Time Ventures back then), explained to me. "When nobody knew where to put it, the launch ended up with us."

At this time, hip-hop magazines were incredibly important in connecting fans and culture. They were a portal into hip-hop's epicenter, New York City, and added depth to the music. Interviews brought artists to life and reporting provided analysis and insights not available elsewhere. Magazines were the monthly way to find out what the tastemakers were listening to, wearing, and thinking.

Jonathan Van Meter was an unlikely choice for the first editor in chief of *Vibe*. He was young—just twenty-eight years old—and a writer, not an editor. He was also white and openly gay. "It was weird. I had sort of been anointed suddenly out of nowhere and I had no idea why," he told me. "I didn't understand how unusual it was." Van Meter moved to New York City and was given plum assignments that journalists dreamed about in *Vogue*, the *New York Times Magazine*, and *Spy*. In 1992, he was approached by Time Inc.'s corporate editor, Gil Rogin, to create a test issue of *Vibe*. Executives believed that his background in fashion and lifestyle offered a unique perspective for a hip-hop publication. Van Meter laughed, recalling what one executive said in approval: "Jonathan Van Meter has the taste of an eighteen-year-old Black girl!"

It was a long interview process that involved flying to Bel-Air to meet with Quincy Jones at his home and many "alcohol-fueled dinners in SoHo." Rogin was convinced of his instincts, but looking back, Van Meter saw the irony. "I was able to explain to [Rogin] hip-hop and urban culture. The idea of a white gay man being the person that they chose is insane, right?!" Outside of the office, he lived a hip downtown lifestyle that was invaluable to a room full of suits. "I was also living a life of going out to clubs, steeped in music. Every part of my existence, except for my work, was about partying and going to nightclubs and concerts. They saw me as the perfect mix of somebody who had the 'right kind' of journalist chops and a deep understanding of some of the culture, not all of it. In today's climate, God, what a weird thing they did by hiring me."

He hired a small staff, which included recruiting other Black people from publishing, and produced the test issue—with a budget of $1 million—in about three or four months. Van Meter credited his then-boyfriend, creative director and stylist Stefan Campbell, for helping create a brand bible that focused on high fashion and diversity. "He, as a fashion person, started tearing any picture out of any magazine that featured a person of color. He created this book for me. Imagine if the demographics were reversed: 80 percent of all the ad pages were the one Calvin Klein ad or the one Ralph Lauren ad with the Black person in it. What if all of it was like that and 20 percent was white people? We presented that book to the higher-ups and said, 'This is what it should look like.'"

Campbell saw the vision of marrying hip-hop and fashion. "I put together all the things that were relevant to me, all things fashion, all things cool," he told me. "Music has always been the basis of anything involved in fashion for me. I told him the motto: 'Where music goes, fashion follows.' I saw myself as a fashion person loving hip-hop music but knowing that I wanted to show hip-hop culture from a different lens. Look what it *could be*." The aspirational ethos was what separated *Vibe* from other publications. The magazine wasn't intended to just feature the hottest artists or trends but it aimed to represent hip-hop culture as a whole and through the lens of prestige. This was the crème de la crème. Fans would pick up a copy of *Vibe* and get a taste of hip-hop at its finest. The paper felt sturdy, the photos were glossy and beautiful, and the writing was top-notch. What *Vogue* was to the fashion industry, *Vibe* would be to hip-hop.

In fall 1992, the issue hit newsstands and it was clear that *Vibe* was different from other hip-hop magazines. Treach of Naughty by Nature was the shirtless cover boy, shot by Albert Watson, and he looked like he was in a high fashion editorial. The muscular rapper was bathed in a shadow that made his dark skin glisten off the paper. *Vibe* had an eye for spotting talent. Treach pursued a modeling career afterward.

Inside, the magazine was diverse and covered different aspects of hip-hop: a feature on Bobby Brown, a photo essay on artists and tattoos, a small piece on supermodel Naomi Campbell, and an editorial about "white people who think they're Black." This was representation in a way that mainstream publications didn't understand. Hip-hop was an all-encompassing *lifestyle*. "The test issue sat on the newsstand for months. It was an enormous success," said Van Meter. He cited a 45 percent sell-through rate that surpassed the industry average of 40 percent.

"One of the questions was, will advertisers like Calvin Klein come into a magazine like this? And sure enough, yes," said Van Meter. Smith, who served as publisher, recalled Diesel and Absolut Vodka being on board. "It was pretty quickly an advertising success. It was pretty impressive who we were able to bring in. We had a nice roster of advertisers." The glossy had an appealing look and layout. Keith Clinkscales, president and CEO of *Vibe* from 1993 to 1999, explained to me: "There was fashion from the very beginning. They had fashion layouts targeted toward the audience. All of the fashion in there was not 'hip-hop fashion.' It was different ways of looking at how young people dressed." *Vibe* attracted hip-hop brands like FUBU, Avirex, and Enyce as well as luxury labels including Polo Ralph Lauren and Emporio Armani. Being able to balance high/low, streetwear, and luxury was a testament to the magazine's overall vision. The *Vibe* consumer mixed and matched their looks; they needed to transition from day to night, from the office to the club. The majority of their wardrobe was likely casual T-shirts and jeans, but they weren't afraid to splurge on a Polo shirt or Armani sweater.

Smith wrote a $10 million business plan, and the official launch was a go. "My pitch to them was, there is this incredible moment happening in music right now. Hip-hop gives you an opportunity for a multicultural magazine," said Van Meter. "All Black magazines are for Black people, no white people read them. *Essence* and *Jet* and *Ebony*, no white people read those magazines. There's a lot of Black people who read white magazines. Shouldn't there be a magazine that is sort of like *Vanity Fair* for a new generation?" Even the paper, which was originally large-format heavy-stock paper left over from *Life* magazine, felt different and elevated. *Vibe* was gorgeous, like a coffee table book that you would be proud to display. Explained Van Meter: "It should be beautiful to look at. The level of photography should be Condé Nast–level for people of color, who never get photographed properly. And it should include everything from disco culture to house music to hip-hop, world music, reggae. My concept was 70 percent hip-hop and R&B, and all of these other genres would be at the edges of it. You would get this amazing mix of what then was euphemistically called 'urban culture.'"

Quincy Jones mainly was laissez-faire in the editorial decisions, but his name provided resources and credibility. "We had deeper pockets than most, and we served up some of the best writing, photography, and design hip-hop has ever seen," said founding editor Rob Kenner. "Yet our multiracial staff and corporate connects were always viewed with some suspicion. We had to earn respect by doing great work." *Vibe* hired bright, young, and diverse talent and gave them a platform for real journalism: long-form and thought-provoking pieces. Its early masthead of editors and writers, such as Danyel Smith, Kevin Powell, Alan Light, Joan Morgan, Emil Wilbekin, and Mimi Valdés, made their impact in the media for decades to come.

The first issue of *Vibe* debuted, with Snoop Dogg on the cover, in September 1993. It was perfect timing. Snoop was the fresh face of West Coast rap as Dr. Dre's protégé and his highly anticipated debut, *Doggystyle*, was to be released a month later. Shot in black-and-white, the young rapper was in a close-up portrait, peering to the side. "The way Snoop is photographed is cleaner, simpler, and less cluttered," said Van Meter. "The design of the magazine was very clean and simple. Let's get the photography to be absolutely stunning. Black faces beautifully shot." The aesthetic was more elevated than that of the other 'zines on the newsstand. "It just emanated class. It was just another level that had not been approached in hip-hop before," said Clinkscales. "It was a brand-new look. It looked like a cross between a Condé Nast publication and if designers had taken over *Rolling Stone*." In comparison, *Rolling Stone* shot a stereotypical "gangsta rap" cover the same month, with Snoop and Dre. Both wore ordinary clothes—the rapper in a flannel and the producer in a black baseball cap—and grimaced into the lens.

Behind the scenes, several people were responsible for shaping the *Vibe* look. George Pitts, photo director from 1993 to 2004, and founding art director Gary Koepke oversaw the clean design and aesthetic. The publication hired several photographers who would ultimately work at the highest levels of high fashion, including David LaChapelle, Ellen von Unwerth, and Mario Testino.

Vibe covers didn't reflect pop culture; they *defined* it. The most memorable covers created commentary around an artist. Tupac Shakur was the crazy genius in a straitjacket in February 1994. TLC appeared as firefighters after Lisa "Left Eye" Lopes committed arson in November 1994. Hip-hop royalty The Notorious B.I.G. and Faith Evans shared their love story in October 1995. What *Vibe* published incited conversation and even controversy. The most polarizing cover spotlighted the rivalry between Tupac Shakur and The Notorious B.I.G. They were once friends, but a litany of conflicts—including Tupac being shot at Quad Studios in 1994 (and blaming Biggie); tension between their respective label heads, Sean "Puffy" Combs and Marion "Suge" Knight; and Tupac's allegation that he slept with Faith Evans—created a bitter back-and-forth. In February 1996, *Vibe* ran "Live from Death Row" with Tupac, Suge, Snoop, and Dre. In September 1996, it was "East vs. West—Biggie and Puffy Break Their Silence." Tupac was murdered in Las Vegas in September 1996, and Biggie was gunned down in Los Angeles in March 1997. The timing left many wondering if *Vibe* was responsible for instigating what happened, but on the other side, the magazine was doing what it was supposed to—cover all facets of hip-hop.

Quincy Jones realized the significance of his covers—it was the first thing people saw in the crowded newsstand—and one misstep could denigrate the brand. The cover with Madonna and Dennis Rodman was pulled before it went to print. "Quincy Jones saw the cover and it was the first time he objected to something I wanted to do," said Van Meter. He said that Jones didn't give him any rationale for pulling it. Perhaps the optics of the hypersexualized white singer, who had a history of sampling music and looks from Black culture, didn't work for a hip-hop publication. Maybe Jones just didn't think Madonna was relevant among *Vibe*'s readership. Van Meter pointed to the idea of the interracial couple as being too controversial. "He couldn't give me a solid answer. There was something about a white woman and a Black man on the cover," Van Meter mused.

Some of the other staff damn near staged a mutiny over the Madonna cover. "We all wanted Eddie [Murphy] over Madonna, so we were upset about it too," said Mimi Valdés, who rose from the ranks of assistant editor in 1993 to editor in chief in 2004. "When [word of the cover choice] started to get out in the industry, we all felt the need to save *Vibe*'s reputation." In his autobiography, Jones refuted that interracial relations were the cause of controversy, pointing to his history in that arena. At this time, genre nomenclature was far more rigid; "urban" was code word for "Black," and there was a limit to risk-taking for a neophyte publication. "It wasn't about Madonna or Dennis: it was about our not having been around long enough to establish a personality as an urban magazine," Jones said. "Because it makes it look as though we're pandering, that we're not sure *Vibe* can be a Black magazine and make it.'"

There were casualties from deciding to kill the cover. Jonathan Van Meter stepped down from *Vibe* after the corporate power play. "I had moved heaven and earth to get Madonna on the cover. That was the moment when I realized what was up and what side the bread was buttered on." He laughed. "That's the moment when I realized that I was not the editor in chief of my own magazine." Madonna wasn't happy either. "See you around, pal," she said. And according to Jones, "Unfortunately, I don't think we've spoken since." At least Madonna and Rodman got *something* out of it. "They fucked that very night," Van Meter revealed. "They met at that photoshoot."

———

Hip-hop purists who wanted something less flashy and more gritty turned to *The Source*. The magazine was known as the hip-hop bible and the publication for true rap fans. Like many successful start-up companies, *The Source* began on the campus of Harvard University. In 1988, roommates David Mays and Jonathan Shecter launched a newsletter—the precursor to the magazine—around their campus radio show *Street Beat*. "I'm talking to hip-hop fans and they all want to know information. 'When's that new EPMD single coming? Who's featured on that new Big Daddy Kane album?' I'm like, there's no information. Let me take this information and share it with my audience," said Mays (then known as "Go-Go Dave").

The newsletter filled a void of journalism in hip-hop. Titles like *Right On!*, *Black Beat*, *Word Up!*, and *Rap Masters* existed, but the content (cute fonts, pull-out posters, crossword puzzles) didn't satiate discerning hip-hop heads. "It was as cheesy as it gets," said Shecter. "That was fine, people wanted that, but there was nobody writing about the music in an intelligent way, with a critical voice. My inspiration at the time was *Rolling Stone*, *Spin*, and the *Village Voice*. I wanted to be like that."

The first few issues of *The Source* were sparse—just a few pages—and free. Eventually, Mays and Shecter expanded the issue and began selling them in independent record stores around the country. Said Mays: "A few years in, we're in over a thousand mom-and-pop record stores in the country. That's where people went to find out about what was going on."

The newsletter evolved into a magazine as Ed Young, who had publishing experience, and James Bernard, a Harvard Law student, came on as founders. "It was a fairly fast but gradual process," said Mays. "The last few issues I did while still at Harvard were probably thirty, forty pages. We added a glossy cover. The inside pages were black-and-white. It was looking more like a magazine. It was being sold all over the country." With graduation and impending adult expenses on the horizon, Mays secured $75,000 in capital by selling yearly ads up front to record labels like Tommy Boy Records and Columbia Records. "*The Source* had become such a valuable outlet for the labels. They didn't have anywhere else to promote their stuff." The team moved to New York City and bought a small office space and expanded the editorial purview to become "the magazine of hip-hop music, culture, and politics." According to *Advertising Age*, *The Source* had a circulation of forty thousand and generated nearly a million dollars in total revenue ($2,000 to $3,000 per page of ad revenue) in 1991.

The Source became the authority on rap. The publication's Unsigned Hype column spotlighted the hottest emcees just below the radar. DMX and The Notorious B.I.G. were early artists who rose from obscurity in January 1991 and March 1992 respectively. In "Juicy," Biggie name-checked the milestone of being published in these pages and how his mom "*smiles every time my face is up in* The Source." The "Record Report" section, home to the five-mic review, could make or break an album. What Siskel and Ebert's thumbs were to movies or Michelin stars were to restaurants, *The Source* mics were to hip-hop. Few albums had received the rarified five mics in the early '90s: Nas's *Illmatic*, A Tribe Called Quest's *The Low End Theory*, Ice Cube's *AmeriKKKa's Most Wanted*, De La Soul's *De La Soul Is Dead*, to name a few. The reviews, which were conferred upon by the editorial staff or "Mind Squad," were always hotly debated in barbershops and the hip-hop industry alike.

In the annals of hip-hop, *The Source* was rarely mentioned in the context of fashion, but its contributions, especially by Black women from inside the pages, were essential. Julia Chance, the magazine's first fashion editor from 1990 to 1994, remembered having to convince the powers that be to feature style in the publication. "Let me tell you, they were not interested," she told me. "Also, fashion was something gay. It's sad, but that was the attitude. Like, *'We're not doing that gay shit.'*" Chance had a different perspective. At twenty-seven, she was older than the founders. She went to Hampton University, a historically Black college, and moved to New York City with aspirations of being a stylist. She was smart, introspective, and outspoken. "I was raised in a Black consciousness household. We always questioned representation and why certain people got to be featured in things." It's no surprise that there were cultural differences behind the scenes. "I remember Dave Mays telling me—you know, Jewish boy from Washington, DC—who okay, you know, he was into rap and before that, he was into go-go. I get it. He might have even said, 'MFers don't care about fashion. They just want a sweatshirt, a pair of jeans, and a fresh pair of sneakers or Timbs. I just looked at him and smiled because you might be around Black people, but you don't get it. What might look like just a pair of sneakers, sweatshirt or whatever to you, do you know how much thought is put into that?"

Hip-hop fashion was not relegated to one look. Yes, there were artists and fans who loved their casual jeans and sneakers, but style was more nuanced. In 1989, Slick Rick was featured on the cover of *The*

Source looking positively dapper in a suit-and-tie combo, complete with pocket square and glasses. Rick had a cosmopolitan finesse and personified how dynamic hip-hop style was. He was West Indian and lived in Britain before moving to the Bronx as a preteen and described his style to me as "ghetto gentlemen swag. A lil' yardie, a lil' Mitcham Surrey blended together." The rapper was known for wearing an eye patch, gaudy baubles, and huge medallions with Brooks Brothers suits and Benetton sweaters. "Britain represented that preppy Catholic school look, like the school-uniform-style gentleman's coat and suits along with the soft shoes. It was cold in England, so our wardrobe represented that environment. We had a high society way of dressing all year round," he said. "I had a London accent; I was half-blind and dressed proper. I drank tea, ate liver, listened to the Beatles and Dionne Warwick. When I migrated to New York, what a difference. There were hot dogs and pizza and music like James Brown. Kids wore sneakers and jeans. For me it was like coming from one world to another. I had to get used to my neighborhood and my neighborhood had to get used to me." Rick leaned into brands less common stateside, like Bally sneakers (from Switzerland) and Clarks Wallabee shoes (from the United Kingdom). He popularized the comfortable and versatile moccasin-like shoes that fell somewhere between dress and casual footwear, with future generations like The Notorious B.I.G. and Ghostface Killah, who would call himself the "Wallabee Kingpin."

In the beginning, there were maybe one or two pages allocated to the style section. Julia Chance bootstrapped the shoots with whatever she had, including pulling resources from her other job as assistant fashion editor at the industry trade *SportStyle*. "Everything was guerilla style. There was no budget for fashion. I just had to make it happen. We couldn't afford to hire models." They outsourced this job to rappers who often had strong opinions on what they would and would not wear—Lauryn Hill refused to wear a skirt in a 1994 shoot with the Fugees—and also scouted regular kids from the streets. Tyson

Beckford was one of those discovered in the pages of *The Source*. Chance remembered the future supermodel being quiet during their first shoot. "When he got in front of the camera, he just came alive. I remember saying [to him], 'Have you ever thought about modeling?'"

Chance leaned on her intern Sonya Magett, who first came in as a hip-hop dancer for a photoshoot, to translate the nuances of hip-hop fashion (i.e., regional differences, subgenres) that only a cultural expositor could explain. "She was a native New Yorker and she knew the streets. She was able to help me hone my eye for borough-to-borough differences or even, you know, there's a certain way the Native Tongues dressed. There's a certain way Run-D.M.C. dressed." In 1992, Magett was the perfect combination of high fashion and hip-hop. She grew up in the clubs and skating parties in Brooklyn and saw how city kids donned outdoor wear like Helly Hansen and Timberland. She knew about the Lo Life movement while simultaneously plastering her walls with images of supermodels. "I basically went to her, 'There's so much stuff that's going on. I have so much knowledge about high fashion and other brands that you guys are not featuring,'" Magett explained to me.

Hip-hop brands like Cross Colours and Karl Kani were on board from the onset and Nike and Reebok booked their first ads in the publication in 1993. Sportswear was the primary focus of the photoshoots—hockey jerseys, baseball jerseys—along with baggy jeans, but the goal was adding chic to the streets. In one shoot, Magett put the female models in tennis skirts. She recalled, "I would always take what was big on the streets and elevate it. To make it more crisp and clear." The budget was tight. "We didn't have a messenger service. I physically picked up the clothing that we would feature on the artists. The company just wasn't there from a business perspective. At a later time, when advertising dollars started to come in—because fashion stories generated advertising dollars—that made them justify the spend." Chance leveraged her valuable trade connections to expand the racks. "I was able to pull for *SportStyle* and say, 'Hey you know, I'm also the fashion editor of a hip-hop magazine,' and I could get things that way."

A hip-hop magazine came with certain stereotypes that extended into the fashion section. "No one ever verbally said outright the obvious," said Magett. "We should approach the designers that the kids are wearing in the streets. Here's an opportunity to educate them on their presence in what they used to call the 'urban market.'" That erudition didn't always translate. "I was pulling Timberland things for *SportStyle* and I would ask them for things for *The Source*," said Chance. "They would send always the most basic thing. It's not that they didn't send me things to shoot. They didn't send me the same caliber or variety that they would send to *SportStyle*."

Timberland, the outdoor company that specialized in rugged waterproof boots, was contending with a new demographic of Black and brown consumers co-opting its brand. "Timberland is wrestling with a sort of, uh, concrete success it has never sought," wrote Michel Marriott in the *New York Times* Style section on November 7, 1993. "In distinct contrast to the company's primary multimillion-dollar market, which buys to the call of the wild—or at least dreams of it—is a newer clientele, one that is plunking down considerable cash to the wildly infectious beat of hip-hop music reverberating from the inner-city canyons of New York, Chicago, Detroit, and beyond."

Heritage workwear and outdoor brands like Timberland, Carhartt Inc., and North Face straddled the fence, not wanting to alienate their core white consumers while quietly enjoying newfound minority money. Jeffrey Swartz, the executive vice president and grandson of the founder of Timberland, described its main consumers as "honest working people." And despite showing record profits, he said: "If you hear that hip-hop kids are wearing Timberland boots and women are wearing Timberland boots with sundresses at a Donna Karan fashion show, that's coin in current dollars. But how in the world is that sustainable?" Brands wanted to enjoy the spoils of this new audience without having to explain them to core consumers who might be offended by assimilation. "The youth market came after us," said Jason Russell, the director of marketing for 104-year-old work-wear company Carhartt. "Fine, they like to wear what we make. But we will never go after that market aggressively . . . we would be walking away from our roots."

The funny part was, these were not prestige brands. They were sold by hunting, fishing, and big-box retailers. The target demographic was white men with construction and factory jobs who subscribed to *Field and Stream*. The brands should have capitalized on the opportunity to align with something as fashionable as hip-hop and, not to mention, the buying power of young people with disposable income. The argument that they wanted to focus on blue-collar consumers was baseless. In fact, in 1985, Timberland tried to appeal to white high-end consumers by taking out ads in the *New Yorker* and selling at Saks Fifth Avenue and Bloomingdale's. The six-inch Timberland wheat Nubuck leather boots (the hip-hop staple) paired well with everything: denim, athletic wear, sweats, skirts, jerseys. Men and women loved them. The boots were just as functional in cold winters in the concrete jungle as in the heartland—and way more stylish.

The dog whistle was loud and clear. Despite touting American values, these brands didn't see value in Black and brown bodies. "I think that they think that if their clothes are celebrated in the Black, urban community, with all its ills, that it will cheapen their brand names," Chance lambasted in the *New York Times*. "I see the stuff on the runways, and I know they are inspired by Black folk, and now some of these companies are saying our dollars don't count."

"This was my opinion. I wasn't saying boycott Timberland," Chance said to me. "We can be just as brand loyal and we are worthy of building brand loyalty with. If it's a good brand, we can be just as brand loyal as anybody." The boots never wavered in popularity. In fact, earlier that year, Timberland launched a public service campaign called "Give Racism the Boot" (that *The Source* had provided free advertisement for), and LL Cool J proudly wore a shirt emblazoned with the slogan.

Chapter Nine

GHETTO FABULOUS

ghet·to-fab·u·lous

adjective **INFORMAL**

adjective: **ghetto-fabulous**

denoting or exemplifying an ostentatious or flamboyant
lifestyle or style of clothing of a type associated with the
hip-hop subculture.

"ghetto-fabulous rappers"

This dude's gonna be a problem," Andre Harrell considered as
he peered through his tortoiseshell frames. Heavy D wanted
him to meet a young hotshot—wearing a white oxford shirt
and polka-dot tie—who wanted this job at Uptown Records.
"This is a really hardworking guy, Dre. You should give him a shot,"
Heavy said. The "Now That We Found Love" rapper never introduced
anybody to the music executive, so this endorsement meant something.
Harrell hired Sean "Puffy" Combs as his intern in 1990. The first
test: *Go pick up tapes from Unique Recording Studios*. The studio was
some ten blocks away and with the snarling traffic and the unwieldy
crowds of Times Square, it would take a good half hour to make the
trip there and back. Harrell figured he had some time to make a call,
but before he could put the receiver down, the kid was back. "How
did you get there so fast?!" Harrell asked, incredulous and impressed.

Puffy, with his tie flailing behind him, said matter-of-factly: "I ran there and I ran back."

Andre Harrell founded Uptown Records in 1986 with a grand vision: "My goal is to bring real Black America—just as it is, not watered down—to people everywhere through music, through films, through everything we do." Even though he grew up in humble surroundings in the Bronxdale housing project, he always felt destined for a life of luxury. "I grew up thinking wonderful things could happen," he said in 1993. "I always believed I'd have a wonderful life." He formed the rap group Dr. Jeckyll and Mr. Hyde with high school classmate Alonzo Brown, and in 1985, they released *Champagne of Rap*. The album embodied their cork-popping dreams and the rappers, looking more mature and sophisticated than their twenty-five years, wore suits and ties as their peers rocked Lee jeans and Adidas tracksuits. "I think it's something that Andre embellished on because our family *dressed*," his second cousin O'Neal McKnight told me. "He was just a walking image of regal and royal Black excellence. He was a well-dressed, outspoken, tailored man." As a rapper, Harrell traveled abroad and became exposed to the cosmopolitan aesthetic and culture of places like Italy, London, and Paris at a young age. "He was doing all these different things. Going international and traveling. He was on the road and he was getting a chance to see those different things."

Despite being from the Bronx, Harrell set his creative compass six hundred miles away toward Motown Records in Detroit. He was enamored by the hit factory that Barry Gordy had built in the 1960s—arguably, the most famous Black record label in the world—with superstars like Diana Ross, the Jackson 5, Smokey Robinson, and Marvin Gaye. Motown artists had a distinctive sound—Gordy dubbed it "the sound of young America"—and a highly curated image that he controlled. The presentation was paramount; the artists had perfectly coiffed hair and wore tailored suits, tuxedos, and formal dresses. They underwent mandatory etiquette coaching. Gordy was painstaking in his desire that his roster be clean-cut and polished so that Black and white audiences alike enjoyed the music.

Harrell brought this same discernment to Uptown Records. "Motown is the first thing that ever taught you about the ghetto as fabulous," he explained. After the New Jack Swing era of the 1980s, which featured zoot suits, silk shirts, and choreographed dancing, the label needed something that spoke to the nascent hip-hop generation.

Harrell remembered coining the phrase "ghetto fabulous" in 1992—based upon lingo he picked up in Harlem when he was a rapper—and his new signee, Mary J. Blige, embodied this confluence of chic and street. Blige signed to Uptown Records in 1988, and her visage was not that of a typical female R&B singer. She was a tomboy, a tough girl from Yonkers. "I was sitting on the shelf because they didn't know what to do with me, because I was not going to put on a gown," she said.

But Puffy saw the vision for what her career could be. Puffy was a Howard University student, dancer, and party promoter who loved the aspirational culture of the label. "It was the champagne lifestyle where you was getting money, you were conscious of what you were wearing, you liked dressing up," said Puffy. "You were thinking upwardly mobile." He quickly became the prized protégé, and his dynamic with Harrell was one of little brother and big brother, prince and king. There was natural synergy; the seasoned executive gleaned valuable insights from his young intern, especially in the fashion department, by seeing Puffy wearing two earrings (which he had "never seen anybody do") or pairing combat boots with a dress jacket. "I knew it was the right move to utilize my fashion sensibilities," explained Puffy. But Harrell served as a buffer between Puffy and the higher-ups at the parent company who had their own definition of corporate propriety. "At that time, those white executives didn't want to see a nigga like Puff Daddy walking in the office," mused McKnight. "They wanted to see Andre. Andre got on a suit. He got on a blazer. He got on glasses. And they were like, 'If we gonna listen to anybody, we're gonna listen to him.'"

Puffy immediately took to Blige and the raw visceral emotion that dripped from her husky voice. She represented girls from the block. By 1991, he was promoted to A&R and unequivocally declared Blige the "queen of hip-hop/soul"—which in hindsight was a rather gutsy label to give a new artist. He was so confident that he leaned into that title sonically and aesthetically for her 1992 debut *What's the 411?* Puffy and his then-girlfriend, stylist Misa Hylton, pulled overall style inspiration for the ingénue from hip-hop (oversized jerseys, backward baseball caps, and menswear) and accented it with feminine luxury (Armani suits, furs, and gold hoop earrings). In her breakout music video for "Real Love," Blige wore a glammed-up, sporty look—white bustier, backward baseball cap, and trousers with an oversized blazer—that balanced the edginess that Puffy envisioned with the classic aesthetic of a soul singer. For 1994's "I'm Goin' Down," she was the forlorn siren in a full-length black fur duster and matching lipstick that offset her honey-blond bob. Blige was sexy, honest, and relatable. "Growing up around drug dealers and the women that I hung out with, they wore furs—long sables and silver foxes—and red lipstick. They were just fly. Men wore them, but when you saw a woman show up in one, you knew who she was," she said. "Ghetto fabulous is just, when you come from the hood, you at your flyest. What can you afford? What can you do with it?"

Ghetto fabulous meant looking good, not in spite of being from the hood but because of it. A variation on high/low fashion, it stripped the word "ghetto" of any pejorative meaning and reappropriated it as something positive. "Fifty percent of fabulous is attitude. You still gotta be who you are," Harrell explained. "I've acquired it."

On a daily basis, Harrell exuded a dapper style. A typical day's look would be a charcoal Armani suit with an Ermenegildo Zegna shirt accented by Robert Marc glasses, Tiffany & Co. sterling cuff links, and Ralph Lauren suede shoes. He was one of the first hip-hop executives, along with Def Jam Records founder Russell Simmons, who lived a true mogul lifestyle. "Russell and Andre were the only two niggas in New

York that had Bentleys," remembered McKnight. "Andre had a black Bentley. Russell had a green one. And people didn't even know what kind of car it was. They was like, What, what kind of shit is this? Like some presidential shit." These men moved about in spaces predominantly inhabited by wealthy white music executives, like Saint Barthélemy, Ibiza, and the Hamptons, the ritzy seaside enclave for celebrities and summering New Yorkers, nearly a decade before other rap neighbors moved in.

An important aspect of ghetto fabulous that differentiated it from simply wearing luxury was understanding adversity; knowing what it was like to start from the bottom. The credibility component was paramount. As fashion critic Robin Givhan noted in the *New York Times*: "But just slipping into designer duds does not make one ghetto fabulous. The clothes must be accompanied by an 'I'm-gettin'-paid' attitude. One must have arrived at an impressive level of wealth and prestige, but memories of the old neighborhood and the old struggles must linger vividly." It was not about fetishizing struggle, although that would inevitably happen as outsiders distorted the lifestyle into a trend. "Middle-class girls can't be ghetto-fabulous," explained Harrell. "They step straight to fabulous. If a middle-class girl gets long, frosty black nails, she's pushing it. She's doing something not natural."

Initially, getting past gatekeepers at fashion labels and publicity houses to gain access to clothes—referred to as "pulling"—was difficult in an industry based on relationships and quid pro quo. "For me, pulling clothes was almost nonexistent in the beginning," Misa Hylton told me, about finding clothing for photoshoots, music videos, and other appearances. "Early on we had many strikes against us, as far as being African American, young, and unknown. There weren't many doors that were open. Luxury designers weren't willing to create relationships with me." Hylton often resorted to creating custom looks for Mary J. Blige and other artists like The Notorious B.I.G. and bad-boy group Jodeci. "I decided to design and create garments that I wanted, and that I knew my clients would love." Because there was no blueprint, they created one in real time. "We would just brainstorm and think about ideas. What would look hot. Things that we liked. It was really organic because we were paving the way," Hylton said.

Ghetto fabulous would become synonymous with hip-hop luxury throughout the decade. It was the hood meets high fashion. When urban and urbane collided. As Givhan explained in 1999: "Ghetto fabulous now refers to a style that merges ethnic eccentricities with runway chic. It is inner-city attitude mixed with Milanese glamour. Chanel meets Kangol. Thugs in platinum and diamond rings sipping Cristal champagne. Three-inch-long fingernails painted to match the latest offerings from Dolce & Gabbana." Harrell may have lit the match, but Puffy threw gasoline on it and spread the lifestyle worldwide. The plucky intern would metamorphize into hip-hop's greatest showman—rap's P. T. Barnum—and spearhead an era of unprecedented decadence and luxury. What the originator started, the protégé would take to the next level.

———————

The same thing that made Sean "Puffy" Combs an asset at Uptown Records would ultimately get him fired. His ego was growing and nobody at the company could check it. "My full-time job became managing Puff," said Andre Harrell. The two got into arguments and had very different opinions on how to solve their conflictions. "Puffy wanted me to fight every second of the day. But what he didn't realize is that you have to pick your battles," remembered Harrell. The young executive admitted that he would cross the line, throw his weight around, and even insult his boss. "Dre created a monster. The whole company hated me—I was aggressive. I would trash the office. I'd call Andre a wimp and a house n*****." The final straw occurred when Uptown Records' parent company MCA Records wanted to shelve The Notorious B.I.G.'s album, a rapper Puffy had signed, because of the explicit subject matter.

"They wanted me to tell him he had to change his tone," Harrell said. "I knew it wasn't gonna work." Harrell fired his protégé and implored him to seek greener pastures. Despite his hubris, the termination hit Puffy hard. "It was like leaving home. I ended up on the stoop of his brownstone that night, crying my eyes out. I wish that I'd never left." Andre continued to be a mentor—he kept Puffy on payroll until his next gig—and advised him to get a deal with Clive Davis and Arista Records, which he did in 1993. "I told [Puffy], 'I'm really letting you go so you can get rich,'" Andre said.

"Puffy Takes Paris" was shot by veteran photographer Annie Leibovitz for the October 1999 issue of *Vogue*. The editorial followed Puffy and supermodel Kate Moss traipsing through the City of Light in a smorgasbord of excess: hounded by paparazzi; posing alongside designers Karl Lagerfeld and John Galliano, creative director at Dior at the time; dancing in a sexy orgy of models; and striking a contemplative pose on the Pont Alexandre III bridge over the Seine River.

In one image, Puffy sat shirtless in black leather pants with a diamond crucifix laid askew on his chest. He wasn't paying attention to one of the world's most famous women a few feet away—instead completely enthralled by a scene from *Scarface* playing on a flat-screen TV. Kate Moss peered at the distracted rapper as tendrils of smoke circled from her cigarette into the atmosphere. Her waifish frame, only five foot seven and the emblem of the emaciated "heroin chic" era, peeked through a translucent beaded gown. "The energy felt like *Guess Who's Coming to Dinner* with Sidney Poitier," reflected Puffy years later. The reference to the landmark romantic comedy about the mores and taboos of interracial relationships in America was a deliberate analogy. "Just seeing Kate Moss with a Black man on a bridge and watching *Scarface* in a hotel room—the provocativeness of it. That was crazy and before its time." Said Puffy: "Coming from Harlem, your style is everything;

you can't compromise on your style. It was unapologetically Black and unapologetically hip-hop in *Vogue*."

Sean "Puffy" Combs was born on November 4, 1969, into Harlem street style. He earned his childhood nickname from a friend due to his propensity for losing his temper and "huffing and puffing." It would be a personality trait that would follow him throughout his life—sometimes an asset, other times a hindrance—and earn him a professional reputation as somebody not to be crossed. As he embarked on his rap career later, he would assume several other monikers, including Puff Daddy and P. Diddy. His father, Melvin, an associate of famed drug dealer Frank Lucas, was murdered in connection to his heroin dealings when his son was only three years old. "I don't have a lot of memories of my father. They say you can't miss something you never had," said Puffy. "My father was a hustler. He was a drug dealer. I learned early in life that there's only two ways out: dead or in jail. Maybe that [made me] work even harder." His mother, Janice, moved the family to Mount Vernon. She didn't speak about Melvin's demise (she told her son that he was killed in a car crash) and worked multiple jobs to provide the family with suburban comforts, like a swimming pool. "I wasn't going to be homeless," she said to the *New York Times*. "I wasn't going to be on welfare, if I had to work all day and all night. Never, never."

Melvin and Janice were a striking pair in their youth. In one photo of the couple, he's in a suit and tie and she's in dazzling drop earrings and a sultry front-tie ensemble, holding a baby Puffy. Grandmother Jessie Smalls was a homegrown fashion maven who designed clothing for her daughter, like a coat cut and sewn out of a repurposed brocaded slipcover. Janice would later become a hip-hop industry fixture of her own—known affectionately as "Mama Combs"—and become recognized for her signature platinum-blond locks and lavish wardrobe of spiked-heel ankle boots, furs, and diamonds. As a child, Puffy modeled in *Essence*. And by fourteen, he was wearing a suit and tie every day as a student at Mount St. Michael Academy in the Bronx.

Longtime stylist Groovey Lew met Puffy at the age of fourteen at the Modernistic barbershop in Mount Vernon. "We used to just all hang out in front of the barbershops," he said. "All the barbers used to dress in the top suits and *GQ* clothing and ties and have the freshest haircuts and manicures and shoes." They were raised during that pivotal time as hip-hop was emerging. "We were born in the '70s. And so all that good energy of the Black power movement and style and the afros was everything. Learning through the elders and you know, being raised by the community. Having block parties. Music was a part of our everything. Whether you played instruments in school or just being at family functions or talent shows. All that was a part of our growing up."

Puffy and Lew ran with a group of guys, the Seven Up Crew, and made trips into New York City to go to concerts, block parties, and the famed Roof Top Roller Skating and Disco in Harlem. Despite his later sartorial braggadocio, Lew said that his friend wasn't a style icon initially. "He was just regular. He's just basic. But we didn't, we didn't look at each other for that. It was more about your spirit and your energy. We didn't look to each other for clothes, but we know who was fresh and who had what." As they got older, dressing became essential. They headed to stores in SoHo on Wooster or Prince Street to find luxury items like WilliWear and "thousand-dollar blazers." "As teenagers, we knew what was cracking early. That was a part of our whole energy running around just looking for different stuff." They recognized the necessity of generating discretionary income independent of their parents. From the age of twelve, Puffy amassed multiple paper routes and created a lucrative cottage industry. Said Lew: "If you want beautiful things, you must work for them. So we knew that."

Puffy attended Howard University in Washington, DC, for two years before dropping out to pursue a career in the music business. He was fired from Uptown Records in 1993 and founded Bad Boy Records the same year. The Notorious B.I.G. was the marquee artist, but the label would discover a formidable roster of hip-hop, R&B, and pop artists, including Craig Mack, Faith Evans, Ma$e, 112, Black Rob, The Lox, Shyne, and Danity Kane.

Most record labels outsourced creative decisions to specific departments, like music to the A&Rs (artists and repertoire) or wardrobe to stylists, but Puffy was hands-on with his artists (micromanaging them, some would argue) in sonic and aesthetic direction. He was a multihyphenate: he was the executive, the producer, the hype man, the wardrobe stylist, the guest feature, and the creative director. On The Notorious B.I.G.'s 1994 debut, *Ready to Die*, Puffy was credited as executive producer but he also appeared on several tracks talking and/or ad-libbing (he was not a rapper yet), and he co-starred in music videos for the album's hits, "Juicy" and "Big Poppa."

Biggie and Puffy were inseparable as music collaborators and best friends. They often wore coordinated ensembles: Biggie in a black blazer accented with gold buttons and Puffy in a black fur at the Billboard Music Awards in 1995, Biggie in a black silk suit and Puffy in a contrasting white one (both accessorized with Jesus piece pendants) at the Soul Train Music Awards in 1997, and both in flowing Versace silk shirts in the music video for "Hypnotize" in 1997.

As a man of considerable size, it was hard for Biggie to find designer clothing that fit his 6'2" and 395-pound frame. "'I wanna dress like a skinny nigga. I wanna dress like you!'" Puffy remembered the rapper complaining when he couldn't buy off the rack. Offerings for the "big & tall" gentleman were often unflattering, in dark colors, boxy, and devoid of style. Certainly no high-end European designers were making clothing with this demographic in mind. Biggie turned to Hylton as well as specialty tailors 5001 Flavors (run by husband-and-wife duo Guy Sr. Wood and Sharene Wood) to create a size-inclusive but still aspirational wardrobe. Biggie's look elevated from guy-next-door (colorful COOGI sweaters and Kangol hats) to kingpin (Versace sunglasses and silk shirts, tailored suits, and Homburg hats). He evolved, as he put it, from "ashy to classy." He knew that he wasn't empirically attractive, but Biggie brought a playful energy and irresistible charisma—as proven by the roster of famous women vying for his attention—that complemented his God-given gift for rap. "I know I ain't no pretty nigga," he said. "But I got a little, a little style to me. I don't know what it is. I just think I'm cool to be with." Singer Faith Evans was immediately enamored after meeting him and they were married just months later. "He was playing on all that," she said, and did her impersonation of him: "Like so what? I'm fat. I'm extra dark. And I got a cock-eye. But guess what? You're gonna love me."

Puffy envisioned Biggie as a sex symbol and made sure he had the record to prove it. Producer Poke of the Trackmasters remembered Puffy telling him, "'We need a sexy record. My fat dude is sexy. He ugly and sexy.' We're like, 'Really?'" That song ended up being 1995's "One More Chance/Stay with Me (Remix)." The hip-hop and R&B hybrid sampled DeBarge's "Stay with Me" and featured Biggie rapping about being both a player as well as a tender lover.

The Notorious B.I.G., along with his predecessor Heavy D, redefined plus-size menswear in hip-hop. Big Poppa and the Overweight Lover looked sharp and dressed like their "straight size" peers. In the future, artists like Big Pun, Rick Ross, and Fat Joe benefited from this paradigm shift and were seen as fashion plates wearing exuberant colors, patterns, and tailored silhouettes. Decades later, Italian house Dolce & Gabbana made a bold step into size inclusivity with a capsule collection of Miami-meets-Mediterranean ready-to-wear with artist/producer DJ Khaled that went up to an Italian size 60 (or XXXL in U.S. sizing).

1997 was a turning point for Puffy. Biggie lost his life in a drive-by shooting in Los Angeles after attending a party for *Vibe* on March 9, 1997. This came just months after Tupac Shakur had died from a drive-by shooting in Las Vegas. Authorities could never conclusively connect these tragedies, but they would forever be correlated to the East Coast–West Coast rap beef. Losing these icons cast a dark cloud over hip-hop. Puffy had lost his best friend, his headliner, and his musical inspiration.

Biggie had been encouraging him to become a rapper and wanted to manage him for his debut, *Hell Up in Harlem* (later renamed *No Way Out*). But Puffy, like the Lazarus piece he wore around his neck, rose from tragedy. He emerged as Puff Daddy the superstar.

In May 1997, he released "I'll Be Missing You" with Faith Evans and 112 as a dirge for The Notorious B.I.G. Critics called the track, sampling the Police's 1983 hit song "Every Breath You Take," a "maudlin 'tribute'" and "somewhat turgid," yet it spent eleven weeks atop the Billboard Hot 100, reached number one in fifteen other countries, and won the Grammy Award for Best Rap Performance by a Duo or Group.

No Way Out sold over seven million copies in the United States alone and marked the era of Puff Daddy. He was the ringmaster overseeing the greatest party. It didn't matter that he wasn't a trained musician or rapper in the pure sense. "Don't worry if I write rhymes, I write checks!" he bragged. In August 1997, Puffy appeared on the cover of *Rolling Stone* in full ghetto fabulous regalia: he was shirtless, wearing a brown fur coat, Chicago White Sox baseball cap, and Versace boxers (an ode to the recently slain designer Gianni Versace). A placeholder tattoo of "B.I.G." was inked onto his chest. He replaced his mourning attire with shiny suits, which he and Ma$e debuted in the music video for "Mo Money Mo Problems" in 1997. Stylist and costume designer June Ambrose, who once interned at Uptown Records, pulled inspiration from her Caribbean heritage and the bright colors of Carnival when creating the red leather metallic suits. "That was one way of me incorporating happiness, spirit, fire, and a jubilation that was so out of this world," she said.

Bad Boy was the label of celebration. Their upbeat soundtrack— produced by in-house team the Hitmen—featured catchy hooks and infectious samples. A-listers like Mariah Carey, Jay-Z, Busta Rhymes, and Foxy Brown clamored for the sound and the opportunity to get a hit from Puff. And everything was packaged in glossy big-budget music videos that aired nonstop on MTV, BET, and VH1 from directors like

Hype Williams and Paul Hunter. The eight-minute-long visual for 1998's "Victory," which featured Puffy in a dark dystopian thriller, featured cameos from A-list actors Dennis Hopper and Danny DeVito and cost upward of $2.7 million, making it one of the most expensive music videos of all time.

This next generation of ghetto fabulous was also referred to as hip-hop's "jiggy" era. Decadence was hip-hop's escapism from trauma and loss. Puffy was the young mogul, juggling multiple cell phones and yacht hopping from Paris Fashion Week to the Oscars. He dated beautiful women like longtime love Kim Porter and English model Emma Hemming and was rumored to be with countless more. His relationship with actress turned singer Jennifer Lopez from 1999 to 2001 made him a tabloid mainstay and household name. The two were fashion soul mates, always causing a commotion. Puffy predicted that Lopez's plunging, nearly naked green Versace silk chiffon dress would mark her coming out as a fashionista. "We were just stepping up our game as far as what we were wearing and how we were gonna use fashion," he told *Entertainment Tonight*. "I thought it was gonna really change the game as far as for her and fashion."

It was such a game changer that the dress became known simply as "The Dress." Google invented the Image Search function because everybody wanted to see photos of it. "After all, people wanted more than just text," wrote former Google CEO Eric Schmidt. "This first became apparent after the 2000 Grammy Awards, where Jennifer Lopez wore a green dress that, well, caught the world's attention. At the time, it was the most popular search query we had ever seen. But we had no surefire way of getting users exactly what they wanted: *JLo wearing that dress*. Google Image Search was born."

Puffy loved throwing lavish parties as the "modern-day Gatsby," punctuated by his annual white party in East Hampton beginning in 1998, which was full circle for the intern who had made fun of Andre Harrell for hanging in that tony scene. At the exclusive July Fourth soiree, bold-faced names from hip-hop, fashion, and culture commin-gled. Young and old. Black and white. New money and old money together. "I remember the first party he threw in the Hamptons," so-cialite Paris Hilton said to the *Hollywood Reporter*. "It was iconic, and everyone was there." *New York Post*'s Page Six and the *New York Daily News*' Gatecrasher gushed over the details: who was there, who came with whom, and who wasn't invited. It wasn't uncommon to find Puffy sip-ping Cristal straight from the bottle while Leonardo DiCaprio watched, women in bikinis on swings, and an original copy of the Declaration of Independence on display (borrowed from TV producer Norman Lear). The dress code was strict—head-to-toe in white—and everyone put their spin on it: Paris Hilton in a fit-and-flare sundress and diamond necklace, Jay-Z in a striped button-down shirt and white shorts, Salman Rushdie in a loose-fitting button-down shirt, Ashton Kutcher in Alain Mikli sunglasses (aka the shutter shades popularized by Kanye West), Mary J. Blige accessorizing in Gucci, and Al Sharpton in shiny white pants. According to rumors, anyone in beige or black shoes was turned away. "Having an entire party all dressed in white was a stunning sight," remembered Martha Stewart, a guest at the first party. "And it helps that Diddy looked very handsome in white."

As rappers kicked it with the rich and famous, hip-hop purists were worried about the ramifications. Hip-hop was mainstream and by the aughts, the majority of the audience was white teenage boys. Now that the voice for the voiceless was speaking to the suburbs, was this selling out? In his book *Somebody Scream!: Rap Music's Rise to Prominence in the Aftershock of Black Power*, author Marcus Reeves noted the "hyper-materialistic theme of ghetto fabulousness" was detrimental to the craft and the culture. "With a reduced concern for shouting down (or at least giving a cursory mention to) social justice, the primary focus of rap stars was reciting a laundry list of possessions (*my* car, *my* jewels,

my clothes, *my* women, and most important, nigga, *my* money)," wrote
Reeves, who was the deputy music editor of *The Source* from 1998 to
1999, ". . . valuing mindless, catchy, simplistic rap styles over prodigious
(or even semi-prodigious) rhyme skills in order to consistently sell hip-
hop music to a mass audience . . ." Ghetto fabulous had crossover
appeal—a term in the music industry that referred to reaching broader
white audiences—because it was catchy, feel-good, and fun. Therefore
these types of rappers were getting signed, developed, and promoted
by record companies.

Backpack rap was the response of artists rejecting the "money,
hoes, and clothes" rap. The slang term for underground or alternative
rap conjured up images of rap fans who walked around with backpacks. In New York City, the etymology was associated with the popular
JanSport backpacks. Backpack rappers saw themselves as true emcees,
authentic lyricists who valued the art of the rhyming over strictly the
financial returns. Backpackers were the descendants of a long history
of conscious and Afrocentric rap from artists like Public Enemy and the
Native Tongues. The music, which drew inspiration from jazz, blues,
and soul, prioritized lyricism, cultural pride, and social responsibility,
and was an alternative to the gangsta rap and ghetto fabulousness that
dominated the airwaves. Backpack rappers were intellectuals and nerds,
not gangsters, hustlers, or moguls. They valued austerity when it came
to their aesthetic and dressed in accessible attire like T-shirts, hoodies,
and knit caps.

In 1996, the Roots released "What They Do" as a warning against the
current rap trends. *"The principles of true hip-hop have been forsaken / It's
all contractual and about money-makin','"* rapped Black Thought. *"Exact
replication and false representation."* In the music video, the Philadelphia
group created a "Rap Video Manual" and poked fun at commercial rap
tropes and the veneer of keeping up appearances: luxury cars (leased
by the mile), mansions (rented for the day), and scantily clad video
vixens (hired to look like they cared). "We couldn't compete with the

then-over-bloated two-million-dollar budgets, so it was more like the indifference," the group's drummer, Ahmir "Questlove" Thompson, said to me. "We simply didn't care. We were a motley, unsexy-looking bunch in the era of Hype Williams and Matthew Rolston making these epic clips." Questlove never thought that the video would offend anybody because of the group's low profile. "I know it's hard to believe, but back then, my self-esteem was so low I never watched our videos 'cause I just hated the way we (I) looked. So I'd just approve and shrug, 'cause *ain't nobody gonna see this shit anyway*." But they were on the radar of Bad Boy Records' biggest artist. "It wasn't until a mutual friend of Big's let me know he didn't like it and took it personal. That's when I was like 'oh shit.'"

Indie label Rawkus Recordings and the Lyricist Lounge popularized key figures of the underground sound like Talib Kweli, Mos Def, and Pharoahe Monch, who explained to me the delicate balance conscious rappers had to strike in looking good while staying authentic. "It's a line that you had to learn back then. At the core of being an artist is how you dress to represent what your music sounds like, you know, outside of the fuckery," he said. "Back then, that was something that I guess more serious artists described themselves." After breaking out as a solo artist in 1999 with the high-impact "Simon Says," his biggest hit to date, Pharoahe Monch witnessed the influx of resources and expectations around success in the stripped-down genre. "It all switched. I had a publicist. A stylist. The people who I was working with at the time would make sure that if I had three photoshoots that day, that I wasn't wearing the same thing."

The nomenclature of backpack rap carried a negative connotation, and some rappers would shun the label despite having success. Many dismissed the music as boring, preachy, and simply not commercially viable. It was technical "rappity rap" for a narrow audience of self-righteous guys who hung out in cyphers and argued on the Okayplayer message boards that launched in 1999. Selwyn Seyfu Hinds remembered how controversial it was to put Black Thought, Mos Def, and Pharoahe Monch on one cover of *The Source* in November 1999. "I fought like hell for that cover," the former editor in chief told me. Backpackers weren't sexy or aspirational. Their music videos weren't being played 24/7. Would an average reader even know who was on the cover? "Where do we plant our flag? What are we aspiring to and why are we aspiring to it? Who's hip-hop?" he wondered. "That was the question for a good couple of years, that particular aspect of what is underground or what is not underground."

Q-Tip was the other cover that month, and his styling—exposed chest, come-hither look, glistening skin—matched his professional move from A Tribe Called Quest to "Vivrant Thing" leading man. Albeit subtle, Q-Tip and the shiny-suit maven shared an underpinning. "Q-Tip's articulation doesn't necessarily look like Puffy's. Right? But it's still rooted in the same place," said Hinds. "It's rooted in: We are bigger, bolder, and brighter. We wanna reach further and higher and faster."

Ghetto fabulous and backpack rap were very different presentations of hip-hop, but they shared the same ambition, the pursuit of excellence. For commercial artists like Puffy, that meant opulence and propagating conventional trappings of wealth. The underground vied for artistic mastery and respect—and the commercial success aligned with that. And a select group of artists, like Q-Tip, could successfully straddle both worlds. Hip-hop was not a monolith. As time went on, there would be more subgenres, regions, and emerging scenes that would continually expand what hip-hop was and what it could be.

Chapter Ten

LADIES FIRST

n Greek mythology, Medusa was the original femme fatale, with hair made up of venomous snakes. Those who gazed into her eyes were petrified into stone for eternity. The seductive image of Medusa fascinated Gianni Versace as a kid playing in the ancient ruins of his hometown, Reggio Calabria, a region of Italy with breathtaking seaside vistas and verdant green mountains, once known as Magna Graecia or Greater Greece. Gianni brought the apotropaic symbol—deadly but protective to its wearer—to his eponymous house in 1993. "When I asked Gianni why he chose Medusa's head," his sister Donatella Versace explained, "he told me he thought that whoever falls in love with Medusa can't flee from her."

Founded in 1978 in Milan, Versace championed femininity with exuberant and sexy designs incorporating Baroque motifs, colorful prints, and daring bodycon silhouettes. Inspired by art and pop culture, the designer pushed the limits of convention and propriety with cutouts of skin; dresses held together with safety pins; and the use of chain mail, leather straps, and metal. "I think it's the responsibility of a designer to try to break rules and barriers," the designer once said, according to the *New York Times*. "I'm a little like Marco Polo, going around and mixing cultures."

Gianni loved to surround himself with celebrities both in his professional and personal life. He kept a cadre of supermodel muses and encouraged them to bring their personalities to the runway, which helped launch some into stars beyond fashion. "Before [Gianni], I don't think many designers let models have personality," said his sister Donatella, whom he hired as head designer in 1994. "The models should wear the clothes, be very serious, not smile, look in front of you, almost no soul. This was totally opposite: it was about the girls, what the girls were thinking, who they were dating. It wasn't just about the clothes, but about who was wearing the clothes." Versace's Fall 1991 runway finale featured the elite class: Naomi Campbell, Cindy Crawford, Christy Turlington, and Linda Evangelista lip-synching to George Michael's "Freedom! '90." Unlike other brands, the designer embraced celebrities from all genres—high- and lowbrow—and even those embroiled in controversy, like Madonna, Prince, Princess Diana, and Mike Tyson, had a place at his table. "He was the first to realize the value of the celebrity in the front row, and the value of the supermodel, and put fashion on an international media platform," said Anna Wintour, longtime friend and editor in chief of *Vogue*. "He relished media attention and masterminded it, and everybody followed in his footsteps."

On July 15, 1997, Gianni was gunned down outside his Miami mansion by serial killer Andrew Cunanan. There were conflicting reports as to whether the two men had known each other or the designer had been targeted at random. No motive was proven and news outlets reported various theories about Cunanan being obsessed with Gianni and wanting his fame and success. The designer left 50 percent of his company to his eleven-year-old niece, Allegra, who was too young to lead at the time. Donatella took over as artistic director of Versace in a haze of grief while battling cocaine addiction. She was catapulted into a role she never wanted—stepping into the footsteps of her famous brother. Overnight, she was the face of a brand valued at $807 million with 130 stores worldwide. Her imposter syndrome manifested itself in a recurring nightmare: "In my dream, Gianni . . . yells at me, saying, 'Donatella, what are these ugly clothes? That's supposed to be Versace? How could you have forgotten everything I taught you?' Then he knocks the clothes racks over."

Donatella could never be Gianni, but she could be a more fabulous version of herself. Versace was selling fantasy and that started with her. "I was the new face of Versace. Who buys fashion from a weak, unstable designer who's out of her mind because she takes drugs and therefore can't stand herself? Nobody! So I created a second Donatella: cold and aloof, aggressive and scary," she said. She branded herself as the boss bombshell with long bleach-blond hair, heavy eyeliner, and a deep tan. She looked like a woman on perpetual vacation, sipping Campari in Capri or yachting in Sardinia, but still in charge. She spoke her mind in a muddled and extravagant accent that she became known for. When asked about comfort in fashion, she was blasé: "What is comfortable fashion? To be comfortable, that can't be in the vocabulary of fashion. If you want to be comfortable, stay home in your pajamas." And she was fiercely independent as a woman and single mother running a company. "Why do women need men nowadays? Certainly not to prove strength, determination, and independence anymore. Men are needed only for love affairs and for physical relaxation."

Donatella Versace would continue her brother's legacy and become a fashion icon in her own right. As the face of the house, she accomplished what few designers could, by being as famous as the names she dressed. She appeared in photoshoots, graced global magazine covers—*Vogue, GQ, MFF, Attitude*—and was even satirized on *Saturday Night Live*. And the next generation of the family dynasty brought with it a new rap muse.

———————

Lil' Kim's *Hard Core* album—two million copies sold worldwide—was a fun, raunchy romp distilled into one famous image: the diminutive rapper wearing a leopard-print bikini and a fur-lined robe and squatting with both legs opened. Plastered around New York City, the soft-core promo had pedestrians doing double takes. In 1996, the image incited parental debates over whether the rapper was destroying the moral fabric of the country. The TV show *Rolanda*, hosted by Rolanda Watts, aired an episode titled "Is Lil' Kim sexualizing our children?" "The poster is vulgar and I think it misrepresents Black women," said a young woman on the daytime show. "She made people feel like that's all we about. That's all women are about. Showing our body," said another.

Behind the salacious visual and lyrics about diamonds, stilettos, and fellatio, Kimberly Jones was a young woman trying to exert her power in a man's world. "Lil' Kim is what I use to get money," she explained of her stage persona to the *Washington Post*, "a character I use to sell my records." The rapper was born in Bedford-Stuyvesant, Brooklyn, on July 11, 1974. Following her parents' divorce, she moved to an all-white neighborhood in New Rochelle, New York, where she was teased and bullied for not looking like everyone else. Eventually, she returned to Brooklyn to live with her volatile father, whom she described as violent and verbally abusive. One incident in particular was the turning point in how she would frame her self-image in adulthood: He called her a "bitch" and "whore" for liking a boy when she was thirteen. "If he hadn't said what he said to me, I probably would have stayed a virgin until I was twenty-one. But after that I rebelled." By fourteen, Kim left the house and men became her lifeline as a means of survival and self-worth.

At seventeen, she met The Notorious B.I.G. while rapping in their neighborhood. "As far as the neighborhood, they thought it was fly. They thought it was hot!" she remembered of her verse. He became her great love and masterminded her career. He coached her on the mechanics of rap, teaching her about how to control her flow and cadence, and encouraged her to use a softer, more feminine voice. He selected the photo that solidified Kim as rap's sex kitten. "He threw the negatives on the table and pointed to the one with my legs open and said, 'That's the one right there,'" she said to XXL. Kim was the standout member of Junior M.A.F.I.A., a collective of local rappers mentored by Biggie, and exuded a natural star quality in the group of guys. She dropped song-stealing verses on "Get Money" and "Player's Anthem" that displayed a razor-sharp delivery and risqué bars, like pulling out a gun on her cheating lover (while wearing Armani suits and Chanel lime boots). Many rap fans believed that Biggie wrote her rhymes—they were shocked that a girl could go so hard—but Kim refuted those claims and pointed to several hits created on her own after The Notorious B.I.G. was killed in 1997.

Kim harnessed the power of her image despite ongoing criticism that she was too raunchy. "What makes me any different from a model?" she asked on BET Talk with Tavis Smiley. "What makes me any different from Madonna?" Despite this outward confidence, the rapper internally suffered from body image issues and the pressure to live up to Anglocentric beauty standards. "I have low self-esteem and I always have," she told Newsweek. "Guys always cheated on me with women who were European-looking. You know, the long-hair type. Really beautiful women that left me thinking, 'How I can I compete with that?' Being a regular Black girl wasn't good enough." Many speculated that Biggie's relationships with singer Faith Evans (whom he cheated on with Kim) and rapper Charli Baltimore, both fair-complexioned and blond, compounded this insecurity. Despite naturally striking eyes, full lips, and a heart-shaped face accented by a beauty mark, she embarked on a long transformation into what appeared to be a living Barbie doll. She was one of the first hip-hop artists to allegedly undergo multiple plastic surgery procedures, including breast implants and liposuction.

Lil' Kim's willingness to be a shape-shifter made her an exciting fashion muse. She had close relationships with designers and called Donatella Versace, Marc Jacobs, and Alexander McQueen her personal friends. "Donatella is my girl. We've loved each other from the moment we first saw each other," said Kim. The pair were seen schmoozing as early as the Versace "Versus" fashion show in March 1998. The next year, Kim was the first rapper at the Met Gala as a guest of Versace, and only Kim and Sean "Puffy" Combs, who attended with girlfriend Jennifer Lopez, represented hip-hop on the red carpet. Kim's interpretation of the "Rock Style" theme was a ghetto-fabulous homage to hot pink: a bespoke mink coat over a studded bra and hot pants. She accented the look with a two-toned pink ombre wig and snakeskin boots. It was a bold choice among the boring gowns and demure looks on the red carpet. *Vogue* lauded the outfit, stating that "it helped to kickstart the trend for fearless and body-conscious style on the Met Gala red carpet."

Lil' Kim and her rap contemporaries in the late '90s and early aughts—Foxy Brown, Eve, Trina, Charli Baltimore, Vita, Amil—rejected the gender norms of their predecessors. Many women in hip-hop in the '80s and early '90s assumed the clothing of men—baggy jeans, loose shirts, and menswear—as a way to fit in, protect themselves from sexual harassment and unwanted advancements, and to garner respect. MC Lyte released the first solo album by a female rapper titled *Lyte as a Rock* in 1988. On the album artwork, Lyte was fully covered in a sweatsuit and hanging with the guys while a woman in a miniskirt and red heels was shunned to the side. Lyte was the serious rapper, not to be confused with some random groupie. Queen Latifah wore African outfits befitting her regal name, like headdresses, Africa medallions, and dashikis. "By wearing African clothes, African accessories, not only am I supporting my African brothers and sisters who have these businesses, but it brings me closer to my ancestors," she said in 1989. "I just feel inner power. Fashion is power, y'all!"

But to Kim's generation, rap credibility didn't require stripping away or downplaying femininity. Women leaned in to their beauty and leveraged the male gaze. Musically, they were sex-positive trailblazers who rejected the standard Madonna-Whore Dichotomy, where women were either chaste and "good" or promiscuous and "bad." If men could rap about "bitches and hos," they could rap about their sexuality. Furthermore, these artists saw how seduction could be an asset: Lil' Kim's "How Many Licks?" was an anthem for cunnilingus. Foxy Brown titled her debut album *Ill Na Na*, which was also a slang term for her sexual prowess. Trina called herself "da baddest bitch." And Amil warned men in "Can I Get A . . ." that she stayed in "the Gucci name" and she wouldn't entertain any man who couldn't afford her. Female rappers garnered female fan bases who finally felt that they were being represented. They also appealed to men who tuned in because these artists looked hot—and ended up staying because the music was too.

David LaChapelle turned Lil' Kim into the epitome of sex and luxury. In 1999, the fashion photographer known for his colorful, exaggerated pop art lens shot the rapper completely naked—save for Louis Vuitton logos airbrushed on her skin—for the cover of *Interview* magazine. "When I did that image, it was about the skin as a luxury item," said LaChapelle. The next year, he shot Kim and Donatella Versace along with Missy Elliott and Rose McGowan for *Interview*. The photos displayed how comfortable and happy Kim and the designer were with each other. They were nearly identical, with long, flat-ironed blond hair, perky noses, and fox eyes. In one look, Kim held a glass of champagne in one hand, and her other rested on the designer's chest. The two seemed to be in their own little world.

Kim and Donatella had more in common than being famous platinum blondes who loved fashion. Their origins were worlds apart, but both came from humble beginnings and understood what it was like to be self-made. They were strong women in male-dominated professions. And most of all, they shared the connection as survivors who had to carry on the larger-than-life legacy of the men they lost.

In a career of memorable looks, Lil' Kim's most famous was when she arrived at the 1999 MTV Video Music Awards (VMAs) in a lavender sequined jumpsuit with her left breast fully exposed except for a strategically placed pastie that kept censors from having a total meltdown. This was still basic cable. Missy Elliott helped conceive the idea when she jokingly told stylist Misa Hylton: "If I was Kim I would always just have one titty out and be like, fuck it." Elliott was a fashion rebel herself after she put on an inflatable plastic bag suit in her music video for "The Rain (Supa Dupa Fly)" in 1997. "I loved the idea of feeling like a hip-hop Michelin woman. I knew I could have on a blow-up suit and still have people talking. It was bold and different," Elliott said years later. The look by June Ambrose challenged the paradigm of female body positivity in rap, decades before the term was popularized.

For Kim's VMAs look, Hylton used Indian bridal fabric—what could originally be for a lehenga or saree accented with traditional sparkles and shimmery appliqués resembling a peacock's plumage—to create the fitted one-piece suit. The front of the suit featured an asymmetrical scalloped collar and flared sleeve and the look was finished with a matching purple wig, a diamond ring, and mauve lipstick. But of course, no one could pay attention to anything but Kim's exposed breast. Even Diana Ross grabbed and jiggled it onstage—five years before Janet Jackson's infamous Super Bowl "wardrobe malfunction"—and put Lil' Kim in the pop culture hall of fame. Kim laughed at what became colloquially known as "the boob incident." "I think it was more of a friendly, 'Oh my God! You look sexy, girl, but do you know you have a boob hanging out?'"

Lil' Kim was hip-hop's premier fashion influencer and that's who Kimora Lee Simmons enlisted to help launch Baby Phat. In 1999, Kimora started her brand with bedazzled logo T-shirts that she gave to Kim and supermodels Naomi Campbell and Christy Turlington to wear. Baby Phat was originally supposed to be a spin-off of Phat Farm, Russell Simmons' line of T-shirts, argyle sweaters, polos, and knits founded in 1992, but in women's sizes. "I would never wear this," Kimora said, looking at a shirt. The former supermodel, who was eighteen years younger than her husband, wanted something more appealing than the uninspired blueprint. "I didn't want to wear a football jersey from a man. That was not what I wanted in the sense that it was like your boyfriend's clothes, like his jerseys," she said.

Kimora had an instinct for clothing. She had been walking European runways since the age of thirteen. She knew about fit, cut, and fabric, and understood a woman's body. She came on as head designer of Baby Phat and created a line with herself as the underserved demographic in mind. "I was paying homage to the feminine form, body, and shape, and the references that I was using, the materials, the finishings, the metals and so on and so forth." She wanted her consumers, young women of color like her, to feel sexy and confident. Baby Phat's "baby tee" was a fitted T-shirt that hugged the shape of its wearer with the brand's diamanté feline logo. Baby Phat jeans were the other tentpole of the brand, with stretchy fabric accentuating the derrière—a decade before it was mainstream—instead of flattening it like most other denim lines. "I had the best jeans in the world," Kimora bragged.

Kimora's life as a hip-hop socialite, which she described as a "never-ending whirlwind," was ingrained into the DNA of Baby Phat. As the only Black and Asian woman heading a luxury fashion line, she bottled and sold the essence of "fabulosity" (also the title of her empowerment book). The *New York Times* described her as "a flamboyant ex-model with the proud carriage of a Masai warrior and the flirtatious charm of a geisha" (a regrettable reference). She could be seen dealmaking on her pink Baby Phat–bejeweled Motorola flip phone. She also opened up her personal life, something most designers kept private, and made it part of her brand. Baby Phat ads starred Kimora and adorable daughters Ming Lee and Aoki in various fantastical but intimate setups. They could be seen playing in their expansive mansion while a maid watched on or jumping into a Rolls-Royce for afternoon tennis. Kimora represented a lifestyle and made fans feel like they were a part of it.

Baby Phat was on trend with the Y2K fashion of the aughts (low-rise jeans, baby tees, bedazzled logos, velour, and bare midriffs). The brand was visibly more inclusive than its contemporaries Juicy Couture, True Religion, and Ed Hardy, which served a very specific rail-thin white archetype. Not everyone looked like the It girls in *Teen Vogue* or *Laguna Beach*, like Paris Hilton, Britney Spears, or Lindsay Lohan. In contrast, Kimora had gorgeous multiethnic features, shiny hair, and feminine curves. As an Indian teenager in the Midwest who didn't look like anybody else—and was always called "exotic"—Kimora represented everything that I wanted to be.

"I want to be a role model before being a fashion model," Kimora said. She was an early proponent of inclusivity by hiring diverse models and executives, vendors and partners. Diversity was present in every Baby Phat fashion show during New York Fashion Week both on and off the runway. In 2000, Lil' Kim walked the lingerie show in a sheer bikini—with the cat logo naughtily placed over her bottom half—under a fur coat and diamond crucifix chain. For the 2003 show, supermodels Carmen Kass and Eva Herzigová wore big hoop earrings and even bigger hair as they modeled denim bustiers, shiny lamé capris, and wraparound tops that let more than one nip slip through. It was a celebrity scene and the paparazzi were there to capture it. Celebrities flocked to the front row. "It's stylish. It's sexy. I think that's what's hot about it," said Aaliyah. "I'm here to support Kimora . . . and to see some pretty women," added Roc-A-Fella Records founder Dame Dash. Rapper Cam'ron told me that he debuted his outrageous baby-pink fur jacket and hat at the 2003 show specifically hoping that the Page Six gossip column would run him in their celebrity sightings the next day. And they did.

In 2004, Russell Simmons sold his fashion portfolio, which included Baby Phat, to the clothing producer Kellwood for $140 million. Kimora remained on as "principal creative arbiter" and eventually became president of Baby Phat in 2006. She took a page from hip-hop's multihyphenate playbook and became one of the few supermodels turned fashion moguls.

Chapter Eleven

THUG LIFE ALTA MODA

t was over fifteen years since David McLean photographed Tupac Shakur walking down the Via Gesù in Milan. He still remembered the otherworldly energy emanating from him. "Some people just have an aura," he said. "They stand out from the crowd." The rapper wore a leather vest that accentuated his tattooed biceps and accessorized with a gold watch, likely a Rolex. He stared pensively at the ground. "Tupac was very sexy, very attractive: he was wearing this fierce Versace waistcoat with his tattoos and beautiful eyelashes. That's what the aura was. I ran after him, and I got three shots."

Tupac Shakur was often believed to be prescient, and he embraced this with his Makaveli alias, a nod to Italian philosopher Niccolò di Bernardo dei Machiavelli. But it was Versace who saw the future. Designer Gianni Versace personally invited Tupac to be in the Fall/Winter menswear show in 1996 and perform his hit "California Love" just months before the rapper's death. Tupac, in a gold velvet suit, and girlfriend Kidada Jones, in a gauzy pink slip dress, were flanked by two beefy bodyguards as they made their way down the runway. From his walk, he seemed nervous, or at the very least self-conscious, as he intermittently looked down at his feet.

Hip-hop was still relatively new in Italy. "I was one of the only kids in Italy that was listening to hip-hop music. I was getting clothes and music from my friends who were getting the opportunity to go to New York and buy them," remembered Riccardo Tisci, who designed for Givenchy and Burberry. "It was not yet popular in Europe."

As seen during the 1991 shows, some designers exploited hip-hop as aesthetic inspiration, but few were interested in including—and compensating—the artists behind it. "Nobody in fashion was working with Black artists then," said Donatella Versace. "Nobody was working with rappers. It was not inclusive at all." Versace went beyond cultural fetishism by forging genuine relationships and long-term goodwill.

Gianni and Tupac shared a kindred connection. Both men were brilliant artists and iconoclasts. There's some fashion lore that Gianni called Tupac "the most beautiful man in the world." And each battled adversity in his own way. Gianni publicly came out in 1995 when homo-sexuality was still taboo, and Tupac was outspoken about his experiences with racism. Frank Alexander, Tupac's bodyguard who walked in the show, was surprised to learn that Gianni's life had been threatened and that the family needed heavy security (even more than the rapper). "It gave me an eerie feeling because they seemed like such kind people," he remembered in *Got Your Back: Protecting Tupac in the World of Gangsta Rap.*

"I always loved rap music," Donatella said. "And I always thought that community was so important. That culture was important. That pain that the culture was going through, because they were not accepted." The men's struggles were parallel but their interactions weren't without uneasiness, especially with hip-hop's narrow views of masculinity at the time. While they were in Milan rehearsing before the show, Alexander felt awkwardness—and implicit homophobia whether he realized it or not—by Gianni's physical affection: "He walked to our table and gave each of us a kiss and a hug. He gave Pac one of those European kisses. He went along about it, but I could tell he wasn't thrilled with it. I was quick to stick my hand out, because I don't play that shit. Not even with Versace."

Vibe magazine was instrumental in bringing Tupac to Milan. "We put him in the show," said Keith Clinkscales, president and CEO of *Vibe* at that time. The publication took the rapper as its ambassador to sit in the front row and walk the menswear shows. According to Karla Radford, *Vibe*'s executive director of Events & Artist Relations, Tupac was hesitant to participate in the Versace show and needed help understanding the gravity of the opportunity. "Tupac had never been out of the country before . . . He had to get a passport," she said. "I had to work this magic in order for him to say yes and get on a flight, fly across the country . . . That was a tough sell . . . He's like, 'Why am I doing this?'"

Stateside, the rapper was flourishing into a bona fide star. His unique vantage point in both music and film made him appealing to the glitterati. He transcended genres. In 1994, he was spotted hanging out with his girlfriend at the time, Madonna, and screen siren Raquel Welch at a celebratory dinner for Gianni Versace. With charisma, sex appeal, and famous people enamored by him, Tupac was poised to be an icon.

———————

Lesane Parish Crooks was born on June 16, 1971, in New York City. And at the age of one, his mother, Afeni, a Black Panther, renamed him after Peruvian fighter Túpac Amaru II and stepfather Mutulu Shakur, a prominent Black nationalist. "I wanted him to have the name of revolutionary, Indigenous people in the world. I wanted him to know he was part of a world culture and not just from a neighborhood," she said. At thirteen years old he moved to Baltimore and developed a love for Shakespeare and acting at the Baltimore School for the Arts. "The empathy, the mimetic instinct, the emotional connection, the vulnerability. He had all of that," remembered his theater teacher to the *Baltimore Sun*. As a teenager wearing ripped jeans and Africa medallions, he relocated to Marin City in 1988 and connected with Digital Underground as a roadie, background dancer, and rapper on the group's "Same Song." Tupac the solo artist was passionate about social and political issues and rapped on themes of family, community, and legacy. "Brenda's Got a Baby," from his 1991 solo debut 2*Pacalypse Now*, tackled teen pregnancy with the nuance of a poet. He could be both sensitive and an outlaw. He was one of the faces of gangsta rap—symbolized by a "Thug Life" tattoo across his torso—and signed to controversial label Death Row Records. Tupac loved being in controversy and relished in the East Coast–West Coast rivalry with The Notorious B.I.G.

Milan was a different world, and transformative for the twenty-five-year-old. "His eyes opened to a world he had never seen before," said Radford. "He was enlightened in a way that totally took him by surprise. The way the Italians loved him, knew him. I think that was a fear too . . . He didn't know who was listening to him . . . He didn't know how his energy had preceded him . . . Every fashion show they wanted Tupac to sit front row and dress in their garments . . . The men and women loved his eyelashes. It was him." He went to Gianni Versace's castle and couldn't believe he was being gifted thousand-dollar pants and shirts. He attended several fashion shows—including Romeo Gigli, Fendi, Valentino—and got starstruck at seeing supermodel Naomi Campbell in the flesh. He saw Tyson Beckford backstage. He partied and did Ecstasy. He was enraptured by the beautiful women, groupies, half-dressed models, regular women on the street. Despite being in a relationship with Kidada Jones, the rapper was acting like a kid in a candy store. "You couldn't help but notice how beautiful the women were in Italy. Not just the supermodels, but the Italian women," said Alexander. "Pac loved them, and the one thing he kept pointing out was their eyes . . . They came in colors [he'd] never seen before, and combined with their skin tone, so many of them were drop-dead gorgeous." Pac was floating, ready to move immediately. "This shit is cool. I could do this all day long."

West Coast rappers wanted success in the bastions of hip-hop, which was dominated by New York City, but they wanted it on their own terms. One way in which West Coast rappers differentiated themselves was by wearing regional fashion. Legendary group N.W.A. dressed like regular guys from Compton in Raiders gear, Air Force 1s, baseball caps, and jackets. They were the everyman, while New York City peers like Eric B. and Rakim were wearing large gold rope chains and intricate Dapper Dan jackets that cost thousands of dollars. Gang culture was prevalent in the West and permeated the style with colors representing specific sets, bandanas, Dickies, or khaki shorts. Even the use of black letter typeface—which would later be appropriated by brands like Vetements and Gucci with the rise of streetwear—came from gangs. The phenomenon of wearing loose and sagging pants—that sit below the waist or butt—was also attributed to gangs (and prison, where wearing belts was prohibited). Police officer Victor Vinson warned parents in 1988 that sagging pants indicated gang affiliation. "Kids today are dressing for death," he said to the *Los Angeles Times*.

The significant population of Mexican Americans (or Chicanos) added a unique cross-cultural dimension in shaping the look of West Coast artists. The "Cholo look" reflected the tastes and socioeconomic status of the descendants of immigrants. It was affordable and included staples like plain white T-shirts, flannels, chinos, and workwear. "The brown people were generally the poor people. We shopped for clothes at Kmart once a year and made that shit last as long as we could," explained Fresno-born designer Willy Chavarria, senior vice president of Design at Calvin Klein. "We treated our $12.00 Dickies chinos like Givenchy and pressed them and tailored them and hung them with routine precision. A pressed white T-shirt, oversized khaki chinos, a black belt, and shiny black shoes . . . I mean it doesn't get any more chic than that."

Because of the year-round good weather, shoppers went to flea markets or swap meets like the massive Rose Bowl Flea Market or Del Amo Swap Meet. Rapper Crooked I, a native of Long Beach, explained to me how these markets attracted all spenders. "It was about what level of money and what was your taste. Some big ballers never came out of the swap meet," he said. "It's like, 'Yo, I go to the swap meet. I don't care how much money I make. I got a Bentley parked outside but I have on a white T-shirt, LA Dodgers hat. Some Dickies and my favorite pair of sneakers: Converse Chuck Taylor All-Star, K-Swiss, Nike Cortez.' You would see these ballers wearing these items and you would want to get them yourself."

Crooked I remembered the one-stop shopping appeal of the swap meet: "Swap meets is where you would go to get Dickies work pants, the shorts. You would get the white T-shirts. Pro Club T-shirts. You could get clothes. They had jewelry pieces," he said. The West Coast had its more affordable version of Dapper Dan's customization, like overlaying a pair of sneakers in the logos of luxury houses (e.g., the Nike swoosh replaced by Gucci print or Adidas's three stripes covered with the Louis Vuitton monogram). This was both a form of affordable luxury and tribalism. "You could put your street name on the side of your hat. Your neighborhood. That was an advertisement to let everybody know where you were from."

One of the most famous pieces of luxury that originated on the West Coast and spread nationally was the eight-ball jacket. In 1990, San Francisco designer Michael Hoban created the jacket with a cue ball on the back after being inspired by the size numbers on the heels of bowling shoes. He sold the jackets at North Beach Leathers. Its associations with winning and cocaine ("eight ball" was slang for an eighth of an ounce) and high price tag of $775 made it a coveted item for drug dealers, athletes like Darryl Strawberry and Bobby Bonilla, and the hip-hop generation. "It had a connotation in the dope world . . . cocaine. But that was not my intention," Hoban said. The jackets spread to New York City and

Dapper Dan created his upscale version for $1,200. "As fast as you could make them, you could sell them," he said to the *New York Times*. "I had a version for workers and a version for bosses."

Pimp culture also influenced West Coast fashion, and pioneers like Too $hort and Ice-T valued being well-groomed in hats and tailored suits. "I used to get my hair done. I had a perm, and my nails manicured," Ice-T told *Esquire*. Snoop Doggy Dogg (who would later go by Snoop Dogg) lauded pimps for influencing his look. "The game is this, though: a real pimp focuses [on making] sure he's manicured, he's pedicured, his hair is done, his face is right, his outfit is cold, his car look good, got a pocket full of money, conversation strong, smell good. These are pimp traits and characteristics that have been hard for me to relinquish," he said. The rapper was known for his perfectly laid hair (he wore Shirley Temple curls in 1999's "The Next Episode" music video), and he rejected the idea that preening was reserved for women. Pimps were hypermasculine by default and therefore they were secure in their manhood. "As males we all have feminine ways, just like women have masculine ways, so it's okay to tap into those inner ways. We have certain characteristics, values, and traits that our mothers gave us. I'm a man that can tap into my feminine side and still know that I'm a masculine man with a manicure. Cause it's called a manicure, not a bitchicure."

Death Row Records played up to the reputation as the most feared rap label on the West Coast with mafioso style. Founder Marion "Suge" Knight was a hip-hop don in tailor-made suits in blood red, a homage to his affiliation with the Bloods gang. He had a menacing look and could be seen with a Cuban cigar in hand or diamond-and-ruby ring that spelled out M-O-B (likely a reference to the Bloods). At 6'4" and 315 pounds, Suge understood the power of using clothing to amplify his status and strength. "Suge could get whatever he wanted because people were so intimidated," said Alex Roberts, former head of business affairs at Death Row Records, in *Changes: An Oral History of Tupac Shakur*. "Everything was over the top." Fear and intimidation were the corporate mission statement, and artists who signed to the roster—Snoop Dogg, Tupac Shakur, Tha Dogg Pound—took on the gangster look of tailored suits, fedoras, bowler hats, button-up shirts, and ties.

Tupac signed with Death Row Records on September 16, 1995. It was Snoop Dogg's idea that Tupac join Death Row, but the rapper was incarcerated for a sexual abuse conviction. He maintained his innocence but was unable to post bail. Suge came to the rescue by bailing him out of prison for $1.4 million and giving him a new home at the epicenter of gangsta rap. "Whether the odds are in your favor or appear to be stacked against you, the Death Row Records family sticks with you and sees you through," said Suge. "The kind of success we have is about more than selling records, it's about relationships."

The newly emancipated rapper was taking fashion risks. He wore a leather vest with metallic buttons (fitted to almost be corset-like) and suspenders over a white T-shirt on the cover of the *New York Times Magazine*, which featured Suge in a red double-breasted suit and Snoop Dogg in a black suit. Tupac accessorized with his signature bandana and the Death Row Records chain. It would be one of his most iconic and duplicated looks. T.I. wore the same ensemble while inducting Tupac into the Rock and Roll Hall of Fame in 2017 and was mercilessly taunted. Later that year, Portland Trail Blazers star Damian Lillard commemorated a game against the Los Angeles Lakers by wearing a suit and vest shirtless as a homage to the rapper. "I had a shirt to wear under here, but I just decided not to," he said with a laugh. The NBA star, who is also a rapper, told me that he liked how the look highlighted his tattoos, in the same way that Tupac showcased his "Thug Life" body ink. "Pac was bold. It seemed wild sometimes, but because he did it with confidence and not trying too hard it was cool."

Tupac was a fan of Versace years before he hit the Milan runway. "He slowly transitioned away from the gangster clothes to Versace," remembered his stylist Kenya Ware. The fashion evolution—from West Coast casual to hip-hop and finally high fashion—was seen in his public appearances: In 1993, Tupac came to the Minority Motion Picture Awards in Dickies overalls and a backward baseball cap. At the *Poetic Justice* premiere that same year, he was head-to-toe in a Karl Kani denim look. In 1996, he wore a double-breasted Versace suit to the Grammy Awards. "How you like this Versace hookup? The swap meet was closed," he joked. "You know I go all out for the Grammys." At the MTV Video Music Awards in September of that year—after the Milan trip—he was sophisticated as ever in a graphic Versace vest layered under a beautiful gray single-breasted suit.

Versace also had a mention in the East Coast–West Coast rivalry between Tupac and The Notorious B.I.G. The beef involved several incidents and disses, including Tupac getting shot in a robbery at Quad Studios and Suge Knight taunting Puffy and the entire Bad Boy Records onstage at the Source Awards in 1995. In 1996, Tupac released the searing diss "Hit 'Em Up" and hurled a multitude of insults and vitriol. Most fans remember the lyrics that Biggie was a cuckold: "*You claim to be a player, but I fucked your wife / We bust on Bad Boys, niggas fucked for life.*" Few probably recall that Tupac called his rival a fashion poser: "*Now it's all about Versace, you copied my style.*" It's unlikely that Tupac was the sole inspiration behind Biggie's penchant for Versace. Puffy was Biggie's mentor and was exposed to luxury before Bad Boy. The scion of ghetto fabulous knew Versace; even his alma mater, Howard University, shouted out the brand in the campus newspaper in 1993.

Fashion influence was not something in a vacuum. Inspiration, credited or otherwise, went between the coasts. Jacques "Haitian Jack" Agnant, a Brooklyn gangster, had a flashy and flamboyant style that Tupac admired. "People gravitate to a gangster," said Jack. "People say Tupac was infatuated by Jack. He wanted to be like the gangster." Jack was a high roller who wore silk shirts, dated Madonna, and hung with Gianni Versace in Miami in 1994. The rapper drew from this persona for his role in 1993's *Above the Rim* and in his personal life. Jack claimed that he instructed Pac to ditch baggy pants for more sophisticated looks. "I think he liked that my style was different . . . the elegance that I bought to his life . . . I bought him a Rolex. I wanted to see that I could groom him and educate him to how he needs to behave to make it." The two had a falling-out around the 1993 sexual assault case they were both charged in. For Jack, this was proof that the rapper was not the gangster he postured as. "I'm gonna ride or die with you, homie. I expect you to do the same," he said, pointing to Tupac's lack of loyalty. "I tell people, you don't really know Pac. Because Pac don't really know Pac." Like the enigmatic rapper, who should be credited for introducing Versace to hip-hop remains a mystery.

Tupac Shakur was fatally gunned down in Las Vegas on September 7, 1996. Footage from the MGM Grand hours before the incident showed him wearing a yellow-orange silk shirt that could very well have been Versace. At 11:15 p.m., the rapper was ambushed with bullets in the passenger side of Suge Knight's black BMW 750. According to Chris Carroll, a retired sergeant with the Las Vegas Metropolitan Police Department and first responder on the scene, the rapper's last words to him were: "Fuck you." He was pronounced dead on September 13, 1996, at the age of twenty-five. Despite countless conspiracy theories and confessions, the murder would remain officially unsolved. The assassination of Tupac—and that of Gianni Versace the following year—indelibly changed culture forever and cemented the men as legends.

Chapter Twelve

POPPIN' TAGS

Dress for the job you want, not the job you have. But how do you dress for the unbelievable, once-in-a-lifetime job you never expected? It was after six p.m. in the waiting area at Bad Boy Worldwide and I was there interviewing for something. Nobody had told me, so I just showed up. In the summer of 2005, I interned in the street team promotions department, which consisted of late nights and a crash course in egos and music industry politics they don't teach you in school. At this entry-level point in my career, I would have been ecstatic to take any job: assistant, dog walker, weed carrier. The air inside 1710 Broadway was noticeably good. Probably *Unforgivable by Sean John*, with notes of bergamot, basil, and tonka bean. Sitting next to me was an overly confident guy from LA in a suit and a girl in ripped jeans and a crop top. And then me: in a black pin-striped blazer from Express that I could barely afford. If I had known whom I was there to meet, I would have splurged on a Sean John T-shirt.

Hours later, I was led into a room and Sean "Puffy" Combs walked in—with my résumé in hand. *Bugging out* doesn't begin to describe it. The reason nobody had told me what the interview was for was because it was for the job. *The job everyone wanted.* He asked one or two questions, got his gut read, and left. Just like that, I was moonlighting as his fourth or fifth assistant. Those late nights bleed together in memory, but what I remember was the mogul's effect on everybody around him. It was palpable. Everyone sat in their seats a little taller. Female assistants put on high heels otherwise stored underneath their desks. He was "Mr. Combs." He embodied his indefatigable "can't stop, won't stop" mantra—powered by four hours of sleep—and demanded excellence.

Sean John was founded in 1998 with the "goal of building a premium brand that shattered tradition and introduced hip-hop to high fashion on a global scale." The late '90s and aughts were the height of rapper-fronted fashion brands. The blueprint followed in the footsteps of predecessors like Karl Kani, April Walker, and Cross Colours to create casual and athletic wear. Puffy wasn't looking to appeal only to the audience that knew his music. That was a short-term vision. He coined his brand after his government name, taking a page from eponymous American luxury houses with staying power like Ralph Lauren and Tommy Hilfiger. Sean John began with logo T-shirts and expanded with their best-selling premium denim and velour tracksuits. In 2000, Sean John made its debut on fashion's main stage: New York Fashion Week. "I feel like I had something to offer to the fashion world. I just threw myself in as a designer," Puffy said from backstage.

Puffy brought the same strategy to fashion that had made him successful in hip-hop. As an artist, he didn't pen lyrics or play instruments, but he was the visionary who left his signature on everything he touched. In the same way, he was the DNA of Sean John despite not designing or fabricating clothing in the traditional sense. "Puff is the ultimate producer," Dao-Yi Chow, creative director and vice president of marketing at Sean John, explained to me. "He was also super involved on the design side of things. Certainly he didn't have enough time to be in every design meeting, but was the muse and provided the inspiration of aspiration for the design team." The mogul pushed the Sean John team as he would his artists. "He worked 24/7, and a lot of people couldn't handle that and were burnt out. But the people that could hang, you know, he got the most out of them and made them want to work just as hard as him. That certainly was his gift."

Sean John fashion shows were like their namesake: an outrageous and ostentatious convergence of hip-hop, fashion, and celebrity. Stars from music to Hollywood and high fashion—Lil' Kim, Luther Vandross, Stephen Baldwin, Ellen Pompeo, Anna Wintour, Tommy Hilfiger, Helena Christensen—came out to sit in the front row. Everyone wanted an invite. Chow remembered working behind the scenes and likened the chaos and adrenaline to being backstage at a concert. "The energy was high and it was intense, but he knew how to motivate people. It was pretty infectious." Puffy curated the vibes, even backstage, to be a sensorial experience. The champagne was flowing and the air smelled like black currant and roses from Diptyque Baies candles (which Sean John employees were told to burn days before the actual show). With a hip-hop superstar at the helm, the soundtrack for the runway was impeccable. "Make sure the music is at *that* level," Puffy instructed firmly before the inaugural show began.

The runway shows were extravaganzas. The venue could be at Manhattan staple Cipriani or the Santa Monica Airport's Barker Hangar. The clothes were ghetto fabulous but elevated: lamb suede hooded sweatsuits, striped silk suits, lynx tail scarves, and coats with fox-edged hoods accessorized with diamonds and crucifixes. Sean John cast gorgeous and noticeably diverse models. There were established supermodels like Tyson Beckford, Karolína Kurková, Adriana Lima, and Liya Kebede, as well as fresh faces such as future star Channing Tatum, Will Lemay, and film producer Datari Turner.

Puffy was the most powerful ambassador for the brand. He reinvented himself over and over—changing his name to P. Diddy and Diddy—and added to his repertoire of creative endeavors that continued to expand his reach. He hosted MTV's hit reality competition *Making the Band*, ran the New York City Marathon, and starred in the 2004 revival of *A Raisin in the Sun* on Broadway. In the same way that Puffy was a renaissance man, so was the Sean John consumer. This was a man who aspired to be a mogul. He was at the office during the day, but then hit the clubs at night. He loved hip-hop and attracted women effortlessly. Whether he was running the company or was an employee, in his mind, he was a boss.

With a history as a marketer, Puff was able to leverage splashy and creative ideas to differentiate Sean John in the marketplace. In the early 2000s, he purchased a giant billboard in Times Square with a revolving gallery of him wearing the brand. The billboard could be seen when standing outside his office at Bad Boy Worldwide. The marketing campaign also featured social commentary that got people talking. In the image, Puff raised his fist as an ode to John Carlos and Tommie Smith at the 1968 Olympics. They broke barriers as Black athletes on the world stage, as Sean John would in fashion. "Puff was always about big moments," said Chow. "I think it was the allure of owning that space over Times Square and being able to see from the [Bad Boy] building."

The Sean John lifestyle was spread through several creative collaborations and brand extensions. In 2003, Ford Motor Company released a limited-edition Sean John Navigator, which was a popular sport utility vehicle model favored by rappers and celebrities. Puffy was a fragrance connoisseur (as seen in his obsession with candles at the Sean John shows) and in 2005, the brand launched the Unforgivable cologne, in partnership with Estée Lauder, as a limited-edition eau de parfum at Saks Fifth Avenue. It became a runaway success at retailers like Bloomingdale's and Macy's and made $150 million globally. The fragrance industry was also impressed, and Sean John won the FiFi Fragrance of the Year Award in 2007.

Within two years of its launch, Sean John was carried in 1,200 stores and had sales of $200 million. By 2016, the annual retail sales were $450 million. This was a line that could take consumers from the block to the boardroom and anywhere else. "Sean John really pushed *fashion*

fashion," said Deirdre Maloney, a buyer for Bloomingdale's at the time. "They had the full-length shearling coat and the button-downs. They represented that cool guy on a yacht."

Sean John received acceptance into high fashion in the biggest way possible. In 2004, Puffy was named the Menswear Designer of the Year by the Council of Fashion Designers of America (CFDA). It was a first for any hip-hop brand. He was also the first Black designer to win the accolade, which is considered the Academy Awards of the fashion industry. Puffy beat out veterans Ralph Lauren and Michael Kors for the honor. In front of an audience that included womenswear designer of the year Carolina Herrera and *Sex and the City* style icon Sarah Jessica Parker, the impresario, wearing a white tuxedo jacket, couldn't believe that he had beat his idol, Ralph Lauren. "I am living the American dream."

"I'm putting them outta business," said Damon "Dame" Dash. The co-founder of Roc-A-Fella Records wanted to forge a partnership with Iceberg and his biggest artist, Jay-Z. The Italian luxury house known for knitwear, leather, and denim was popular in hip-hop, so much so that it was analogous to Gucci at the time. The rapper was already a fan of the brand. It was a natural fit. But when they asked for free clothing samples, the brand was dismissive and told them to hit the sample sale. "They were really, really rude," Dame said to me. "So at that point I was just like, I'm putting them outta business."

In 1995, Dame, Jay-Z, and Kareem "Biggs" Burke founded Roc-A-Fella Records. Even before the fame, they shot music videos in St. Thomas, played Monopoly with real money, and used the Mercedes-Benz E-class 320 (known as the "buggy-eyed Benz") as their throwaway street team car. "When three young Black men out of the projects suddenly had the world at our fingertips, it was hard to convince us that anything wasn't possible. I guess that included opulence," Biggs told me. "Dame and I are from Harlem, where luxury is a state of mind. Jay just so happens to have the talent to paint that picture in his music." Jay-Z's debut, *Reasonable Doubt*, in 1996 was the sonic manifestation of this luxury street life. Songs like "Can't Knock the Hustle," "Can I Live," and "Feelin' It" were glossy hustler anthems about enjoying ill-gotten gains. Jay-Z's lyrical dexterity and wordplay were enhanced by his credibility—he lived the life he rapped about.

Despite that, Roc-A-Fella experienced friction when dealing with luxury brands. Iceberg wasn't the only company that wasn't interested in working with them. No record label wanted to sign Jay-Z, so they created their own. Belvedere Vodka dismissed them, so they started Armadale Vodka. The reasoning remains unknown, but it's possible that established brands simply didn't understand—or didn't want to understand—Jay-Z. "They ain't want nothing to do with it," remembered Biggs about their detractors. Roc-A-Fella turned rejection into opportunity. "That's how Rocawear started. Every time somebody closed the door, we went and did it ourselves."

Rocawear was founded in 1999—with Dame and Jay-Z as co-owners—and brought street aspiration to the masses. Most fans couldn't afford the private jets, penthouses, and yachts that Jay-Z rapped about, but they sure could buy a logo T-shirt, tracksuit, or satin baseball jacket with raglan sleeves. Fashion was the transfusion of the lifestyle. As Roc-A-Fella's entertainment empire expanded, they leveraged the roster of artists including Memphis Bleek, Dipset, and State Property to serve as brand ambassadors.

The vision of Rocawear was derived from Dame. "I've always been fresh. I've taken pride in my skills," he said. He was hands-on and spent significant time at the Rocawear offices. Dame explained to the *New York Times*: "Every sketch, every sample of clothing has to have my approval—and that's three million signatures. When you first get into a business like fashion, you have to run it from the bottom up, know what I'm saying?" The Harlem native was braggadocious. "I remember one time I ran into Ralph Lauren and you know, I'm a very arrogant, cocky guy. I'm thinking I'm all that and he's like, not saying too much, but he grins and when he walked away, I realized I was wearing a [Ralph Lauren] Purple Label suit and that shit burnt my soul. I immediately went to study with tailors on how to create a suit."

Rocawear benefited from the fact that its roster of rapper models was diverse. Jay-Z represented the quiet guy from Brooklyn who wasn't a fashionista but liked to look clean and attract hot women. *"Young don't mess with chicks in Burberry patterns / Fake Manolo boots straight from Steve Madden,"* he rapped on 2003's "La-La-La (Excuse Me Miss Again)." His girlfriend Beyoncé Knowles wore Manolo Blahnik "Okla-mod" booties (inspired by Timbs) in their "'03 Bonnie & Clyde" music video. The boot, which retailed for around $650, became a celebrity favorite and was knocked off by the Steve Madden Hijo for $149.

Dipset (aka The Diplomats) brought high energy and a colorful, flashy aesthetic that reflected their home borough of Harlem. They weren't a rap group, they were a *movement* in the early aughts. Cam'ron, Juelz Santana, Jim Jones, and Freekey Zekey were childhood friends and loved bold looks with patriotic motifs like the American flag and bald eagle. Despite being a collective, each member had his own style: Cam'ron was the rebel in a baby-pink fur coat that matched his Range Rover, Juelz loved bandanas, and Jimmy popularized True Religion jeans. As Santana explained: "We was just doin' it. Anywhere we went . . . all eyes was on the boys!"

Cross-promotion was the watchword. Rocawear showed up on album covers (e.g., Jay-Z wearing a denim suit for *Vol. 3 . . . The Life and Times of S. Carter*) and song lyrics, like the Young Gunz' *"You know, powder blue Rocawear suit, white Nike her."* One 2004 promo photo featuring Cam'ron and Juelz Santana in Rocawear denim suits could very well have been a layout in a magazine had it not been for the tag that the brand was available at Burdines, Macy's, Filene's, and Marshall Field's.

Dame wanted Rocawear to have a universal appeal—to be

"colorless and accessible to everyone"—and he cast models outside of rap, like British socialites Victoria Beckham and Samantha Ronson. "People look at Victoria Beckham and think, 'That's fashion forward.' She would never affiliate herself with anything unless it was hot. People who didn't know about Rocawear before will at least be curious about it because of Victoria." The former Spice Girl helped launch Rocawear at Selfridges in the United Kingdom and recorded a hip-hop album with Roc-A-Fella that was shelved. From the outside, the pairing may have seemed strange, but Dame was a risk-taker and to his credit, he was dogged in his belief—and he made everybody else a believer.

Getting into retail was compulsory for every fashion brand and the retail buyer had the important role of selecting which designers and items would be stocked based on consumer preferences and forecasting trends. Hip-hop lines, in particular, often relied on young buyers like Deirdre Maloney. Dame called her his "plug" and advocate at the luxury retailer. "Bloomingdale's wields big buying power and certainly at that time for the market, with twenty-six stores, you could write really big orders if you thought it was going to work," she said. "You're like a scout looking for what's new and what's next." She was a hip-hop fan and understood Rocawear's cultural influence. Even if the buyer was sold on a designer, whether it would actually sell was the question. "Buying for Bloomingdale's—in what was the more progressive silo of fashion in menswear—it wasn't an indictment of the designer. It was an indictment of what the customer was ready for."

Each retailer buyer approached the process differently. Some relied more on data over gut. "It's a lot more analytical than one may think. I don't just go in and I'm like, 'Hey, I think my customer would like this, this, and this and buy it," Deric Humphrey, assistant buyer at Macy's, told me. "I'm looking at everything, like what colors are selling; maybe blues did really well or red did really well in this particular category.

I'm looking at silhouettes. I'm looking at stuff like that." He planned six to seven months out and made buys twice a year. "Just as much information I can gather to make educated decisions when I head into market and place my buy."

By 2003, Rocawear had surpassed $300 million in sales. The line jet-setted on runways around the world—New York City, Milan, London, and Paris—but the toughest competition happened inside the Roc-A-Fella Records office. Every day was a fashion show. Or more accurately, a fashion showdown. Employees meticulously planned their outfits because everyone wanted to outdo each other in looking fresh. You had to come correct or risk getting clowned. "Yeah, I ain't gonna lie. I got killed once or twice. Murdered," said Lenny "Lenny S" Santiago, SVP of Roc Nation, who climbed the ranks from street team director. "I developed tough skin there. It was almost like school. It wasn't bullying but you had to have tough skin." LaTrice Burnette, executive vice president of Def Jam, started as an intern in 1999 and experienced the gaffe of inadvertently dressing like rapper Cam'ron in a pink-and-white Rocawear sweatsuit with matching Nike Dunks. "I'm gonna smash this outfit," she thought. "Just as I thought I was doing something, who literally wore the same outfit I was going to wear a couple days before? Cam." He negated her chance of stealing the look because nobody wanted to be a copycat or style "biter." "I remember having a conversation with someone at the office like, 'Damn. I was gonna kill this 'fit. but now I can't even do it anymore because Cam did it.'"

Cam'ron's fashion sense didn't come from how much he spent. It was more about confidence and an inner swagger. "It don't matter how much your clothes cost. Your sneakers cost, whatever. If you don't rock it the right way, with a certain swag, it don't matter," the rapper explained to me while shopping at Avianne & Co. Jewelers in the Diamond District. You could have all the hottest designer labels but if you didn't have the attitude to wear them the right way, what was the point? "Listen man, I don't care how much bread you got or how much designer shit you got. If you don't wear it right, you're gonna look stupid. Like, my nigga Jim [Jones] never wears designer sneakers. He thinks they don't look right on him. You ain't gonna catch him in no Balenciagas or Alexander McQueens or anything like that. Some niggas just flossy and it's like, 'Yo. You look dumb.' You have no swag on you. No drip."

The new kids on the block had authenticity that couldn't be bought. "Tommy Hilfiger and Ralph Lauren capitalized on the fact that there wasn't any competition for the urban market—well there is now," Dame said. "The fact of the matter is they're not living it. They don't appreciate it and they don't understand the culture. They exploit." Everyone wanted a piece of the action.

———————

"How easy is this?" LL Cool J smiled. He had just finished his rap for his commercial with the Gap. Directed by Mark Seliger, the 1997 spot for the Gap's easy-fit jeans had a hip-hop twist, with the rapper in a white T-shirt, jeans (with one leg rolled up), a FUBU cap, and Timberland boots. The Gap must have thought it was a coup to partner with LL Cool J and add edge to their classic American image. But while his pillowy lips rapped "Fall into the Gap," in actuality, he sent a subliminal message that only those in the know could hear: *"Jeans popping in every mall and town and city / G-A-P gritty / Ready to go / For us, by us, on the low."*

For us, by us. That was the tagline for hip-hop brand FUBU. The Gap had no idea that LL Cool J had dropped the shout-out for another company. "They spent $30 million basically airing a FUBU commercial," said Daymond John. According to the founder, the rapper wasn't happy with the blasé and stereotypical way the retailer had approached him initially to collaborate. "The Gap called him and he didn't really feel good about the way they addressed him: 'C'mon in and shoot one of those rap videos.' He didn't really feel good about it." FUBU had been around since 1992 but nobody at the Gap knew about it until weeks after the commercial premiered. "Because they didn't have anybody in the company or the marketing agency who loved hip-hop or was of color, they didn't pull that ad for five weeks until they finally found out what happened," said John.

LL Cool J remembered the experience in a more sanguine way. "I was a partner in [FUBU] and I wanted to support what we were doing," he told Oprah. "I felt like, honestly, Gap was big enough to handle that and not be hurt by it. And it worked out for everybody . . . It made them cool." Although the rapper implied that the Gap was "perturbed" initially, he credited them for not nixing the spot altogether. "They didn't pull it. They didn't go into a crazy tailspin about it once they did find it out. Whoever those executives were, because we didn't talk much back then, thank you. They helped out a fledgling company. They gave back." That was an understatement. According to John, FUBU finessed the opportunity and became bigger than ever. The brand's sales rocketed and turned FUBU into a $350 to $400 million brand.

The late '90s and aughts marked the gold rush for hip-hop clothing lines—interchangeably referred to as "urban" fashion—and everyone was a prospector. Some brands like Enyce, Akademiks, Avirex, and Pelle Pelle incorporated elements of hip-hop culture. For instance, they favored large logos, baggy silhouettes, and using rappers in their marketing campaigns. Rappers saw a lucrative opportunity and artist-led clothing lines became ubiquitous. Regardless of whether the lines were organic or not, they were a part of the artist starter pack. Drop an album and then release a clothing line.

Music videos provided 24/7 promotion for these brands. Ralph McDaniels launched *Video Music Box*, an early video platform airing in New York City, in 1983. In 1988, hip-hop videos went national when MTV released *Yo! MTV Raps*. The late '90s marked the height of hip-hop videos, especially high-budget visuals by directors like Hype Williams, Paul Hunter, and Little X. Music videos were especially impactful because fans didn't realize they were being marketed to. We were just watching our favorite artists. From the time I came home from school, I would channel surf between *MTV Jams, Total Request Live, Planet Groove,* and BET's *106 & Park. Total Request Live* and *106 & Park* were especially astute at harnessing viewership with fan voting (regardless of whether our votes accounted for anything).

MTV realized how brands were using music videos and not paying the network like a traditional advertiser. The channel blurred fashion logos that weren't cleared or, more accurately, weren't cutting them a check. "We blur logos in every video we play," said an MTV spokesperson to the *Chicago Tribune* in 1996. "We don't (blur)," countered Kevin Taylor, music researcher and record label liaison for BET. "MTV does it because they say they're concerned about that whole label thing. But it opens up ad revenue. If they go after a shoe company (such as Nike) for sponsorship, Nike knows its competition isn't getting any free advertising." A former MTV insider confirmed this fact to me.

Fashion became a viable programming option and both MTV and BET launched several stand-alone shows. MTV's *House of Style* premiered in 1989 and capitalized on the supermodel craze and made hosts like Cindy Crawford, Amber Valletta, Shalom Harlow, and Daisy Fuentes pop culture staples beyond the runway. The show featured interviews and footage from fashion shows. In 1999, host Rebecca Romijn interviewed Jay-Z as he debuted Rocawear at the MTV Video Music Awards. In 2005, BET launched *Rip the Runway*, which featured a runway show with a variety of designers from Sean John and Baby Phat to emerging names like LaQuan Smith and Simon Rasmussen.

Sean John and Rocawear were paragons of successful artist clothing lines. However, the graveyard of failed clothing lines—some never getting off the ground beyond the announcement press release—was longer than the success stories and littered with platinum names: DMX and DMX Signature Clothing (DMX), David Brown (Young Buck), Bushi (Busta Rhymes), Soji (Common), OutKast Clothing Co. (OutKast), Shago (Lil' Bow Wow), Snoop Dogg Clothing (Snoop Dogg), 24/7 Star

(Lil' Kim), FJ560 (Fat Joe), Nostic (Jim Jones), Pink Diamond Couture (Trina), No Limit Clothing (Master P), just to name a few.

Hip-hop lines were dominated by male artists but two prominent brands were run by women. Fetish by Eve and J.Lo by Jennifer Lopez, launched in 2003 and 2001 respectively, had a better chance at success because the artists sold a lifestyle beyond music. They targeted the multicultural audience of women who looked like them and were more inclusive in putting out body-positive images. Both Eve and Lopez had high visibility as multihyphenate actresses/artists and therefore had more opportunities to get their clothes exposure. The bedazzled tees, mega-hardware handbags, low-rise jeans, and colorful tracksuits fit well within the zeitgeist of the aughts but eventually fell out of favor. Eve ended Fetish six years after it launched due to business issues like production and delivery problems, and shifted her focus to acting. J.Lo's brand, which went through several reincarnations, was more expansive with a top-selling fragrance (Glow by JLo), clothing, accessories, and home goods. But its draw came from positioning toward a mass audience.

One reason why most artist fashion lines failed in the long run was the inherent disconnect between designer and consumer. Jennifer Lopez the fashion icon wore high-end designers like Versace, Giambattista Valli, and Valentino but her line found success at department stores like Kohl's and T.J.Maxx. This begged the question: Would famous people wear these clothes if they weren't financially motivated to do so?

Furthermore, a talented musician couldn't necessarily convert their fans into fashion buyers. Having a five-mic album in *The Source* meant you were a good rapper and not necessarily an aesthetic influencer. The best example of this was Eminem. The rapper from 8 Mile was a cultural phenomenon who hit the coveted trifecta: a skilled lyricist with pop star appeal and radio hits. He had teenyboppers in the suburbs and hip-hop heads alike loving him. He broke the curse of jejune white rappers and became the biggest rapper of all time, according to several Guinness

World Records. In 2002, Eminem starred in *8 Mile*, a loose biopic of his life that generated over $240 million worldwide and garnered an Academy Award for Best Original Song. With millions of fans worldwide, a clothing line was the next step. In 2003, he launched Shady Ltd., a nod to his rap alter ego, Slim Shady, that resembled concert merch more than fashion. The T-shirts, hoodies, and jerseys were perfect for hard-core fans but had little appeal outside of that narrow niche. Eminem was a rap god, but did anyone want to look like Marshall Mathers? Unlike Rocawear or Sean John, Eminem didn't sell a lifestyle. His white-boy dysfunction was more cautionary than aspirational. Furthermore, the extent of his involvement in the line remained vague. Given the rigors of his day job, it would be surprising if the rapper did anything more than give final approvals on the finished collection and then wear it as promotion or name-check it in songs.

Working with a celebrity designer came with a myriad of challenges, including quelling big egos, scheduling nightmares, and creative fickleness. Many artists also didn't realize the difficulty of launching a brand. Everybody wanted models wearing their clothes down the runway and billboards in Times Square, but the majority of the sweat equity involved less glamorous activities like designing, securing manufacturing, and understanding distribution. Often the artist was merely the "face" of the brand and outsourced laborious and boring tasks to partners with existing experience and infrastructure. It was easy to get bored and move on to more entertaining and lucrative prospects. And if the artist became irrelevant or, worse, uncool, the brand's days were numbered.

Starting and operating a fashion line involved a steep financial burden. According to a 2003 survey of designers by *Women's Wear Daily*, the average annual cost to create, show, promote, and sell a collection was $250,000. This didn't include the cost of actually making and distributing the clothes. "That means designers with sales of $1 million a year or more are barely scraping by," the publication noted. Who was willing to pony up their own money for their line? "To get into the fashion business is just so cash intensive," explained Dao-Yi Chow. "Like, it needs to be like your only thing. And you're throwing everything you have into it." This was fundamentally different from the economics of the music business, in which successful artists were usually signed to major record labels that advanced them funds—oftentimes budgets well into the millions—to record music. The artists had the enviable privilege of spending somebody else's money up front, and the label handled the administrative minutiae.

Even the most successful brands eventually changed hands. Dame Dash planned to form a fashion conglomerate in the same vein as Louis Vuitton Moët Hennessy (LVMH) and invested in brands including Rachel Roy, Charlotte Ronson, and State Property, but he was impeded for several reasons. On *Assets Over Liabilities*, he shared that Tommy Hilfiger wanted to acquire Rocawear for $450 million but Jay-Z squelched the deal to launch his own S. Carter brand. Additionally, he said that Rocawear had purchased button-down shirts to reflect Jay-Z's new grown-up look that he displayed in 2003's "Change Clothes." The shirts didn't sell. Between the financial hits and behind-the-scenes friction, Dame was over it. "So now, [the company] is going down and I'm arguing with them. Like 'yo, sell my interest, man.'" In 2005, Jay-Z bought out Dame's 25 percent share of Rocawear for a reported $30 million, according to *Women's Wear Daily*. Jay-Z's star continued to rise and two years later, he was able to sell Rocawear to the Iconix Brand Group for a reported $204 million in cash. The financial discrepancy would be a sticking point as the two went their separate ways. "Rocawear was my idea, it was my baby," said Dame. "I know business and so if you ask me and you want to revisit it, of course, I'm gonna be salty about it a little because I lost money, but let's move on."

Puffy was also ready to take a back seat at Sean John. In 2016, he sold a majority ownership to Global Brands Group and maintained a minority stake. The brand's influence on the next generation of high fashion was undeniable. In 2007, Chow and fellow Sean John alum Maxwell Osborne founded the menswear line Public School. "When we started our own brand, it was less about not wanting to work for anyone else but more about wanting to be able to have the creative freedom and not have to answer to anyone," Chow said. Following in the footsteps of its progenitor, Public School's ethos was one of disruption and reappropriation. The line won the CFDA Menswear Designer of the Year awards in 2013 and 2014. "When I think about the whole journey, it truly was a fashion revolution from how things were then and to see the impact we had on style," Puffy reflected to the *Washington Post*. "When I'd do a collection, I'd do a mood board and put everyone who inspired me on my board—Ralph Lauren and Tom Ford's Gucci, in particular. And now I'm on other people's mood boards. It's humbling."

Chapter Thirteen

LOUIS VUITTON DON

Kanye West was always ready for his close-up—even when no one was asking for it. It was a chilly, gray day on January 23, 2009, and the rapper was on his way to the Comme des Garçons show at Paris Fashion Week. Inside, Japanese designer Rei Kawakubo, known for her avant-garde taste and unconventional silhouettes, evoked something of a modern streetwear geisha with her collection, with models in veiled face masks, nude tulle, and greatcoats. The looks were exaggerated and, admittedly, had questionable wearability. But that's not what anybody would remember decades later. The real star was outside.

A van pulled up to the venue and a squad of men—a wild, stylish menagerie—emerged. The rapper/producer was at the center of the group and it was strangely quiet. There were no screams from overzealous fans. The usual *click, click, click* of paparazzi cameras was absent. Two lone photographers watched, confused. At thirty-one, Kanye embodied the preppy, hip-hop schoolboy. He wore a blue-and-green peacoat over a buttoned-up blazer, accented by a rose boutonniere. His jeans were a bit baggy. His getup was accented with tan leather gloves, Louis Vuitton sneakers, and Goyard briefcase. A motley crew of friends, who were also curiously fitted, flanked the rapper. First up, then-unknown designer Virgil Abloh, an Illinois native like West, was in a bright blue Moncler puffer vest, Jil Sander marble print shirt by Raf Simons, and red-rimmed eyeglasses. Derek "Fonzworth Bentley" Watkins, known as Sean "Puffy" Combs's dapper right-hand man in a bow tie or wielding an umbrella, was in a tan fedora, smartly tilted to one side, with a matching attaché. Don C, West's longtime friend and collaborator, conjured the spirit of a marching band leader in a dark blazer with red trim, gold sneakers, and Louis Vuitton briefcase. Chris Julian, of luxury boutique Fruition, was the only non-Black member of the squad and wore a red trench coat and layered plaid. Designer Taz Arnold, arguably the most daring of the bunch, was unforgettable in snug leopard-print leggings, a fitted green leather jacket, and wild cowboy hat. Kanye had been to Paris Fashion Week before but this time he wanted to make a statement.

Kanye had made inroads in high fashion—he was known as a stylish dresser—but he had yet to garner the respect of gatekeepers that he would need as a designer. "We knew that we weren't fully received in the world quite yet, but we were at the door," Watkins said to me. "Kanye was working on his Louis Vuitton shoe collection at the time. So we saw it as being superheroes. It was the Olympics and we were representing the United States. Putting a flag down in Paris [was] saying, 'Okay, we're taking territory.'" Being there was the rapper's way of saying that he took this fashion shit seriously. He knew that this stylish cohort of men of color was groundbreaking in Paris. "I remember Kanye saying: 'We're going to look back on this and it's going to be similar to the civil rights movement, because we're standing up to have a voice,'" recalled Don C to GQ.

Peacocking was a necessity. Instagram hadn't been invented and street-style photography was in its nascence. "Niggas in Paris," Kanye's mega-hit with Jay-Z, was two years away. It would be five years until he married paparazzi magnet Kim Kardashian, and several more before he renounced hip-hop for Jesus and embarked on two catastrophic runs for president (in 2020 and 2024). But he knew how to create conversation. And the megalomania that would come to define him was already hardwired.

Kanye West rapped to the beat of his own drum since day one. He was born to Donda West, an academic, and Ray West, a photographer, on June 8, 1977. The couple separated and mother and son moved together to Chicago when he was three years old. He would see his father during summers, but he was the consummate mama's boy. While his haters described their relationship in a pejorative, they-need-to-cut-the-cord type of way, his mother said it was a loving harmony. She was his rock and he was her proudest accomplishment.

In her book, *Raising Kanye*, Donda West realized her son was remarkable at seven. "He looked at me with eyes that spoke. And I knew, like the old folks sometimes know when they see certain babies, 'He was an old soul,'" she said. She gushed about his talents, his ability to pick up Chinese when they lived abroad for a year in Nanjing, and his nature to see beyond boundaries and societal constraints. "The one thing your child must know is that he is loved above all else. You give him security and confidence when you let him know that no matter what, he will always be loved . . . This love is eternal."

Donda's unconditional support created, perhaps to a fault, a self-assured, outspoken, and opinionated adult. "My mama's my best friend. I talk to her every day," he said. "If parents could be more open-minded to their children, more open to what their children are into—like their music, their clothes, and their interests—maybe they could raise children who become open-minded adults. That's how my mom was. And I was open to what she told me because she always valued what I had to say."

Kanye started his career as a producer in the mid-1990s. His first single was Jermaine Dupri's "Turn It Out" (featuring Nas) in 1997, but it was Beanie Sigel's "The Truth" in 2000 that turned hip-hop heads. It was grimy street rap, markedly different from the heavy melodies and sped-up soul samples that would become the producer's calling card. The following year, he produced several tracks for Jay-Z's *The Blueprint*, including the Nas diss "Takeover," "Heart of the City (Ain't No Love)," "Girls Girls Girls (Remix)," and "Izzo (H.O.V.A.)." The latter, an exuberant anthem that sampled "I Want You Back" by the Jackson 5, reached number eight on the Billboard Hot 100 in the U.S. and was Jay-Z's first top 10 single as a lead artist.

Kanye became fully embedded as an in-house producer for Roc-A-Fella Records, but the cocky kid from Chicago was itching to emerge from behind the boards and into the spotlight. It wasn't unheard of to straddle the lane between producer and rapper: Dr. Dre, Sean "Puffy" Combs, Jermaine Dupri, and Pharrell Williams had all done it with significant success. But Kanye didn't have their brand of swagger and lacked street credibility, something hip-hop prioritized back then.

He made the rounds and tried to get signed to a record label, but no one was biting. He experimented with clothing, but his wardrobe was more suburban than hood; colorful Polo shirts—with the collar popped up—rugbys, cardigans, fitted khakis, and his signature Louis Vuitton backpack. Meanwhile, his peers wore Rocawear, XXXL T-shirts, and Mitchell & Ness throwback sports jerseys. When Jay-Z instructed men to evolve their style on the track "Change Clothes" in 2003, men translated that into boxy blazers and loose button-downs with New York Yankees baseball caps. "Kanye wore a pink shirt with the collar sticking up and Gucci loafers," said Dame Dash, founder of Roc-A-Fella Records. "It was obvious we were not from the same place or cut from the same cloth." Jay-Z also expressed apprehension. "We all grew up street guys who had to do whatever we had to do to get by. Then there's Kanye, who to my knowledge has never hustled a day in his life. I didn't see how it could work."

The music didn't resonate either. Hip-hop was replete with songs about drug dealers and popping bottles at the club. Kanye wanted to make a provocative and bold song about Jesus. "I played them 'Jesus

Walks' and they didn't sign me," the rapper recalled of pitching himself to executives at labels. At the time, a song praising Jesus Christ was blasphemous for a secular rapper to release. They shouted Jesus out at awards show acceptance speeches. He was too different, a risky investment for a record label. A record deal was a commitment of finances and resources. Executives wanted to back a sure thing, an artist with the potential to sell millions of albums and singles, to recoup these significant up-front costs.

But Kanye was undeterred, obsessively convincing everybody of his genius. He garnered a reputation for being a self-indulgent asshole with zero social awareness. Kanye would rap at the drop of a dime, even when people around him were not listening. In the documentary *Jeen-Yuhs*, which followed him for twenty-one years, there's moments in which Kanye was desperately vying for recognition from Roc-A-Fella staff and executives, who appeared visibly bored or annoyed. He was known to beat his chest and jump on conference tables as he tried to convince the powers that be that *they needed him*. Sony Music passed. Capitol Records supposedly had a deal in the works that was squashed last-minute. Eventually, Roc-A-Fella Records signed him. It was a tainted win. Some believed that the offer was a smart ploy to retain the label's hot producer.

In 2002, Kanye marked his arrival when he received his Roc-A-Fella chain in his hometown as part of Jay-Z's Dynasty tour. Every record label—Bad Boy, Death Row, Cash Money, No Limit—had chains, but the Roc-A-Fella medallion stood above the rest. It featured the logo of a vinyl record with a bottle of champagne and a cursive *R* (designed by the late Adrian Vargas) and originated with Dame. "I just wanted to create a chain that represented who we are," he told me. He doesn't recall exactly when he started having chains made—Kareem "Biggs" Burke remembered 1997 or 1998—but he designed them mostly with Jacob Arabo aka Jacob the Jeweler, rap's beloved diamond dealer. For someone like Kanye, who hadn't made it yet, "jewelry can make it look like you have a lot more than you do." According to former Roc-A-Fella employees and close associates, getting the original chain required approval from at least two out of the three founders. It wasn't something you could (or should) *ask* for. "I'm the only person who ever gave Roc-A-Fella artists a chain," said Dame. "If you notice, I took the chain off my neck to give that to Kanye. I was supposed to get that back, but I never got that back," he said with a laugh.

Kanye's "Chaining Day" was commemorated in his "Through the Wire" music video the next year. "Now, I'm the newest member of the Roc-A-Fella team," he rapped giddily, excited to show off his affiliation. His debut album, *The College Dropout*, earned back the value of that chain several times over. With the album hailed as a modern classic, he created a new blueprint for rappers. Instead of hiding his true self, he championed everything that was different about him.

On "Through the Wire," he rapped through a wired jaw after a 2002 car accident. At times, his voice was slurred and the enunciation off, but it was refreshingly honest. On the track, which featured a sped-up sample of Chaka Khan's "Through the Fire," he humorously rapped about not being able to eat solid foods: *"I drink a Boost for breakfast, an Ensure for dizzert / Somebody ordered pancakes / I just sip the sizzurp."* Fans flocked to his everyman appeal. He was unafraid to be weird or sensitive. For a suburban college student like me who was on campus when *The College Dropout* dropped, he was more relatable than his rap peers. He wasn't a drug dealer or a gangbanger. With his average build and apple cheeks, Kanye was no lothario or playboy. He was regular; no different from the guys who lived down the hall in the dorm. According to Donda West, her son dressed differently well before his first album. "Kanye was onto something entirely different when it came to clothes," she wrote. "When *College Dropout* dropped, people started copying, biting his preppy style . . . No rapper had stepped out of the box like that. Who would ever have thought it would work?"

Hip-hop loved Polo decades before Kanye West, but the way he rocked his Lo was different. He wasn't wearing a sporty jacket with huge logos or drawing attention in head-to-toe Polo gear. Instead, Kanye brought a preppy sensibility. He liked Polo sweaters and striped rugbys and would wear his Polo shirts with the collars popped up or accessorized with a backpack.

Kanye created his version of Ralph Lauren's cuddly Polo Bear called "Dropout Bear." The anthropomorphic bear was his mascot—imagine a hip-hop Disney character—and a metaphor for the rapper. Dropout Bear was the gentler antithesis to the tough guys in hip-hop. Sam Hansen, the designer behind the bear, explained: "I'm a Polo head and I knew Kanye was also so I was like, yo, we could flip this bear on some kind of Polo shit but make it a little more sporty and so I have this sketch. I remember just kind of, like, on a piece of paper putting sad eyes and sketching out and making it look more collegiate and putting a thick stroke around it and that's what we did . . . We took the head off the picture of the cover and turned that [into the logo]." It was rumored that people in the entourage took turns donning the suit. Hansen admitted to me that he wore it once for a photo and his colleague Albert Naugle had it on during Usher's Truth Tour. "They got random people to be in the suit for different shows."

The College Dropout was a critical and commercial success, debuting at number two on the Billboard 200 and selling 441,000 copies in its first week. It would sell over 3.4 million copies by 2014, certified triple platinum by the Recording Industry Association of America (RIAA). "Jesus Walks" went double platinum and Jay-Z called it his favorite. Critics lauded *The College Dropout*: *XXL* and marveled that it was a "revolution." The *Village Voice* elevated Kanye to a philosopher. *Spin* called him a "full-service hip-hop artiste." The lore of Kanye as a genius had begun.

Sonically, the rapper combined his sound, which was known as "chipmunk soul" because it was like Alvin and the Chipmunks on Speed, with smart, witty lyrics that reflected his educated middle-class upbringing and the confidence that his mama instilled in him. "*First nigga* with a Benz and a backpack," he dubbed himself on the track "Breathe In Breathe Out" (featuring Ludacris), a nod to his penchant for his Louis Vuitton backpack. The backpack added to his characterization as a thoughtful rapper who was vulnerable and sensitive. In "All Falls Down," he rapped about his dangerous obsession with consumerism: "*Man I promise, I'm so self-conscious / That's why you always see me with at least one of my watches.*" In the music video, West lost his lady (actress Stacey Dash) because she chose material things over love. "*The prettiest people do the ugliest things / For the road to riches and diamond rings,*" he rapped.

Kanye was unapologetically himself. His first prominent magazine placement was the cover of *The Source* in April 2004 and featured the rapper intensely staring in a pink button-down shirt and baby-blue blazer with his Roc-A-Fella chain. At the time, people wondered if the guy in pink Polos should be the face of hip-hop. "It was definitely a risk," Kim Osorio, editor in chief of *The Source*, said to me. "To me, he was so forward-thinking." She remembered how meticulous the rapper was in curating his image. "Kanye was conceptually involved in everything he did. He was involved in this cover. He picked everything and put it all together. He was huge on style. I remember him talking about his aspirations in fashion at that point." In the generation before him, fashion was a business venture to branch out into *after* being a successful rapper. Kanye was already thinking about his style empire now. Said Osorio: "It was totally different from the look of a Roc-A-Fella artist. But Kanye was very high fashion. It was always a Polo sweater, with the teddy bear. Always looking sharp."

Five years later in Paris, Kanye was standing in front of photographer Tommy Ton. The young Canadian creative had his fashion blog, *Jak & Jil*, and covered style for outlets like *Style* and *GQ*. Ton wasn't just a whiz behind the lens; he lived fashion and was a fan of Japanese streetwear line Visvim and Nike Flyknit sneakers. Being captured by Ton was good exposure. Kanye and his Paris Fashion Week crew created a human fashion wall and ensured that the photographer wouldn't miss them. "Some may think that this is the ultimate street style peacocking image," said Ton. "But this was actually before street style had become such a phenomenon and you could really see how much Kanye loved fashion and clothes, and Virgil did too. I saw Kanye and his posse walk from their car toward us and there was no paparazzi. They saw me and the one other photographer there and just stopped to assemble in formation in front of us."

Kanye's statement piece was the Goyard briefcase, which at the time wasn't in the hip-hop vernacular. But for high fashion, the House of Goyard was prestigious, exclusive, and mysterious since 1792. Its DNA was handcrafted in beautifully built trunks, boxes, and leather goods. The emblematic piled-up dot pattern was minimalist but recognizable to the discerning eye, and the world's richest consumers; French aristocrats, Coco Chanel, Jeanne Lanvin, Pablo Picasso, the Rockefellers, and the Maharaja of Kapurthala made up some of the clientele who spent thousands for a single piece. The brand shunned traditional marketing, mass production, and e-commerce. While the rest of the world grappled with the bottom line and economic recessions, Goyard was unapologetically elite. It was meant only for those in the know.

Kanye's own brand was rising in sneakers. He became the first non-athlete to get a collaboration with Nike. In 2009, he released the Air Yeezys, which retailed at $215. The follow-up, Air Yeezy II, came out in 2012 and retailed at $245 (but resold for thousands). That same year, a pair sold for over $90,000 on eBay. The sneakers were the perfect blend of sport and style, with features like a molded rubber heel, faux reptile skin, and gold aglets. "The anaconda-textured side panel, the toe overlay, the articulated tongue, the inscribed lace toggle—everything was truly looked over by [Kanye], crafted specifically for him," said Nathan VanHook, Nike's lead designer for the Air Yeezy II. The "Red

October" version came out as a surprise two years later, and sold out in ten minutes.

Kanye and Louis Vuitton did a high-end sneaker collaboration in June 2009. The designs were inspired by Japanese pop art and science fiction. One decision he made was adding a flap at the back of the sneaker. "The inspiration came from a jacket with a huge collar in the movie *Dune*," Kanye explained. "Most sneakers focus on the tongue, so I wanted to do something different." The idea was ingenious, perfect for tucking jeans into. The sneaker collection, three models, originally retailed from around $870 to $1,140. Sneakers were a *relatively* affordable way to look expensive without breaking the bank. They could be worn with different outfits as a wardrobe staple and mixed with inexpensive items to create a high-low look. "They're a great entry point into a luxury brand," said Kanye. "For people who can't afford to buy $2,000 trousers, they can take these shoes and mix it with jeans from another brand." Yeezys, which later went to Adidas in 2013, became a necessary addition to hip-hop's shoe collection.

"*Don't touch Kanye. He doesn't like being touched,*" the bodyguard flatly instructed. It was September 2013 but still balmy outside. The music industry cognoscenti congregated to celebrate Pusha T's debut album, *My Name Is My Name*, at Industria Studios in New York City's Meatpacking District. Inside, I made small talk with Pusha T. "Yo! Kanye is here!" somebody yelled. Cameras flashed and like the parting of the Red Sea, a pathway was created for Kanye.

Without warning, he grabbed the mic to turn the event into a bully pulpit. "This Yeezy right now, speaking to y'all!" he exclaimed. "We don't give a fuck! I'm a little loose right now!" He rambled about fashion and "culture vultures" who were appropriating his style. "This is that culture! For everybody stealing the culture, all those niggas stealing the camo prints . . . all those niggas stealing ideas for T-shirts . . ." The room vacillated between *woos* and confusion. I recorded what I could on my phone and that footage ended up going viral by the next day. When it came to fashion, Kanye made headlines.

The rapper's first meaningful foray into becoming a fashion entrepreneur was Pastelle, which he teased in his 2007 hit "Stronger": *"So go ahead, go nuts, go apeshit! 'Specially in my Pastellé, on my Bape shit!"* Prior to that, there was a short-lived line called Mascotte that little information is publicly known about. According to Sam Hansen, Mascotte was intended to exist under the Rocawear umbrella. "Mascotte was supposed to be the high-end brand for Rocawear. Not sure how high of fashion they wanted to go," he said based upon his conversations with Kanye, Don C, and Rocawear senior designer Chris Bevans. "At first, it was definitely intended to be a full line produced by Rocawear's manufacturers." Kanye filed the trademark for Mascotte Holdings, Inc. in June 2004. Hansen remembered printing Mascotte sample T-shirts (Kanye wore some publicly) and creating a layout for a sneaker collaboration with Reebok but said that things stalled after Dame Dash sold his shares of Rocawear. "After the split between Jay and Dame, the future of Mascotte got murky."

In 2007, Kanye pulled together a superhuman team of creatives for his next line, called Pastelle. Taz Arnold, who was a creative consultant for the line, called it "the X-Men coming together." The rapper enlisted his inner circle, including Virgil Abloh, Don C, Matt George, and multidisciplinary designer and director Willo Perron, as well as talent for various design and consulting roles, including Kim Jones—who worked with sports line Umbro and would take on director roles at Louis Vuitton, Dior, and Fendi—jeweler Ben Baller, artist KAWS, and Emma Hedlund of CMMN SWDN. Those who got the invite saw a huge opportunity working with the rap superstar making waves in fashion. Kanye had just popularized the Alain Mikli shutter shades in the music video for "Stronger." "Wow. Now we are the kings of street fashion," thought Giorgio di Salvo, one of the founders of Italian brand VNGRD.

Kanye teased Pastelle by wearing a cobalt-blue varsity jacket with the brand name across the back to the 2008 American Music Awards. In a post on his blog, *Kanye University*, he assured that the line would be out by January: "I swear to you guys all I do is work on design when I get off the stage. I want to and will be the real thing. I will not just be a 'celebrity designer.' Shit has to be good!!!" That never happened.

A look book leaked in October 2009 with reasonably priced T-shirts (priced from $40 to $150), appealing bright colors, and vintage motifs. "Pastelle feels more down-to-earth, and more wearable than anything we've seen from West so far," fashion magazine *VMan* noted. The next day, media outlets reported that the line was dead on arrival. The Pastelle varsity jacket became a relic of "the old Kanye" and superfans salivated over it for years. Luxury consignment shop Justin Reed sold one version for $10,000.

The doom of Pastelle remains a mystery. There appeared to be organizational issues with having so many collaborators and micromanagement from the rapper. "The guy wanted to know every little detail, and he came in super-early and left super-late, like this was his priority," said one anonymous designer. Despite his enthusiasm, Kanye's demanding schedule created conflicts. "He was very energetic about [Pastelle], and he loves working in fashion, but his main business is music," said Simon Beckerman from Retrosuperfuture. Some alleged that they did not get compensated for their work. "We worked on the project a lot, but no money and no glory," said di Salvo. This pattern was confirmed to me by others who worked with Kanye throughout the years. He had the habit of becoming obsessed with an idea, calling them at all hours and demanding that they meet him wherever he was in the world. Any one type of pushback could result in being cut from his inner sanctum.

Kanye continued to up the luxury ante in his music. "*What's that jacket, Margiela?*" he famously asked on "Niggas in Paris" (featuring Jay-Z) in 2011. The song was a global phenomenon and sold over fifteen million copies worldwide. On June 1, 2012, the rappers performed it a record-breaking eleven times at the Palais Omnisports de Bercy in Paris. There's no telling how many people learned about the house of Maison Margiela because of that lyric.

Kanye elevated the style of artists whom he signed to G.O.O.D. Music, the imprint he founded in 2011. He was meticulous in curating their image and fostered a community that wanted to be best dressed. "I have to sit around Big Sean, Kanye West, Don C, Virgil. I have to be around whatever friends they have. I pride myself on being different from them. So I had to dial in on what my style was," said Pusha T. "They're wearing Dior. I want to wear Margiela." But it wasn't about simply wearing the most expensive labels. Kanye was discerning about how fashion fit within the artist's repertoire. Pusha T's music was sparse and hard-hitting with intricate wordplay about cocaine. "Ye was like, 'I listen to you. You're a lyricist. Your voice is raw and minimal,'" said Pusha. "So every album cover I've ever done has been in workwear. Like, Carhartt WIP and shit like that. That's always been my aesthetic for my albums."

Kanye was also on a mission to make Kim Kardashian a fashion icon. The rapper and reality star started dating in April 2012 and he gutted her wardrobe of Hervé Léger bodycon dresses in favor of upscale Balmain, Balenciaga, and Givenchy. He likened Kardashian to a modern-day Marilyn Monroe and implored *Vogue* honcho Anna Wintour to give the couple a cover, which she did in March 2014. That controversial decision initiated Kim Kardashian into high fashion and she returned the favor by becoming a walking promotion for Yeezy.

Kanye's first Yeezy collection, called Season 1, debuted at New York Fashion Week in February 2015. The ready-to-wear collection, in collaboration with adidas Originals, was dystopian unisex athleisure with distressed sweatshirts, flesh-toned body stockings, military surplus, and the highlight, the Yeezy Boost 750 sneakers. Kanye found models through an open casting and worked with contemporary artist Vanessa Beecroft for the presentation that drew Jay-Z, Beyoncé, Rihanna, and

Justin Bieber. "It's literally like . . . I know this is really harsh, but it's like Before Yeezy and After Yeezy," Kanye said to the *New York Times*. "This is the new Rome!"

As his God complex grew, Yeezy became a bigger spectacle. During Season 2, the models were dressed in various shades of nude, including Kylie Jenner, whom Kanye was campaigning as the new It girl. In 2016, over twenty thousand people descended on Madison Square Garden for the Season 3 fashion show–cum–album premiere for *The Life of Pablo*. Reality cameras followed the Kardashian-Jenners, who were clad in neutral bodysuits, furs, and knit dresses. Yeezy shows were notoriously dramatic, chaotic, and late. Every season, Kanye wanted to push the envelope to create disruption—no matter the cost. During Season 4, models fainted and had to remove their uncomfortable shoes during the show. The show was lambasted as being cruel and inhumane. For Season 6, Kanye nixed a formal show altogether and had Kim Kardashian create a social media look-book, shot paparazzi-style, in leggings, biker shorts, and bandeau bras.

Kanye West undoubtedly inspired his acolytes from Calabasas to Tokyo to live in neutrals, sweatpants, and Yeezys. But many in the fashion establishment saw his work, especially early iterations, as amateurish and his famous bluster as overcompensation for poor design. "This second round of drab, broken-down basics proved he can't be taken seriously as a designer, but nevertheless many people in fashion *do* seem to take West seriously—they keep showing up expectantly for his performances—and that makes them fools," said noted critic Cathryn Horn about Season 2. "I'm kind of over Kanye," said Fern Mallis, the industry doyenne, creator of New York Fashion Week, and executive director of the Council of Fashion Designers of America (CFDA), in 2015. "I mean, I'm not a fan of his music, and the attitude and the agenda is not my style." Others basically told Kanye to stick to making music. "I think he's fine as a rapper. I think he's a joke as a fashion designer," ripped publicist Kelly Cutrone. "I just think that you should stay focused at what you're good at. Just because you're a good rapper doesn't mean you're going to be a good fashion designer."

As in music, Kanye went after his detractors. He got on Twitter to tell Mallis that "attempting to do clothing has been difficult" and that he was "too famous." "He went crazy on me—tweeting in the middle of the night—and the media was following it worldwide," Mallis said to me. When asked how this compared to the numerous designers she's encountered, she explained: "Designers have a tougher skin or at least they behave better. I mean, it's part of the process. They're used to [showing collections] two to four times a year. They put their things out there for their audience to see and they get criticized or they get complimented. You never know what somebody's gonna say." His rants increasingly become more worrisome and prompted questions around his mental health. "He pissed off as many people as he pleased. And that was fine with him. He had his own vision of what he wanted to do," Mallis said. As time went on, the line between mad genius and someone who needed help became more evident. Nobody could tell him nothing.

Chapter Fourteen

BILLIONAIRE BOYS CLUB

The Ise Jingū (or Ise Grand Shrine) is the most sacred Shinto shrine in Japan and is known as the "Soul of Japan." Millions of devotees visit every year to conduct rituals for prosperity, peace, and abundance. Ten minutes away is one of the most venerated places in fashion: the home of Hiroshi Fujiwara, widely considered the godfather of streetwear. Born in Ise, Mie, in 1964, Fujiwara was always drawn to faraway culture. "The first impact was punk rock, when I was thirteen years old, so I always wanted to go to England or to come to Tokyo to buy those punk clothes. I also think I was really lucky to feel punk culture when I was thirteen years old, because it changed everything. It really inspired me," he said. At eighteen, he moved to Tokyo, where he immersed himself in street fashion, which at the time included preppy, Karasu Zoku (wearing all black), punk, and Parisian styles.

In 1989, Fujiwara launched his line, Goodenough, after meeting Shawn Stüssy, founder of the namesake streetwear giant, and Nick Philip, founder of BMX-inspired line Anarchic Adjustment. Streetwear was a small community and Fujiwara shepherded the next generation of Japanese designers. In 1993, he began helping Jun Takahashi of avant-garde label Undercover, and Nigo, who would go on to found A Bathing Ape (aka BAPE), one of hip-hop's favorite streetwear lines. People would say, "If you want to know what's going on, ask Hiroshi."

Streetwear is defined as "fashionable casual clothes," but that only touches the surface. The aesthetic began in the late 1970s and early '80s and featured elements of punk and Japanese street fashion, hip-hop, skate, surf, and graffiti. Streetwear was counterculture and represented fighting against conventions. As *Hypebeast* explained: "In essence, street-wear involves the production, promotion, sale, and resale of casual fashion . . . in ways that bypass traditional retail channels, often sub-verting the way the fashion industry has long defined and dictated how 'cool' is made profitable. The audience, and therefore the target market, is very young: mostly under twenty-five." The designers were young and employed grassroots means of printing T-shirts and clothes. "We were just making stuff for ourselves and our friends in the beginning," said Will Rowley-Conwy, co-founder of streetwear line Done London. "It was really just a way for us to connect with our peers, and when we eventually started selling our T-shirts, we saw that people actually wanted to support what we were doing because they appreciated the effort we put into making stuff."

Hip-hop had a long history of its own streetwear brands, including Karl Kani, Walker Wear, and Baby Phat. However, the bridge between hip-hop and Japanese designers came from Pharrell Williams. Pharrell and Chad Hugo—the production duo the Neptunes—ushered in their signature "Neptunes sound" of sparse beats, whirring synths, mouth clicks, and Pharrell's falsetto that dominated the aughts. Pharrell was a futurist and experimented with new sounds that pushed artists outside of their comfort zone.

He was a fashion risk-taker as well. The producer turned artist went against the grain in skinny jeans, trucker hats, and graphic T-shirts. "They looked like dorks to me," said Noreaga of the first time meeting Pharrell, who was in tight jeans and a choker. Even before hip-hop,

Pharrell was an outsider. He grew up skateboarding in Virginia—earning the nickname "Skateboard P"—which wasn't considered a popular sport for young Black kids at the time. "I think growing up and being a skater kid in an environment that wasn't friendly to skater kids just gave him a lot of confidence because he just didn't care," Loïc Villepontoux, a longtime business associate of Pharrell, said to me. But not fitting in was the X factor that set Pharrell apart.

Pharrell met his streetwear soulmate through hip-hop's preeminent lapidary Jacob the Jeweler. Thousands of miles away, Nigo of BAPE was a fan. "We were shopping with Jacob the Jeweler one day and he said, 'Hey, there's a guy who's a DJ, I believe, in Tokyo and he loves you. He buys all your jewelry. He knows all you guys' music,'" Pusha T recounted to me. "He was like, 'I have to let you guys meet each other.'" Pharrell made his first trip to Japan in 2003 and the two had an instant connection. Through a translator, they shared the universal language of style. Pusha remembered Pharrell's excitement afterward. "He's got a clothing line and this is the *illest shit* I think I ever seen."

Pusha, who had signed to Pharrell's Star Trak imprint in 2001, was living with the producer and saw the perks of knowing Nigo. "We started getting boxes upon boxes upon boxes of clothes, shoes, shirts, jackets, and hoodies," he said. BAPE was unknown to most hip-hop fans and some weren't ready to trade in their favorite brands for streetwear. "My friends were like, 'Fuck that shit. Man, what are those fake Air Force 1s,'" Pusha said. "Then [later], they ended up stealing my shoes and selling them. Doing all type of weird shit. I was like, 'Oh? I thought you were laughing.'" BAPE grew as a cult brand, as did mystique around its designer. Only those in the know made a requisite stop at his atelier overseas. "I was getting the clothes for so long and hearing these tales about him and then finally meeting him in Japan was crazy," said Pusha T.

The first rapper to wear BAPE was The Notorious B.I.G. During a photoshoot for *Ego Trip* at the Good Luck Bar in Los Feliz on March 7, 1997, the rapper admired the BAPE camo jacket worn by photographer

Shawn Mortensen. According to Maureen Hilbun, Mortensen's mother and the administer of his estate, the jacket was gifted to her son by Nigo. "Shawn asked Biggie if he could take a photo of him wearing the jacket as a surprise for Nigo. Biggie agreed," she told me. "Shawn's jacket was only a size XL, and too small for The Notorious B.I.G.!" That image of Biggie draped in the BAPE jacket, a soft cream shirt, and his signature Versace sunglasses was exhibited at the BAPE Gallery in Japan for Mortensen's book *It's My Life . . . or It Seemed Like a Good Idea at the Time* in 2002 and on limited-edition T-shirts. Biggie was rumored to have requested bespoke BAPE pieces in his size. "He loved it so much that his team got in contact with Nigo, who made a special collection for him," said Kevin Le, brand partnerships manager at BAPE, who heard the story. Since the rapper died only days after the photoshoot, it's unknown how much of this was truth or streetwear lore.

The Beastie Boys were also early BAPE enthusiasts and met Nigo back in 1987 when he opened for them on tour (he was a DJ and rapper). It's unclear when they began wearing the clothing, but Adam "Ad-Rock" Horovitz was spotted in a mustard "Very Ape" shirt in Portugal in 1998 and then on tour in Melbourne, Australia, in 1999. The same year, Nigo created custom action figures of the group around their *Hello Nasty* album. The lifelike renderings of Michael "Mike D" Diamond, Adam "MCA" Yauch, and Ad-Rock in custom BAPE took two years to make, according to an interview with Nigo posted on *Beastie Mania* (the exact interview date is unknown, but it's circa 2000 or 2001, based on Nigo's age). Only one thousand sets were made, and the designer was adamant that they were not safe to take into the bathtub!

The question of who should be credited for popularizing BAPE in hip-hop is a source of ongoing tension. In 2006, Lil Wayne wore a pink camo BAPE hoodie, unzipped and shirtless, on the cover of *Vibe*. Meanwhile, Pharrell rapped: *"Buy yourself some Bapestas / Bulletproof under T-shirts because they hate us"* on Clipse's "Mr. Me Too" in 2006.

Dapper Dan with LL Cool J, 1986.
DAPPER DAN

Big Daddy Kane with
Dapper Dan's MCM
Jeep, 1988.
DAPPER DAN

Olympian Diane Dixon in a Dapper Dan
custom jacket, 1986. DAPPER DAN

Run-D.M.C., 1986. PETER BROOKER/SHUTTERSTOCK

Salt-N-Pepa, 1988.
EUGENE ADEBARI/
SHUTTERSTOCK

LEFT: "Cross Flags": the Lo Lifes (clockwise from top left: Naughty 40, Bek Live, Big Vic Lo aka Thirstin Howl The 3rd, and Disco) in Times Square, 1988. THIRSTIN HOWL THE 3RD

ABOVE: Tyson Beckford. DMI/THE LIFE PICTURE COLLECTION/ SHUTTERSTOCK

LEFT: Karen Mulder walks the Chanel Fall/Winter 1991 ready-to-wear show in Paris. GUY MARINEAU/CONDÉ NAST/ SHUTTERSTOCK

Tupac Shakur in a
Karl Kani ad, 1993.
KARL KANI

Designer Karl Kani,
1992. KARL KANI

LEFT: Designer April Walker in a Fashion in Effect custom outfit, circa 1988–1989.
APRIL WALKER

ABOVE: Aaliyah at Tommy Hilfiger's "Next Generation Jeans" ad shoot, 1997.
ALEX BERLINER/BEI/SHUTTERSTOCK

LEFT: The Notorious B.I.G. and Sean "Puffy" Combs in Versace, 1995.
ERIK PENDZICH/
SHUTTERSTOCK

ABOVE: Foxy Brown, 1999. DMI/THE LIFE PICTURE COLLECTION/SHUTTERSTOCK

ABOVE: Mary J. Blige and Lil' Kim, 1999. DMI/THE LIFE PICTURE COLLECTION/SHUTTERSTOCK

RIGHT: Eve, 2004.
KADZEN/SHUTTERSTOCK

Tupac Shakur wearing
Versace in Milan, 1996.
DAVID MCLEAN

Lil' Kim in Versace
at the Met Gala, 1999.
RT/MEDIAPUNCH/
SHUTTERSTOCK

RIGHT: Sean "Puffy" Combs unveils a Sean John window at Bloomingdale's in New York City, 2000.
DMI/THE LIFE PICTURE COLLECTION/SHUTTERSTOCK

ABOVE: Jay-Z, 1999.
WALIK GOSHORN/MEDIAPUNCH/ SHUTTERSTOCK

RIGHT: Jennifer Lopez, the famous Versace dress, and Sean "Puffy" Combs, 2000.
BEI/SHUTTERSTOCK

Dame Dash, Victoria Beckham, and Kareem "Biggs" Burke launch Rocawear at Selfridges in London, 2003. RICHARD YOUNG/SHUTTERSTOCK

Kimora Lee Simmons and her daughters close the Baby Phat fashion show, 2005. JASON SZENES/EPA/ SHUTTERSTOCK

ABOVE: Kanye West and his Paris Fashion Week squad (left to right: Don C, Taz Arnold, Chris Julian, Kanye West, Derek "Fonzworth Bentley" Watkins, and Virgil Abloh). TOMMY TON

ABOVE: Pharrell Williams and Nigo launch Ice Cream and BBC footwear, 2004. BEI/SHUTTERSTOCK

LEFT: The Notorious B.I.G. in BAPE, 1997. THE PHOTOGRAPHY OF SHAWN MORTENSEN

Virgil Abloh at the Off-White show in Paris, 2018.
PIXELFORMULA/SIPA/SHUTTERSTOCK

Pharrell wearing a Vivienne Westwood Buffalo hat, aka "the Pharrell hat," 2014.
LARRY BUSACCA/WIREIMAGE

RIGHT: Outkast, 2003.
JASON SZENES/EPA/
SHUTTERSTOCK

BELOW: Kanye West
in a Givenchy kilt during
the Watch the Throne
tour, 2011.
SHUTTERSTOCK

ABOVE: Cam'ron in pink at the
Baby Phat New York Fashion Week
show, 2003. DJAMILLA ROSA COCHRAN/
WIREIMAGE

Young Thug, 2021.
STEPHEN LOVEKIN/
SHUTTERSTOCK

Tyler, The Creator at
the Louis Vuitton Fall/
Winter Paris Fashion
Week show, 2022.
PASCAL LE SEGRETAIN/
GETTY IMAGES FOR
LOUIS VUITTON

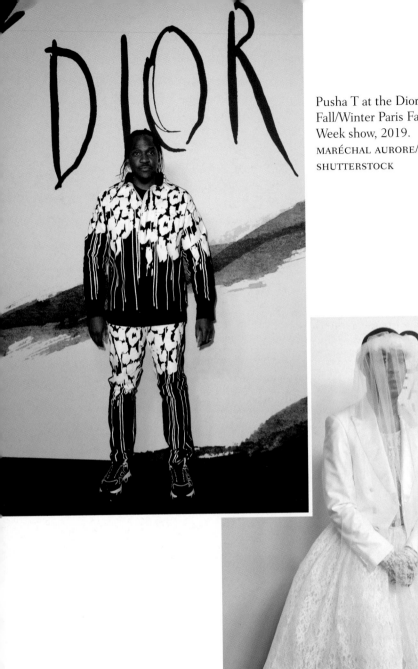

Pusha T at the Dior Homme
Fall/Winter Paris Fashion
Week show, 2019.
MARÉCHAL AURORE/ABACA/
SHUTTERSTOCK

Kid Cudi at the CFDA
Fashion Awards, 2021.
STEPHEN LOVEKIN/SHUTTERSTOCK

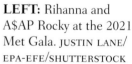

RIGHT: Cardi B in Moschino at the 2018 Met Gala. HECTOR RETAMAL/AFP VIA GETTY IMAGES

LEFT: Rihanna and A$AP Rocky at the 2021 Met Gala. JUSTIN LANE/ EPA-EFE/SHUTTERSTOCK

RIGHT: Future and Naomi Campbell at the Boss Fall/Winter Milan Fashion Week show, 2022. RICCARDO GIORDANO/IPA-AGENCY N/ SHUTTERSTOCK

Cardi B in Custom Schiaparelli
Haute Couture, 2021.
SCHIAPARELLI

A$AP Rocky at the Gucci Fall/
Winter Milan Fashion Week show,
2023. VITTORIO ZUNINO CELOTTO/
GETTY IMAGES FOR GUCCI

Many believed that the song about imitators was a shot at Wayne. "Who the fuck is Pharrell? Do you really respect him? That nigga wore BAPEs and y'all thought he was weird. I wore it and y'all thought it was hot," Wayne said. Meanwhile, Soulja Boy claimed that he was the originator among young fans and wore BAPE in 2007's "Crank Dat (Soulja Boy)" music video. "I mess with Pharrell," he said, giving the producer his props, but explained that he most wholeheartedly embodied the brand. "I really live this!"

"Nigo is just as important and significant to hip-hop as Pharrell, or Slick Rick, or Kanye," said A$AP Rocky. Before becoming a fashionable rapper, Kid Cudi worked at BAPE in New York City. "BAPE is like my generation's Chanel," Virgil Abloh said. "To me, what Nigo did to build this brand is something we may never see in our lifetime again. It represents youth culture, it represents Japanese streetwear aesthetic, it represents American hip-hop. It represents a formative year in our generation's lifetime."

In 2003, Pharrell and Nigo created their own streetwear line, Billionaire Boys Club (BBC), and subsequently Ice Cream. Hip-hop fashion lines like Sean John and Rocawear were dominating the landscape and BBC needed to be different. The name was a play on words on how Pharrell saw luxury as a mentality, not a price tag. "Wealth is of the heart and mind. Not the pocket." The logo of a spaceman represented the brand's forward-looking perspective. "It was crowded, and we knew that if we could find a different angle, we'd have more chance of succeeding," said Villepontoux, VP of Billionaire Boys Club and Ice Cream.

The team turned to BAPE for a blueprint. They set up a staff and design studio in Japan and used BAPE T-shirts for the original samples. "They all had Bathing Ape tags," Villepontoux said. The first collection of T-shirts, hoodies, varsity jackets, and outerwear was so small that it fit into two duffel bags.

Pharrell launched the brand in his music video for "Frontin'" (featuring Jay-Z) in 2003. He wanted fans to see that this wasn't a line he was merely financially backing, but designs he really wore. "Yeah, that ['Frontin'' video debut] was calculated. Not because we were going to launch the brand, but because I just wanted to see that. I wanted to present every-body with my world, because at that time, I was making Billionaire Boys Club stuff for myself," he said. The line of T-shirts, varsity jackets, polos, and sneakers (in collaboration with Reebok) were cut slim and designed in bright colors that fit Pharrell's aesthetic—he wore his own supply. The pricing was more expensive than other hip-hop brands but on par with high fashion: fleeces ($300–$500), varsity jackets ($1200), and special T-shirts (some as much as $550).

There were ten to fifteen early distributors. Villepontoux pointed to Barneys as a significant retailer because it "elevated the brand" with tastemakers. Because Pharrell was an owner, and not just someone getting a check, he was invested in its success. "It definitely helped to have Pharrell showing up to meetings. If Pharrell didn't succeed as a music producer, he could definitely have been a salesman of some sort." Villepontoux laughed. "'Cause he's really good at selling things." BBC implemented its international vision and launched brick-and-mortar outlets globally, including New York City, London, Tokyo, and Miami, which was something other hip-hop lines had not successfully accom-plished. In addition to selling clothes, these stores served as hangout spots and destinations for fans.

As a prolific hitmaker, Pharrell amplified his brand in songs in-cluding Jay-Z's "Change Clothes" in 2003 and Snoop Dogg's "Drop It Like It's Hot" in 2004. In May 2012, Jay-Z's Roc Apparel Group signed a partnership agreement with Billionaire Boys Club/Ice Cream. By 2013, a decade after it began, BBC and its brands generated $25 million to $30 million. The biggest test for BBC was whether it was strong enough to stand on its own as Pharrell focused on other pursuits. "It's a hard business, especially if you're an artist connected to a brand," said Villepontoux. "The minute you lose interest or your fan base doesn't think you're involved in that brand anymore, it just loses traction and it becomes worthless. I think we're one—I can't think of any other brand—that can stand on its own." Pharrell had launched a brand that was capable of flourishing autonomously. He had his eyes set on high fashion, but the BBC base of streetwear fans remained intact.

"Every five years, music completely changes," Pharrell said to me in 2012, his dyed green hair poking out from underneath his beanie. "Then, in the fifth year, something new comes out and everyone turns around and follows that." He constantly reinvented himself in fashion. This was apparent in his choice of chapeau at the 2014 Grammy Awards, when he wore a dimpled brown derby from Vivienne Westwood with a red Adidas track jacket. He was a true urban cowboy. The hat had various names, including the Buffalo Hat, Jelly Mould Hat, and Mountain Hat, but if you asked anybody, it was simply "the Pharrell hat."

The success of BAPE and Billionaire Boys Club laid out a blueprint for Virgil Abloh to start his streetwear line. Born on September 30, 1980, to Ghanaian parents, Abloh grew up in the Chicago suburb of Rockford. He obtained a degree in civil engineering from the University of Wisconsin–Madison and studied architecture at the Illinois Institute of Technology. He and Kanye both shared eclectic tastes and the desire to disrupt. In 2009, they went to the ground floor of luxury fashion and became interns at Fendi's headquarters in Rome. Although they were well past typical intern age, they wanted to be exposed to high fashion in the flesh. "We interned at Fendi but we ain't do shit. We ain't get to do nothing. We were just happy to have a key card," Kanye remembered. "Every day, going to work, walking to work, getting cappuccinos." They made an indelible impression on Michael Burke, chief executive of Fendi at the time, in the six months of the internship. "I paid them $500 a month! I was really impressed with how they brought a whole new vibe to the studio and were disruptive in the best way," said Burke, who would become the chief executive of Louis Vuitton.

Kanye believed that ideas they brought to Fendi were plagiarized, and specifically, leather jogging pants. "Me and Virgil are in Rome giving designs to Fendi over and over and getting our designs knocked down," he said. "We brought the leather jogging pants six years ago to Fendi, and they said no. How many motherfuckers you done seen with a jogging pant?" It was true that several versions of leather trousers were seen afterward on the runways of Saint Laurent, Isabel Marant, Balmain, and Alexander Wang, but how much of that was directly caused by Kanye (or simply a trend that everybody embraced) couldn't be known for sure. Ego hit aside, anybody who has been an intern knows that it's common for companies to source ideas from fresh talent. That's probably why Kanye and Abloh were in the building. And by his own admission, the pair weren't designers in the traditional sense. "We couldn't figure out how to actually make the clothes, so we'd just do it in Photoshop," Kanye said. "And Virgil became the fastest Photoshop artist that I have ever met in my life."

Virgil Abloh was more than a "Photoshop artist." He became the creative director at DONDA, the umbrella company for Kanye's creative work, in 2010 and conceptualized several iconic album covers that were aesthetically interesting and thought-provoking. In 2010, he selected artist George Condo to create the artwork for Kanye's *My Beautiful Dark Twisted Fantasy*, and in 2011, he commissioned Givenchy's creative director, Riccardo Tisci, for Jay-Z and Kanye's *Watch the Throne* artwork. This earned Abloh a Grammy nomination for Best Recording Package. Virgil was a tastemaker with a deep sensibility of who was hot and what was next. He curated his inspirations, daily outfits, and influences on his Tumblr, which became a destination for rappers and creatives.

In 2012, Virgil founded his first brand, Pyrex Vision, by screenprinting on old Ralph Lauren Rugby flannels. He put the phrase *Pyrex* 23, a homage to crack dealers' bakeware of choice and basketball legend Michael Jordan's jersey number, and sold the shirts for $550 each. After he ended the line, he launched his streetwear line Off-White in 2013. The luxury brand was based in Milan, which was a definitive way of showing that Virgil was serious about being seen as a European brand. Off-White encapsulated his cosmopolitan lifestyle: the amalgam of streetwear, music, travel, design, and art. He added quotation marks on his designs, which showed his sense of humor. This wasn't something to be taken too seriously. Virgil leveraged his fame into numerous collaborations, which would become popular with other high fashion brands. French *Vogue* counted at least twenty-six partnerships he did by 2021, from the Mercedes-Benz G-Class SUV to Nike and the National Basketball Association (NBA). Some of these alliances were truly strange, like the Off-White color-block alarm clock with Braun in 2021 or the collaboration with IKEA—including random objects like a brown paper shopping bag with the word "Sculpture" and a welcome mat that read "WET GRASS"—in 2019.

Virgil was a pop culture fixture. In 2013, he directed A$AP Rocky's "Fashion Killa" music video, which co-starred Rihanna, and he became a celebrity DJ. In 2019, he designed Hailey Baldwin's wedding dress when she married pop superstar Justin Bieber. The off-the-shoulder, lace-embroidered Off-White dress had a plunging back and long sleeves that extended over her hands. Her veil read on the hemline, in quotation marks: "Till death do us part." "From day one, I said I wanted Virgil," the supermodel bride said. "I didn't want somebody who was a wedding dress designer. I just feel like my style and my street style is such a part of who I am, and Virgil has always been in my corner since the beginning."

The real brand that people were buying into was Virgil. In 2018, *Time* selected the designer as one of the hundred most influential people in the world. In his profile, acclaimed Japanese artist Takashi Murakami wrote of his impact: "Kids' fervor for the stripe patterns and arrow marks he created for his fashion label, Off-White, is not a passing trend; rather, it shows how Virgil's young followers, with their unclouded eyes, have been seeing right into the core of his creativity all along."

Virgil's arrival at Louis Vuitton in 2018 was one of the most seismic shifts in high fashion. The idea that there was a thirty-seven-year-old

Black man—who came from hip-hop—sitting at the company's head-quarters at 2 Rue du Pont Neuf was mind-blowing. This wasn't a one-off collaboration or some ephemeral love affair. Virgil had a real seat at the table as a decision-maker. "I'm here; I want to show that I'm just a figure with many more behind him. I've cracked open the door. I want to show it's open, to meet people halfway," he said on the eve of his first Louis Vuitton collection. "Laying a foundation, that's what this season is about. I want to speak to the generation presiding. But I also want a young generation to come in and know, hey, there's someone here who's listening and speaking back to them."

Virgil was the cultural bridge for Louis Vuitton. He brought his streetwear sensibility while respecting the legacy of the heritage house. Pieces like the XXL monogram puffer vest, chain-strapped bags, and a shiny Keepall travel bag (called the Prism) made in iridescent PVC were young and fresh. He wasn't afraid to play with fluorescent colors, fabrics, or logos. He also made bold moves that were directed at hype-beasts and the streetwear community. In 2020, he released a capsule collection with Nigo of elevated streetwear with tailored denim, bucket hats, and a delicious tote that featured both Louis Vuitton's monogram and Damier print for a logo overload.

Creatives from all aspects of culture became a part of Virgil's vision. He hired multicultural and nontraditional models, many of whom were his friends from music, for the exuberant fashion shows. For the 2018 debut show, rapper Kid Cudi and musicians Steve Lacy and Dev Hynes walked the rainbow-colored runway at the Palais-Royal. The front row was flanked with famous names whom Virgil had collaborated with over the years, like A$AP Rocky, Rihanna, and Murakami.

Kanye and Virgil tearfully hugged on the runway, although their relationship was now strained. Kanye was insistent that he deserved the creative director position, not his protégé. After all, he was the one who carried that Louis Vuitton backpack all those years ago and he wasn't going to relinquish that sigil without a fight. "I felt like it was supposed to be me," he said. "I was the Louis Vuitton Don." Friends could turn into rivals at any time.

Virgil's appointment at Louis Vuitton correlated with high fashion as a whole embracing streetwear. In 2017, *Vogue* called streetwear "the biggest fashion movement in recent history." *Women's Wear Daily* reported "the once humble aesthetic has successfully moved into the higher echelons of fashion." Streetwear was cozy, flattering, and people were now willing to spend upward of $1,000 on sweatpants and hoodies. This created lucrative opportunities for streetwear upstarts such as Kith and Vetements, co-founded by Balenciaga's creative director, Demna Gvasalia. Heritage houses used collaborations (like Louis Vuitton x Supreme) to work with notable streetwear names and garner authenticity within the culture.

In 2018, private equity behemoth the Carlyle Group made a billion-dollar bet on Supreme, which was acquired by VF Corporation (the parent company of the North Face and Vans) and valued at $2.1 billion two years later. Counterculture was a billion-dollar behemoth. Those who had been in streetwear since the start saw the irony. "Streetwear is never a trend. It was always a movement," Jian DeLeon, author of *The Incomplete Highsnobiety Guide to Street Fashion and Culture* and *The New Luxury*, explained to me. "Like people thought it was a trend but it was just a way of looking at product and connecting it directly to culture. It's just been a natural way for brands and labels who looked at what was happening." Some of the originators from the '90s and aughts saw the space turning into one big cash grab. "Back then, it just felt so fresh and new and exciting. Nobody knew what they were getting into," said Lanie Alabanza-Barcena, designer and owner of Hellz Bellz. "Now, kids have an exact blueprint of what can happen if they get into streetwear. Rather than get involved because they love it, it's about making as much money as possible."

The commercial opportunities benefited hip-hop designers of the past. The lines that were once called "urban" or considered relics were being deified as streetwear icons. April Walker and Karl Kani enjoyed a resurgence as respected OGs in streetwear. They had been early and were getting their due by the fashion industry at large. Kani saw success globally and expanded his brand to twenty-five countries in Europe and thirteen stores in Japan. Kimora Lee Simmons relaunched Baby Phat in 2019 for a new generation who celebrated inclusion and representation in the boys' club of streetwear. "I know this customer so well," she said of her continuing influence. "As women, we are special, exotic creatures. I raised my kids this way, I raised a whole generation of people that way and I want them to know we're still here, we're doing it."

Chapter Fifteen

DEVIL IN A NEW DRESS

Young Thug extended his long limbs to exaggerate the fluidity of the fabric. Baby blue with rows and rows of soft ruffles. At six foot three, the rapper had the proportions of a model, but his heavily inked-up face that included a snake by his hairline and rain cloud below his lower lip would give designers pause (possibly except for Louis Vuitton, given the huge "LV" tattooed on his neck). The garment was a modern take on the Japanese samurai warrior with a reimagined *kosode* cloak and *jingasa* hat that opened up into a full warrior stance. Young Thug wore the dress by Alessandro Trincone on the cover of his 2016 mixtape, *Jeffrey*. It was something only the self-proclaimed thug could pull off. "In my world, you could be a gangsta with a dress or you could be a gangsta with baggy pants," he said. "I feel like there's no such thing as gender."

The rapper first encountered the dress during *V Magazine*'s VFILES Season 7. The runway show championed young talent during New York Fashion Week and Thug was a mentor alongside legendary supermodel Naomi Campbell, makeup artist Pat McGrath, Fear of God's Jerry Lorenzo, and stylist Mel Ottenberg. He was hands-on, literally, walking on the runway to fix a model's look. "I think he is going to have a major impact on the way fashion and music come together in the future as he looks through a lens that is totally unfiltered and not subjected to preexisting paradigms of how one should approach the way they dress," VFILES founder Julie Anne Quay said. "His approach to gender fluidity is a very powerful moment I think for fashion because it is connected to his approach to music and the message he shares through that medium."

"This is the cover for my album *Jeffrey*," Thug said when he first saw the dress, likening it to a character from a popular action-adventure video game. "It's like *Mortal Kombat* . . . Sub-Zero." Wearing a piece of art was an involved process. Garfield Larmond, the photographer behind the cover of *Jeffrey*, said, "When we got on set, it definitely took like an hour and a half to put it on. Then once he put it on, and I started shooting, they noticed a piece was off—like something really intricate. So we had to take another thirty minutes to pin stuff up, get the hat right. It took hours. Hours on top of hours." For the twenty-five-year-old Italian designer of the dress, the widespread notoriety was a total surprise. Trincone explained: "I was literally shocked because Young Thug and me—I don't know. But I said, 'Okay, let's try it.' Then when I saw the cover I was like 'Oh my God. I did it.' I liked it."

Young Thug's background was in sharp contrast to his carefree fashion persona. Born Jeffrey Williams on August 16, 1991, he was raised in the Jonesboro South housing project in Atlanta. "It was worse than struggle—that shit was hell," he said. Growing up poor, he was one of eleven children, and got in trouble from a young age. "I was in the streets at eight, nine years old," he told *Rolling Stone*. "I was going to school so my dad and mom would keep buying me clothes, but when I got out I did what I wanted to do—fighting, all kinds of shit." In middle school, he was sent to juvenile detention after breaking his teacher's arm. "I didn't do it for people to understand me. I did it for the weird ones," he told *XXL* about his desire to rap. He released his first mixtape, *I Came from Nothing*, in 2011 and quickly amassed an expansive discography, including 2015's *Barter 6*, which went gold. His music was vibrant and fun with

weird ad-libs and twisty lyrics—which an actual linguist decoded for
Genius—and he became the leader of modern trap. His first chart-topper
on the Billboard Hot 100 was his feature on Camila Cabello's "Havana"
in 2018—and he sounded even sexier than she did. Young Thug was an
anomaly, to say the least, as a flamboyant street rapper who intentionally
subverted gender norms. "Ninety percent of my clothes are women's," he
told *GQ*. "Because women's clothes are [slimmer] than men's clothes.
The jeans I got on right now, they're women's jeans. But they fit how
they're supposed to fit. Like a rock star."

High fashion heralded the enfant terrible as an androgynous revolutionary. *Dazed* called him "the closest music style icon we have to
[David] Bowie." *Vogue* spotlighted him for his femme style. He named
his cohort and record label Young Slime Life or YSL (a nod to the
French house formerly known as Yves Saint Laurent) and appeared
in a campaign for Calvin Klein, wearing womenswear. "You look hot in
a dress," said a woman in his promo shoot for Calvin Klein. Without a
blink, he responded, "Thanks."

However, pushing gender boundaries in clothing didn't immediately
translate in hip-hop. Instead of its being the precursor to progressiveness,
questions abounded about Young Thug's sexuality and gender identity,
despite the fact that he was very publicly romantically involved with
women. Reddit forums flooded with rumors and heated fan discussions
on topics like "Young Thug, gay or not?," "Since when is he gender
fluid???," and "Is young thug a part of the LGBT community?" Internet detectives scoured his old tweets and lyrics in search of a smoking
gun about his preferences for men, women, or both. "He's a hip-hop
cross-dresser," said radio shock jock Charlamagne Tha God, pointing
to parallels with Prince, rock artists, and hip-hop artist CeeLo Green,
who wore a wedding dress for a 2008 photoshoot with his group Gnarls
Barkley. The latter was more of a publicity stunt than a genuine fashion
statement, so perhaps Young Thug also intended to cause commotion.
"I think he's part of the new generation of men who have been growing

up under the feminization of society . . . It's a lot of men who didn't have fathers in the house. They just have de-masculated men in a way," mused Charlamagne. "But the other side of the coin is, he may be one of those guys who dresses that way, but he's very much a man. We don't know. I don't know the dude. Or maybe it's just the character."

Jerrika Karlae, Thug's then-fiancée, went on the offensive: "He's not gay. There's nothing gay about him . . . You really think I'm desperate enough to have to go with somebody that's gay?" Young Thug seemed blithely unconcerned by the rumors and relished in all of the attention. "I like everything that people say," he told the *Guardian*. "No matter what they say. You gay, you a punk. You got a nice girlfriend, you're ugly, you can't rap, you're the hardest." His manager underscored that the rapper resonated with Europeans specifically because he didn't embody the usual archetype of a rapper. "Yeah," agreed Thug, "because you're from Atlanta, Georgia, and you're dressed like a fucking European. Of course."

Young Thug was astute enough to realize that being outrageous generated attention and differentiated him in an increasingly crowded landscape. However, he was an aesthetic rebel even when he was younger. There's footage of the rapper as a teenager wearing what looks like True Religion skinny jeans (worn well below the natural waist) and a fitted varsity jacket. His friends laugh and ask him to turn around and show off this outfit, which he does with gusto.

Hip-hop had a complex history with masculinity. As a genre driven by Black men, its heteronormative and cisgender standards have been framed within the context of patriarchy and hegemony. Masculinity meant physical strength, success, style, and sexual charisma. The idea of toxic masculinity, marked by aggression, violence, and homophobia, was encouraged. Misogyny was often parsed into the idea that women were "bitches and hoes" and was reflected throughout the genre's discography—including by female rappers. The commercialization of hip-hop added another layer as record labels, media, and brands prioritized certain avatars of Black masculinity. As Dr. Crystal Belle explained in "From Jay-Z to Dead Prez: Examining Representations of Black Masculinity in Mainstream Versus Underground Hip-Hop Music": "There is a merging of intellectualism and the cliched 'thug' . . . the stereotypical representations . . . that Black men are too aggressive, violent, and angry. Rappers often exploit this stereotype, playing into the gaze of the white mainstream imagination in order to make profit."

Before hip-hop, Black music icons had long experimented with gender conventions by wearing extravagant clothing and makeup and paying meticulous attention to their hair. "R&B is very much about spending a ton of time figuring out your look before you come out in public. Hip-hop played far less into that," Touré, cultural critic and author of *Nothing Compares 2 U: An Oral History of Prince*, told me. "R&B definitely has a long history of the guy with his shirt open, maybe a frilly shirt that he got from the women's section. Before Prince, there's James Brown. So many of these people are the sons of Little Richard." Since the 1950s, rock and roll pioneer Little Richard was known for his signature look—a full face of makeup, dark eyeliner, and his hair done up in a pompadour—and a wardrobe of voluminous capes, billowy sleeves, and enough sequins to make Liberace proud. Throughout his decades-long career, he had a complicated relationship with his own sexuality and vacillated between acceptance and homophobia. He would describe himself in various ways, including gay, bisexual, and omnisexual. "A third degree of gender fluidity or gender play is central to Black masculine sartorial expression," Dr. Jonathan Michael Square, writer and historian specializing in fashion and visual culture, explained to me. "I would say that there's a long history of Black men playing around with fashion and playing around with gender more than playing around with sexuality."

As drug dealers became the driving force of masculinity in hip-hop throughout the 1980s and '90s, rappers took on their streetwise mentality and persona. "What separates hip-hop in that regard is its relationship to drug dealer culture," said Touré, and pointed to rappers invoking the menacing visage of the "drug dealer screw face" in photos and music videos. "Drug dealers have talked to me about this sort of ethos of you would never do anything that would allow somebody to think that they might be able to test you. This leads you to a sort of hyper-masculinity." The paradigm changed to being rough and rugged. Someone in the streets—or inspired by a life of criminality—had the mentality of survival and not fun.

In the South, the drug dealer was the "d-boy" (a slang for dope boy) and the place he was slinging from was the "trap." Trap music as a sub-genre originated in Atlanta during the 1990s and helped propel the region from under the shadow of either coasts, as André 3000 of OutKast predicted at the 1995 Source Awards: "The South got something to say!" His prescience was manifested in the aughts. Trap music's distinct sound of synth beats with pounding percussion and complex hi-hats (influenced by the Roland TR-808 drum machine) was infectious. Trap artists fed the streets by incessantly releasing music in the form of mixtapes. The biggest artists leaned into their d-boy background: T.I. crowned himself the "Kang of the South," Young Jeezy made promo T-shirts emblazoned with a Snowman representing his cocaine ties, and Gucci Mane's 2012 mixtape *Trap Back* featured incarcerated Black Mafia Family (BMF) kingpin Demetrius "Big Meech" Flenory.

Southern rap usually referred to artists from Atlanta, but the region was broader and included Houston, New Orleans, Miami, Memphis, and parts of the Midwest. Initially, the South's fashion was as respected as the music. Rappers dressed like ordinary people, especially when viewed through the critical lens of New York City. Everybody more or less had the same uniform: a white T-shirt that was several sizes too big and baggy jeans accessorized with a chain and grillz. Dem Franchize Boyz made a tribute to this look with "White Tee" in 2004. Even the successful Cash Money Millionaires, which included rappers Lil Wayne, Birdman, and Juvenile, wore this in their breakout music video for "Back

That Azz Up" in 1999. Sports jerseys were also popular and impactful in tapping into regional tribalism. St. Louis native Nelly introduced himself to the world in "Country Grammar (Hot Shit)" in a Cardinals jersey and Air Force 1s in 2000. Southern rappers also loved to be shirtless, which made sense due to the heat, compared to their colleagues above the Mason-Dixon Line. The Southern look was democratic—anybody could throw on a white Hanes T-shirt.

That said, it would be remiss not to mention Pimp C, who famously donned a huge mink coat in the music video for Jay-Z's "Big Pimpin'" (featuring UGK) in 1999. It was ninety degrees in Miami and Jay-Z asked the Texas rapper why he wanted to wear the fur he brought to set in the beachy visual. But Pimp C knew the power of statement fashion. "Man, TV ain't got no temperature," he said, and walked away. That's when Jay-Z, the bigger celebrity by comparison, turned to UGK's Bun B and said, "Your brother's a motherfucking star!" The standout of "Big Pimpin'" was not A-list video vixens and scantily clad hotties—with their assets zoomed in on by the fish-eye lens—but Pimp C, shirtless, in his mink.

The subsequent wave of trap artists would embrace luxury fashion in droves—and the feeling was mutual. The supergroup Migos broke out with 2013's "Versace"—the chorus would name-drop the Italian brand some thirty-six times—and the song would get played that same year at Versace's runway show in Milan. In 2018, the trio wore matching Versace suits to the Met Gala. Future became a fashion darling, with a handsome face and the rare physique that could wear all types of clothing well. "Future long ago mastered the art of personal style, a comfort that enables him to transition from street- to formalwear without a hiccup," lauded The Cut. He was referred to as a "toxic king" because of the promiscuity and emotional maturity that marked his music and private life, and unsurprisingly, he scored points with male fans and rappers. Former trappers cleaned up and used fashion as a way to reinvent themselves. Young Jeezy renamed himself as just "Jeezy" in 2010 and later stepped up his fashion game with his wife, the stylist turned TV personality

Jeannie Mai. Gucci Mane underwent a 180-degree transformation after coming home from prison in 2016. He shed a hundred pounds and began wearing upscale and tailored looks, like a $10,000 head-to-toe designer look to his 2020 *Verzuz* battle against Jeezy and a turquoise tuxedo to the 2017 BET Awards designed by—who else—Gucci.

André 3000 created the blueprint as the Southern rap provocateur both in music and fashion. In 1994, he and Big Boi debuted as OutKast with their first album *Southernplayalisticadillacmuzik*, a fresh and soulful album featuring live instrumentation. Like their group's moniker, they were outcasts. While his partner, Big Boi, preferred an Atlanta Braves jersey and jeans, André took fashion risks that ran the gamut from dashikis to dandyism. The rapper experimented with turbans, colorful wigs, furry pants, and suspenders. In the 2007 music video for UGK's "Int'l Players Anthem (I Choose You)," he played the role of a groom wearing a tartan kilt. "OutKast really broke the mold for Atlanta hip-hop," said Derek "Fonzworth Bentley" Watkins, who also appeared in the video, to me. "They put us on a national and global scale. I was happy 'cause I'm like, you gotta do *something* to make sure to get these folks' attention."

André's lyrical prowess and popularity with women, especially his public relationship with singer Erykah Badu, gave him the green light to push boundaries with the hip-hop establishment. "André was beloved, his masculinity was unquestionable," said Touré. "He had been with many women that we all sort of like, looked up to him for pulling. If he's wearing high fashion, his masculinity is not questioned."

The rapper also had the unique vantage of growing up in Atlanta, the paragon for Black prosperity and empowerment in America. In 1971, *Ebony* exalted the city as the "Black Mecca of the South" and declared: "Some say it's the place where Black dreams are most likely to come true." Activism was embedded into the city's fabric, as it was the birthplace of Dr. Martin Luther King Jr. and had had decades of Black political leadership, beginning with Mayor Maynard Holbrook Jackson Jr. in 1973. The Black church provided the spiritual backbone to the community, but this was juxtaposed with a long timeline of bawdy nightlife. The city was socially free and attracted out-of-towners looking for a good time. The annual Freaknik festival turned the streets into a party with hundreds of thousands of college students in the '90s, and to this day, the strip clubs are a beloved destination. I'll never forget my first trip to Magic City, where I saw both male and female patrons coolly eating wings and listening to the latest rap records—while T.I. walked around unbothered like a private citizen—and nobody was the least bit flustered by the fleshy dancers or dollar bills piling up on the floor. Watkins, an Atlanta native, explained: "Atlanta specifically has always had an interesting relationship with the way sex is celebrated. [The strip club] doesn't have the same connotation as in other places."

Watkins began working with OutKast prior to the groundbreaking double album *Speakerboxxx/The Love Below*. They immersed themselves into the eclectic double album—one side dedicated to Big Boi's Southern rap and the other to André's pop, funk, psychedelic fest—released in 2003. They formed a "Rat Pack" of creatives, including film director Bryan Barber and actor Lukas Haas, who made a cameo in the music video "Roses." In the visual for "Hey Ya!" (also helmed by Barber), André paid homage to the Beatles on *The Ed Sullivan Show* and donned long hair, polo shirts, equestrian helmets, and plaid pants. During this time, André and Watkins created their own lingo, a schtick inspired by comedy duo Abbott and Costello, in which they would speak to each other in posh British accents and say things like "Good day, good sir." You can hear some version of this on the album's interlude of the same name.

Along the same line, André launched his Benjamin Bixby fashion brand with sweaters, corduroys, and blazers for the modern gentleman in 2008. He told the *Observer* during the launch at Barney's that he was inspired by the 1930s because it was an era when "you had rough guys who played football, but they were impeccably dressed." However, there was a schism between listening to his music and being daring enough to dress like him. Benjamin Bixby was proper, straight out of the English countryside. André 3000 had made a line for him—he said that the clothes were his sketches and designs—and the average guy probably had no idea how to pair it with his staples. A fashion line needed wearable pieces with widespread appeal to be commercially viable. The rapper was too early of an adopter—everyone else was at least a decade behind—and Benjamin Bixby went defunct. Dré admitted at Complex Con in 2017 that he took a significant financial hit in launching his line. "I was like, 'Let me take this. Let me not get an investor.' So all of it was me. My own money. Unfortunately, I lost millions, to be honest. It was an expensive lesson. But I can tell you, it was the best times, the best lessons in my life about myself and creating things."

André 3000's spirit endured in future style disruptors. "He's a great bridge between them. Definitely somebody who is able to break down some barriers around, 'Hey, I can wear high fashion,'" said Touré. Young Thug would boast that he wasn't familiar with his predecessor, and even claimed, "I can't rap you two Andre 3000 songs." That was most likely young rapper hubris. The real power was in the subterfuge. He was influenced whether he realized it or not.

The term "metrosexual" is widely credited to journalist Mark Simpson, who wrote "Here Come the Mirror Men" in the *Independent* in November 1994. A portmanteau of metropolitan and sexual, the metrosexual was the modern man who didn't ascribe to old conventions of masculinity. He cared about his appearance, spent money on grooming, and wore top designers like Calvin Klein, Ralph Lauren, and Giorgio Armani. "Nevertheless, the metrosexual man contradicts the basic premise of traditional heterosexuality—that only women are looked at and only men do the looking," wrote Simpson. Despite the etymology, the term had nothing to do with sexual preference. "Metrosexual man might prefer women, he might prefer men, but when all's said and done, nothing comes between him and his reflection." In 2002, Simpson crowned soccer hunk David Beckham as the metrosexual prototype—hot, athletic, and groomed—who would replace the boring man of the past:

"For some time now, old-fashioned (re)productive, repressed, unmoisturized heterosexuality has been given the pink slip by consumer capitalism. The stoic, self-denying, modest straight male didn't shop enough (his role was to earn money for his wife to spend), and so he had to be replaced by a new kind of man, one less certain of his identity and much more interested in his image—that's to say, one who was much more interested in being looked at (because that's the only way you can be certain you actually exist). A man, in other words, who is an advertiser's walking wet dream."

Hip-hop's frame of masculinity correlated metrosexual traits to those of homosexuality, considered to be the antithesis of manhood. In song, the ultimate diss was labeling someone using homophobic slurs, such as in Ice Cube's 1991 "No Vaseline" and The Notorious B.I.G.'s posthumous "Dead Wrong" in 1999. The number of times slurs for gay men had been used was too many to count, but Eminem, Jay-Z, and Nas were some of the illustrious emcees who had used it in lyrics. Rappers proved their masculinity by beating their chests and bragging about sexual conquests and body counts. Hypersexuality was a shield from suspicion, but there were many rumors that the hip-hop industry harbored powerful Black men living double homosexual lives, known as being on the down-low or "DL." Popular radio host Wendy Williams had an entire schtick called "how you doin'?" that implied that a celebrity was secretly gay. Interestingly, unsuspecting viewers would co-opt this into a generic, positive catchphrase when her show went to daytime television.

In this climate of constant paranoia, Cam'ron popularized the term "no homo" in the late aughts as a catch-all shield. Anything that could be construed as homosexual was punctuated with the phrase. "With me, 'no homo' is basically installed in my vocabulary," said Cam'ron to Hot 97. He used it regardless of context, no matter how ridiculous it sounded. "It's like even if I'm in a meeting, I'll be with my lawyer and say something like 'no homo' and my lawyer be like looking at me and I'm like, 'I know you have no idea what I'm talking about, but I need to say that because I said something real homo, no homo.' It isn't about being gay. It's about saying something gay. For instance, my man Jim Jones said, 'I'ma beat you with that 'til all the white stuff come out of it.' That's wild homo." "No homo" and its auxiliary phrase, "pause," would become an annoying suffix used by rappers.

People used certain signalers such as an outfit's fit or color to draw inferences about the wearer's masculinity. Jay-Z questioned men who wore snug looks in 2009's "D.O.A. (Death of Auto-Tune)": *You niggas' jeans too tight / Your colors too bright, your voice too light (That's too far, nigga!)*." As skinny jeans rose in popularity, the older generation held steadfast to their baggy britches, which could be seen as a fight for turf as much as it was over masculinity.

Of course, there was a double standard. Rappers could wear something stereotypically feminine, like bright colors, if they offset it with hyper-masculinity. The scale had to be balanced, so to speak. Cam'ron was the poster boy of pink—spending $5,000 on a signature custom, head-to-toe baby-pink ensemble he wore to New York Fashion Week in 2003—but he was given a pass because of his street credibility. "I'd never seen anybody like Cam with it," said Wayne "Wayno" Clark, who was an assistant A&R at Roc-A-Fella Records. "Pink was always a girl's color. Like, nah, men don't wear pink. I never seen anybody wear pink. Now I own a few pairs of pink sweats." The music executive shared that "nobody was daring enough" or "had the heart" to pull off pink and pointed to Cam's stomping grounds in Harlem as influencing his gutsy wardrobe. "You'll never tell what a dude from the west side will do. That's some west side shit." "Cam was the first hard-core rapper to rock pink," said Emil Wilbekin, former editor in chief of *Vibe*, to the *New York Times*. Anybody who wore pink—Sean "Puffy" Combs, Jay-Z, and Fat Joe—could do so if they were not to be tested. Some laughed at Nas for wearing a pink suit in the 1996 music video for "Street Dreams," but his credibility as a respected emcee and position as a sex symbol protected him from any real backlash. And in his defense, he was playing a role inspired by Martin Scorsese's film *Casino*. What was more masculine than that?

Kanye West's sexuality was questioned because of his colorful Polo shirts and propensity to surrounded himself with gay creatives like Givenchy's Riccardo Tisci and Balmain's Olivier Rousteing. Despite the fact that Kanye was married to Kim Kardashian, the tabloids continually tried to out him for these friendships. By 2009, he told the *Guardian* that he was "secure in [his] manhood" and he could "go to Paris [and] have conversations with people who are blatantly gay." Kanye also became a trans ally when his father-in-law, Caitlyn Jenner, transitioned in 2015, including encouraging the Kardashian family to accept her. "I think this is one of the strongest things that's happened in our existence as human beings," said Kanye to Caitlyn. "You couldn't have been up against more."

In 2011, Kanye wore his most daring look: a leather Givenchy kilt. The vision—pleated kilt, long T-shirt, leather pants, and Yeezy sneakers—was courtesy of Tisci. "I know from the meeting that Ricardo, Virgil [Abloh], and Kanye had in Paris, he just knew he should be wearing a kilt," said stylist Renelou Padora. Backstage at the Watch the Throne tour, Kanye asked his inner circle, including longtime friend Don C, Virgil Abloh, and producer Mike Dean, to give him feedback on the pleats before the next show. The rapper stared at himself in the mirror, admiring the kilt. "I just love this . . . I just like the silhouette, it's really modern."

The fashion progeny of Kanye shared his perspectives. A$AP Rocky admonished young fans for succumbing to outdated definitions of masculinity and cited fashion as a vehicle for change. "In the criteria of the small state of mind of the urban community, you're 'gay.' Different is 'gay.' Weird is 'gay' where they come from. But they're slowly learning because of a guy named A$AP Rocky," he said. "As I got older, I don't discriminate against anybody . . . I'm wise enough to know that it's stupid and wrong."

Rocky ushered in a new wave of New York City hip-hop with 2011's *Live. Love. A$AP* and combined uptown flair with downtown sartorial sense. His A$AP Mob collective—including A$AP Ferg and A$AP Yams—was the next generation of Harlem after Dipset. Rocky called himself "that pretty motherfucka" and leveraged his photogenic good looks into working with DKNY, Calvin Klein, Ferragamo, and Dior Homme. He was unafraid in his style and one of the first adopters of brands like Raf Simons, Maison Martin Margiela, Christian Louboutin, and Jeremy Scott in hip-hop. Early on, Rocky would also be plagued by gay rumors. He didn't care and continued to boldly wear ankle-grazing hems, cropped cuts, and headscarves. His stance was defiant toward his haters. "I did a magazine cover with a gay designer, Jeremy Scott, which was an idol of mine. I admired his fashion and I admired his art since I was a late teen. I don't give a fuck about street people . . . I don't care."

Tyler, The Creator took another approach. The Odd Future front man was blatantly homophobic, violent, and sexist at the start of his career. *NME* reported that his 2011 debut studio album, *Goblin*, had the word f****t and its variants a total of 213 times. He was unapologetic in his homophobia and told the publication, "My gay fans don't find my language offensive." It seemed like Tyler was repeating the mistakes of his rap forefathers, but in reality, he was masking his truth. "*Next line will have 'em like, 'whoa' / I've been kissing white boys since 2004,*" he rapped on 2017's "I Ain't Got Time." Many were confused. The *Guardian* asked: "Is Tyler, The Creator coming out as a gay man or just a queer-baiting provocateur?" This marked a rebirth in terms of his public image and music. His *Flower Boy* album was a wistful and meditative exploration of love and sexuality that was critically and commercially applauded and nominated for Best Rap Album at the 2018 Grammy Awards.

It wasn't clear what Tyler's sexual orientation was, but Gen Z (anyone born from 1997 onward) didn't care. They were writing the new rules of identity. In 2020 Pew Research reported, "Ideas about gender identity are rapidly changing in the U.S., and Gen Z is at the front end of those changes." From a macro perspective, a record 7.1 percent of U.S. adults self-identified as lesbian, gay, bisexual, transgender, or something other than heterosexual, according to a 2022 Gallup poll, and Gen Z was driving those numbers. They were more open-minded and didn't need categorizations. Gender and sexuality were a vast spectrum—as seen by the plethora of pronouns surfaced in the zeitgeist—and whom their favorite artists slept with (or how they identified) was not relevant. When Kid Cudi wore a custom bridal dress from ERL and held the designer's hand at the 2021 CFDA Awards, it was just fashion. The rapper, who was known for streetwear, was celebrated for wearing a floral sundress on *Saturday Night Live* that year as an homage to Nirvana's Kurt Cobain, who wore a similar outfit on the cover of *The Face* in 1993. There was nothing more to read into it. In fact, when Offset misused the word "queer" in a 2018 song and Da Baby made homophobic comments at Rolling Loud in 2021, both were immediately censured and forced to apologize. Rappers who defended them, who were, unsurprisingly, older men, were viewed as antiquated dinosaurs.

Lil Nas X became hip-hop's most prominent openly gay rapper when he came out in 2019. His flamboyant style and openness would offend some in hip-hop. "Honestly, I don't feel as respected in hip-hop or many music places in general," he said. "But these are communities that I am a part of, whether people would like it or not . . . I am a rapper. I am a pop star. I am a gay artist. But it's like, I belong in these places, you know?" Detractors did nothing to slow his momentum. He resonated with young fans, and his debut, "Old Town Road," pushed boundaries as a rap-country hit that went on to sell ten million copies. He then made history at the BET Awards by kissing a male dancer while performing "Montero (Call Me by Your Name)" in 2021. When asked if he was actively pushing to normalize homosexuality, he was adamant. "You know what? Yeah. That's actually what I'm trying to do."

Hip-hop was approaching middle age and things were changing. The teenagers who listened to DJ Jazzy Jeff & the Fresh Prince's "Parents Just Don't Understand" in 1988 were now parents themselves. What was once rebellious was now regular. And even boring. For youth culture to survive, it had to evolve with new behavior and totems that would piss off its predecessors. "It's gonna rub people the wrong way, and that's what makes it fun and interesting," said Dr. Jonathan Michael Square. "You don't want to do something that your parents or grandparents like. You want to flip the script." "You can count on hip-hop to do the thing that will shock the parents," said Touré. "The kids are like, yeah, you're going in the right direction." The anathema of cool was becoming uncool and dated—an old head. The ante had to be upped again. Rappers had worn dresses . . . what was next?

Chapter Sixteen

DRIP GODS

D apper Dan's return to Harlem originated halfway around the world. Model Alana Henry walked down the runway in Florence, Italy, wearing a fur-paneled bomber jacket with balloon sleeves covered with the double-G logo. The look was one of 115 that Gucci showed as part of its cruise collection. To many, it was innocuous, but eagle-eyed watchers immediately spotted the offense. The bomber was a dead ringer for a custom Louis Vuitton jacket that Dapper Dan created for Olympian Diane Dixon decades earlier. Dixon posted side-by-side images on Instagram juxtaposing her version in mink and Gucci's knockoff with the caption: "'Bish' stole my look! Give credit to @dapperdanharlem He did it FIRST in 1989!"

Dap wasn't surprised that a luxury brand had pilfered his designs. "They ain't let me in the fashion world. I had all this anger in me," he said. "I didn't expect nothing but appropriation and exploitation from the fashion industry." The designer had gone underground since being raided by Fendi in 1992. But the social climate was different. There was dialogue about racism and appropriation being amplified on social media and consumers, especially millennials and Gen Z, valued social consciousness, responsibility, and transparency from brands more than did their predecessors.

The side-by-side comparison that Dixon posted went viral, and fans and critics harangued Gucci for plagiarism and appropriation. "We still struggle to garner a seat at the table. Even though we've oft built the table ourselves," wrote Faith Cummings in *Teen Vogue*. Dap was surprised by the outpouring of support from strangers, and pointed to Black women on social media as especially vocal in his defense. "I was shocked like everybody else when Black Twitter stood up for me because I had no voice . . . I'm still shocked," he said. "What surprised me the most, people who didn't even wear Gucci or logo-mania were more concerned about the story and what I went through."

On May 31, Gucci posted that the jacket was meant to be an "homage to Dapper Dan." The public perceived the apology as perfunctory and doing nothing to compensate the originator. Gucci realized they needed to give more than lip service and contacted Dan. The haberdasher and the Italian house began conversations. By September, Gucci's design team personally visited Harlem and they agreed to open an atelier together. Dap was insistent that the new shop had to be located where his story started. "Anybody I do any collaborations with has to have a footprint in Harlem."

Dapper Dan's of Harlem opened its doors in January 2018. "A 'dream deferred' is not a dream denied," he shared on social media. It was the first time a European luxury brand had invested a real stake in the neighborhood. "Let the fashion industry take note—though terribly overdue, this is how to begin to right your wrongs," wrote Cummings. "This is what Black creators and fashion lovers deserve for their years of creativity and innovation, their years of boosting house's profits." Dap's comeback was overwhelmingly celebrated. *Vogue* called him an "innovator." Publications that had never covered him during his original run featured him on their covers. In 2021, the Council of Fashion Designers of America (CFDA) bestowed Dapper Dan with its highest honor, the Geoffrey Beene Lifetime Achievement Award. For the fashion industry who had literally run him out of the game, this was a chance to rewrite history.

High fashion brands were realizing that they needed to do more than sell to hip-hop, they needed to collaborate with them. Pharrell Williams had forged an intimate relationship with Chanel over the years. In 2015, he penned a track called "CC the Word" and made history as the first man in the brand's handbag advertisements in 2017. Two years later, the producer and French heritage house deepened their bond with the "Chanel Pharrell" capsule collection. The landmark collaboration, which was named by Karl Lagerfeld before he died in 2019, celebrated Pharrell's streetwear aesthetic with vibrant unisex hoodies, terry cloth bucket hats, and sneakers. Chanel valued Pharrell's talents as a designer and visionary. "Gabrielle Coco Chanel didn't see partitions, and it's interesting because neither did the brand when it came to giving me a shot," said Pharrell. "There doesn't need to be boundaries as long as you can hold on to the heritage and continue to push it . . . We don't need walls, we need bridges."

Another European brand that built a bridge was Kenzo, who hired Nigo to take the helm as artistic director in 2021. Nigo was instrumental in bringing Japanese streetwear to hip-hop—and subsequently the world—and was the perfect person to reinvigorate the brand following the death of founder Takada Kenzo. Both men had attended the same fashion school in Tokyo and had experience in creating universal East-meets-West fashion. "Maybe it's a Japanese thing, but the idea of taking in a lot of disparate influences from various cultures and in some way, managing to fuse them into something that feels like it has its own identity is something that I recognize in the way that Takada worked, and it's something I'm very close to," Nigo said. "The inputs may be different, but I think the process is similar."

There was no one way to create the perfect collaboration. Nicki Minaj connected with Fendi while shooting the cover of *ELLE* in 2019.

The spread, photographed by the house's creative director, Karl Lagerfeld, showed the exuberant rapper looking stylishly tamed and tailored. One look featured a modern tuxedo made from a Chanel stretch-cotton velvet jacket and cotton piqué vest. In another shot, Nicki cozied up to Lagerfeld while wearing a sumptuous Fendi glazed-canvas belted coat, nylon tights, and suede pumps. "He was always someone I wanted to work with, and I was just counting down the moments [until it happened]," the rapper told *ELLE* Fashion Features Director Véronique Hyland. The chemistry between the two was palpable and led to the rapper creating her 127-piece collection for Fendi the next year, which included a hot-pink curve-hugger dress—accentuating Nicki's bodacious figure—as well as futuristic metallic bodysuits and silver bomber jackets covered in the house's logo. "They really got close during that, and that's when the seeds of [the collection] began," Hyland told me. "It's really cool that from the story we did came this bigger thing: two people that come from music and fashion meeting up. It was a very contemporary way to meld hip-hop and fashion."

Lagerfeld never saw Nicki Minaj's Fendi capsule collection come to fruition, but his spirit was omnipresent throughout the design process. "I just wish he'd gotten a chance to see this come full circle, because I remember how supportive he was of me on the [*ELLE*] shoot, and it made me feel really good," she said. While shooting the editorial around the campaign, she thought of his discerning eye. "While I was on set, while I was taking the pictures, I definitely was thinking to myself, 'Would he be proud of this look? Would he be proud of this pose?'"

The pairing of the right designer with the right artist created something truly magical. High fashion fell in love with Cardi B, the hip-hop Cinderella, when she shouted out red-heeled stiletto godfather Christian Louboutin on 2018's "Bodak Yellow": "*Said little bitch, you can't fuck with me if you wanted to / These expensive, these is red bottom, these is bloody shoes.*" "Bodak Yellow" topped the Billboard Hot 100 chart for three consecutive weeks and Cardi B became the first female rapper to have a diamond-certified song (the equivalent of ten million units). Cardi B was an audacious personality who was outspoken and unapologetic about her past as a stripper and reality TV star, and her propensity to experiment with fashion made her exciting to designers.

Jeremy Scott was known as "fashion's last rebel" for his quirky and outrageous looks. As the creative director of Moschino, he invited Cardi as his guest to the Met Gala in 2018. Cardi was the glorious embodiment of the theme "Heavenly Bodies: Fashion and the Catholic Imagination" in a cream wool long-sleeve Moschino dress and ostentatious headdress. And to be clear: Cardi B wasn't going to be the Virgin Mary or subscribe to some puritanical maternity dress code. "When you see my look, I feel like you don't just see a pregnant woman," she said. "I feel like you see royal-goddess-woman-motherhood." The dress took approximately 33,600 hours to complete and featured a thigh-high slit and plunging bodice neckline. Her pregnancy bump was on full display and encrusted with pearls, crystals, and gems "inspired by tapestries and embroideries from ecclesiastic vestments."

Cardi B made history as the first female rapper on the cover of American *Vogue* in January 2020. The twenty-seven-year-old emanated a maternal glow in Cartier earrings and a ring from Tiffany & Co., but the best accessory was her adorable daughter, Kulture, who matched her mother's Michael Kors Collection dress. The baby gave a sweet smile, and photographer Annie Leibovitz captured the perfect moment. Cardi was invited into the venerated world of haute couture, where designers could create extravagant custom looks inspired by her daring personality. In 2021, the rapper wore eight custom looks to host the American Music Awards, including a Schiaparelli black crepe jersey column dress with a black tulle veil, enormous gold chandelier earrings, black gloves with pierced golden nails, and a custom gold face mask featuring Swarovski-crystal anatomical features. To accept her award for Favorite Hip-Hop Song, she changed into a high-neck chartreuse Jean Paul Gaultier gown, her waist snatched and gathered by a rose of fabric, and her voluptuous chest enhanced in gauzy accents. "Can you believe I'm getting custom Jean Paul Gaultier?" she tweeted with a visual of the dress's creation. "I can't fuckin believe!!! Im [*sic*] literally living a dream."

This was a time of reckoning across the fashion industry. The Black Lives Matter movement following the murder of George Floyd in 2020 and countless instances of police brutality in America forced companies to examine their biases and blind spots around diversity and inclusion. Even high fashion, intrinsically an industry of pleasure and escapism, had to come to terms with its behavior. There was a lack of diversity in corporate leadership, in design, and on the runway. Dapper Dan's knocked-off look was just one offense. There was a constant barrage of looks that ranged from tone-deaf to blackface that somehow nobody in the room thought were an issue. "Blackface is white supremacy as fashion—and it's always been in season," wrote Robin Givhan in the *Washington Post* in 2019.

The responses from brands ran the gamut: Some made desultory statements on social media with hashtags and black squares and others hired diversity, equity, and inclusion (DEI) task forces. A few brands—including Gucci, Pyer Moss, and Vince—offered to donate proceeds to racial causes. Designer Aurora James founded the Fifteen Percent Pledge, an advocacy organization partnered with retailers to commit 15 percent of their shelf space to Black-owned businesses. "People have realized you cannot pretend this stuff is going to go away—people are not going to go away," said Dr. Nelarine Cornelius, professor of Organisation Studies and associate dean, People, Culture and Inclusion at the Queen Mary University of London. "Luxury brands were caught off guard by the Black Lives Matter movement, and they were not prepared to respond."

In June 2020, Anna Wintour, editor in chief of *Vogue*, acknowledged that the esteemed publication had been "hurtful and intolerant" and not done enough to promote Black designers and staff. In a historic letter she wrote: "I want to say this especially to the Black members of our team—I can only imagine what these days have been like. But I also know that the hurt, and violence, and injustice we're seeing and talking about have been around for a long time. Recognizing it and doing something about it is overdue."

Systematic change required action beyond nice words. Scott Galloway, thought leader and professor of marketing at the New York University Stern School of Business, criticized brands in general as being performative around social justice. "Firms stating what is basic political orthodoxy is not leadership but performance. Words are meaningful, but actions are profound—speak louder. So far, the actions have been anemic," he wrote in the *Business Insider*. For disruption to take place, the most powerful names had to be taken to task.

Kanye West had the most successful hip-hop fashion line and was forced to take accountability. He had courted controversy throughout his career and it had finally caught up to him. In 2022, he lost lucrative partnerships with Adidas, Balenciaga, and the Gap after making numerous anti-Semitic and racial remarks, including presenting a "White Lives Matter" T-shirt at his Yeezy show in Paris and making disparaging remarks about Black Lives Matter and George Floyd. What had been excused as freethinking in the past was scrutinized through a new lens. Kanye refused several chances for contrition and was clouded by his own hubris that he was impervious to consequences. He was wrong. Optics were important, and once the bottom line was threatened, his partners and allies disappeared. The fallout was fast.* The goodwill he had worked so hard to build was gone (as was his status as a billionaire) within weeks. By the end of the year, he was a veritable pariah. Never before had a hip-hop fashion icon fallen so far—and so fast. Nobody could save Kanye from himself, but himself.

*See Appendix.

Dapper Dan Harlem is open for business. It was a warm fall afternoon in 2022 when I headed to the atelier for the first time. Located inside a brownstone, the shop was not too far from the original store on 125th Street. The showroom was on the main floor with VIP fittings upstairs. Production was being handled in the basement and a tailor was intently focused at a sewing machine. On the main floor, the décor was luxe with deep burgundy fabrics, plush velvet chairs, and gold accents. Dap's illustrious history was everywhere. A living museum. There were re-creations of his most famous pieces, like the Louis Vuitton snorkel he made for drug dealer Alpo Martinez. The atelier was by appointment, but celebrities stopped by whenever. A$AP Ferg recently came through with Kendrick Lamar. Unreleased creations hung on racks—I was instructed not to photograph them—and Puma sneakers lined the floor, with his logo in rhinestones.

A photo of LL Cool J in a Gucci crisscross jacket hung on the wall. Nearby, a coffee table book opened to a page of Run-D.M.C. The multitude of magazines tastefully displayed—*Don Diva, Business of Fashion, Surface,* the *New York Times Magazine*—chronicled a spectacular comeback.

The godfather of hip-hop luxury was home. The seventy-eight-year-old outlaw was on the inside and had a place to call his own. "The whole journey I've been on has been part revolutionary, part fashion, and part social justice," he said. "I don't like to dictate culture. I like to translate culture." When he wasn't running the atelier or working on his next collaboration, he liked to spend time connecting to the next generation. It was common to find him sitting outside on the stoop, looking dapper in a suit, Gucci scarf, and pocket square, and talking to those who passed by. He wanted his hip-hop progeny to study his legacy and to appreciate the importance of autonomy and evolution. Stay true to yourself and the validation would come. Be so good that the luxury brands wanted to *knock you off*.

Hip-hop was entering its next phase of high fashion. In 2023, Louis Vuitton appointed Pharrell as its new men's creative director. The position was previously held by Virgil Abloh, who died on November 28, 2021, after battling cardiac angiosarcoma. There was much debate and speculation on who was worthy to fill the lofty role and honor Virgil's legacy. Several names floated around, including British designers Grace Wales Bonner and Martine Rose, and young disrupters Telfar Clemens and Colm Dillane, better known as KidSuper. Some argued that the coveted position should have gone to an unknown designer, like a young person of color who could benefit from the exposure, or a creative already inside the Louis Vuitton organizational structure. However, there was no competition. Pharrell was the embodiment of the role. His heart was in hip-hop and his reverence for high fashion was undeniable. His role in popularizing streetwear reverberated on runways across the world. There was nobody better to take the heritage house into the future.

The lane was wide open for hip-hop's next haberdasher, fashion line, and revolutionary. If you asked Dapper Dan where to find inspiration, he would point right outside. "Make sure you come get the next Dapper Dan off the street corner. Because that's where he came from." Whether it was from the streets, on the runways, or something nobody had seen yet, there was no right way to make it. Hip-hop had shown that there was no single blueprint for success in high fashion. Everything was possible.

Appendix

KANYE WEST TIMELINE

September 15, 2022

✦ Kanye (or Ye, as he renamed himself) terminated his deal with Gap, claiming that he didn't have creative control. "Everyone knows that I'm the leader, I'm the king," he said. "A king can't live in someone else's castle. A king has to make his own castle."

October 3, 2022

✦ A surprise YZY show at Paris Fashion Week ended in an uproar when the designer came out in an oversized shirt with the phrase "White Lives Matter."

✦ The rapper sparred with his critics, including global *Vogue* contributing editor Gabriella Karefa-Johnson and her supporters, supermodels Hailey Bieber and Gigi Hadid.

October 4, 2022

✦ Ye claimed that LVMH CEO Bernard Arnault "killed my best friend," referring to Virgil Abloh, who had passed away on November 28, 2021. Abloh was immensely private about his personal life, and friends of the Off-White designer were offended. "KEEP VIRGIL NAME OUT YOUR MOUTH," said Tremaine Emory, Supreme's creative director. "Your [*sic*] not a victim your [*sic*] just an insecure narcissist that's dying for validation from the fashion world."

October 6, 2022

✦ Ye doubled down on his "White Lives Matter" shirt with right-wing sympathizer Tucker Carlson. "I do certain things from a feeling," Ye said. "It's using a gut instinct . . . just brilliance . . . I thought the idea of me wearing it was funny."

✦ Adidas announced that it would put its partnership with Kanye under review. "After repeated efforts to privately resolve the situation, we have taken the decision to place the partnership under review. We will continue to co-manage the current product during this period," the company said in a statement.

October 7, 2022

✦ Ye declared "war" on Sean "Diddy" Combs and claimed Jewish people controlled the mogul. "This ain't a game," Ye texted. "Ima use you as an example to show the Jewish people that told you to call me that no one can threaten or influence me. I told you this was war. Now gone get you some business." He was banned from Instagram.

October 9, 2022

✦ Ye posted more anti-Semitic comments: "I'm a bit sleepy tonight but when I wake up I'm going death con 3   On JEWISH PEOPLE]   The funny thing is I actually can't be Anti Semitic because Black people are actually Jew also   You guys have toyed with me and tried to black ball anyone whoever opposes your agenda." He was banned from Twitter.

October 15, 2022

+ Ye continued his anti-Semitic remarks on the *Drink Champs* podcast and dared Adidas to hold him accountable. "I can say anti-Semitic things, and Adidas can't drop me. Now what? Now what?" he asked.

+ In the same interview, he tried to undermine Black Lives Matter and falsely claimed that George Floyd died due to a fentanyl overdose, not at the hands of a police officer as had been ruled. The Floyd family filed a $250 million lawsuit in response for "harassment, misappropriation, defamation and infliction of emotional distress."

October 21, 2022

+ Balenciaga cut ties with Ye. "Balenciaga has no longer any relationship nor any plans for future projects related to this artist," said parent company Kering.

October 25, 2022

+ Following public pressure from consumers, celebrities, and business leaders, Adidas announced it would sever its relationship with Ye after almost a decade.

+ "Adidas does not tolerate antisemitism and any other sort of hate speech," the company said in a statement. "Ye's recent comments and actions have been unacceptable, hateful and dangerous, and they violate the company's values of diversity and inclusion, mutual respect and fairness."

+ Adidas said that this decision would cost it $246 million. According to *Forbes*, Ye was no longer a billionaire.

Acknowledgments

M om, you've been a part of this since the first word. There aren't enough words to show my appreciation. Dad, you're the reason I'm a writer. Thank you for encouraging me to pursue this against the odds.

My editor, Rebecca Strobel, and everyone at Gallery Books/ Simon & Schuster, William LoTurco, Robert Guinsler, and Sterling Lord Literistic.

Everyone whose words were a part of this story: Dapper Dan, Dr. Jonathan Michael Square, Pusha T, Bimmy Antney, Bill Adler, Thirstin Howl The 3rd, Just Blaze, Charlotte Neuville, Véronique Hyland, April Walker, Karl Kani, Big Daddy Kane, Tuma Basa, Tommy Hilfiger, Andy Hilfiger, Datwon Thomas, Jonathan Van Meter, Stefan Campbell, Carol Smith, Keith Clinkscales, Julia Chance, Sonya Magett, Michael Gonzales, Slick Rick, Misa Hylton, O'Neal McKnight, Groovey Lew, Pharoahe Monch, Selwyn Seyfu Hinds, Ahmir "Questlove" Thompson, Cam'ron, Crooked I, Damian Lillard, Dao-Yi Chow, Damon Dash, Kareem "Biggs" Burke, Deirdre Maloney, Deric Humphrey, LaTrice Burnette, Lenny S, Kim Osorio, Derek "Fonzworth Bentley" Watkins, Sam Hansen, Noreaga, Jian DeLeon, A$AP Rocky, Loïc Villepontoux, Pharrell Williams, J. Cole, Fern Mallis, Kevin Le, Maureen Hilbun, Kyle Luu, Touré, and Wayno.

Dapper Dan, Thirstin Howl The 3rd, Karl Kani, April Walker, David

McLean, Tommy Ton, the Estate of Shawn Mortensen, and Schiaparelli for their incredible photos.

Everybody who played a part along the way: A$AP Ferg, Alicia Loehle, Andrew Barber, Ariele Elia, Bara Ndiaye, Capricorn Clark, Carlito Rodriguez, Dan Charnas, Darnell-Jamal Lisby, Dave East, Debbie D, Derek Roche, DJ EFN, Estevan Oriol, Ice, J. Period, Janette Beckman, Jermaine Hall, Jill Demling, Joe Avianne, Jonathan Mannion, Julia Beverly, Juliette PICQ, Kangol, Karam Gill, Koe Rodriguez, Lionel C. Martin, Lisa Cortés, Mandy Aragones, MCM, Meek Mill, Michael Gonzales, Naima Cochrane, Ornella Humler, Parrish Smith, Raekwon, Ralph McDaniels, Robin Newland, Robin Wolaner, Sarika Rastogi, Steven Victor, Vikki Toback, and Zoe Dupree.

My friends and colleagues: Aaron Busby, Aisha Ali Parker, Aliya S. King, Amanda Seales, Amir Abbassy, Amy Odell, Andreas Hale, Andrés Tardio, Andrew Steinthal, Angela Yee, Annie Chen, Anuja Madar, April Bombai, April King, April Pope, Aqua Boogie, Archie Dixon, Ari Melber, Aroop Sanakkayala, Ashley Kalmanowitz, Austin Miller, Awista Ayub, Brandon "Jinx" Jenkins, Brent English, Brian McManus, Brian "B. Dot" Miller, Carl Lamarre, Carlos Larkin, Charlamagne Tha God, Cheo Hodari Coker, Chris Atlas, Chris Brickley, Chris Huth, Chuck Creekmur, Cipha Sounds, Clover Hope, Coreen Uhl, Courtney Lowery, Craig Jenkins, Dan Rys, Dana Meyerson, Danielle Noriega, Danyel Smith, Dave Gordon, David Drake, David Noles, David Turner, Dela, Devi Brown, Dharmic Jain, Donald Hobson, Drew de Leon, Ebro Darden, Eddie "Stats" Houghton, Elliott Wilson, Emmanuel C.M., Eric Diep, Erik Parker, Erika Montes, Erin Ashley, Famlay, Freeway, Gabe Tesoriero, Gary Suarez, Gee Spin, Georgette Cline, Gerrick Kennedy, Harry Fraud, Hen Roc, Ibrahim Hamad, Insanul Ahmed, Ivie Ani, Jada Gomez, Jai Dior, Jamal Jimoh, Jana Fleishman, Jason Davis, Jay Gatzby, Jayson Rodriguez, Jennifer Yin, Jerry Barrow, Joe Coscarelli, Joél Leon, John "Young JFK" Kennedy, John Ochoa, Johnny Nuñez, Joi-Marie McKenzie Lewis, Jojo Brim, Joseph Patel, Justin Tinsley,

Karin Neubauer, Karlie Hustle, Kasia Sawicz, Kathy Iandoli, Kazeem Famuyide, Kevin Liles, Kid Scoob, Kirdis Postelle, Kisha Scott, Kozza, Krystal Rodriguez, Laura Stylez, Lawrence Stuart, Lea Miller, Leroy Benros, Leslie Hall, Leslie Rosales, Letty, Lisa Evers, Lola Plaku, Low Key, Lyndsey Havens, Marat Berenstein, Marcus J. Moore, Marissa DeVito, Mark Richardson, Matt Fastow, Mecca, Melody Carter, Metro Boomin, Michell Clark, Michelle McDevitt, Mike Dean, Mike Navarra, Mikey Fresh, Nadeska Alexis, Nakia Hicks, Natalie Espinosa, Navjosh, Neena Roe, Nessa, Nicole Platin, Niles G, Nina Parker, Paul Cantor, Paul Pennington, Pete Sim, Peter Berry, Phylicia Fant, Premium Pete, Rae Holliday, Rahim the Dream, Rashaun Hall, Reggie Miller, Renata Muniz, Rich Westover, Richa Chandra, Richie Abbott, Rob Kenner, Rob Markman, Rob "Reef" Tewlow, Robbie Sokolowsky, Roberta Magrini, Roberto Caiaffa, Roderick Scott, Roger Krastz, Ron Stew, Russ, Sachin Bhola, Sam Ewen, Sara Anwar, Sara Gilbert, Sarah Cunningham, Scott Hurwitz, Scott Rosenblum, Sean "Puffy" Combs, Sean Malcolm, Selam Belay, Shaheem Reid, Shanita Hubbard, Shawn Prez, Shawn Setaro, Shiv, Sickamore, Sidney Madden, Sree Sreenivasan, Steve Carless, Sumit Sharma, Steve Scibelli, Sway, Sydney Margetson, Tamar Juda, Tiffany Lea, Tina and Chris Sampson, Todd Moscowitz, Torae, Tracy Garraud, Trent Clark, Ty Hunter, Vanessa Satten, William Ketchum III, Won Park, Young Sav, and Zack O'Malley Greenburg.

Rohan, Shruti, Amara, and my family.

RIP Andre Harrell and Virgil Abloh.

If I forgot anyone, please blame my head and not my heart.

Notes

PREFACE: BACK TO SCHOOL

ix *August 11, 1973, was the hot*: Michael A. Gonzales, "The Holy House of Hip-Hop," *New York* magazine, September 22, 2008, http://nymag.com/anniversary/40th/50665/.

ix *He loved to spin James Brown's "Give It Up or Turnit a Loose"*: Frank Broughton, "Interview: DJ Kool Herc," Red Bull Music Academy Daily, January 31, 2018, https://daily.redbullmusicacademy.com/2018/01/kool-herc-interview/.

ix *"And once they heard that"*: Jeff Chang, *Can't Stop Won't Stop: A History of the Hip-Hop Generation* (New York: Picador, 2015), 79.

ix *"When you go back to school"*: Ibid., 67–68.

x *Herc originated a technique*: Ibid., 79.

x *The "get-down" was*: Gonzales, "The Holy House of Hip-Hop."

x *"The music was just, it was slammin'!"*: "Kool Herc 'Merry-Go-Round' Technique," GoodStuff79, August 3, 2012, https://www.youtube.com/watch?v=7qwml-F7zKQ.

x *"This was a breath of fresh air"*: Ibid.

x *"Rap music is rooted"*: Geneva Smitherman, "'The Chain Remain the Same': Communicative Practices in the Hip-Hop Nation," *Journal of Black Studies* 28, no. 1 (July 2016): 4.

xi *"postmodern African griot"*: Ibid.

xi *From these ashes*: *Fresh Dressed*, directed by Sacha Jenkins, CNN Films, 2015.

xi *"Hip-hop is the study"*: "KRS Gives 9 Elements of Hip-Hop at Harvard," Cliff Blaze, May 21, 2008, https://www.youtube.com/watch?v=4tUaGFI2m5Y.

xi *The song was the first*: T. Rees Shapiro, "Sylvia Robinson, Producer of

Sugarhill Gang's 'Rapper's Delight,' Dies at 75," *Washington Post*, October 1, 2011, https://www.washingtonpost.com/local/obituaries/sylvia-robinson -producer-of-sugarhill-gangs-rappers-delight-dies-at-75/2011/09/30 /gIQAdsGRDL_story.html.

xi   *Billboard's Top 40 chart*: "29 Black Music Milestones: Sugarhill Gang Pioneers Hip-Hop," *Billboard*, February 10, 2011, https://www.billboard .com/music/music-news/29-black-music-milestones-sugarhill-gang -pioneers-hip-hop-473110/.

xi   *"Basically, it's a record"*: "A History of the 'Big' Business of Hip-Hop," NPR, December 9, 2010, https://www.npr.org/2010/12/09/131932127 /a-history-of-the-big-business-of-hip-hop.

xii   *In 2017, hip-hop became*: "Billboard Explains: How R&B/Hip-Hop Became the Biggest Genre in the U.S.," *Billboard*, August 11, 2021, https://www.billboard.com/music/music-news/billboard-explains-rb -hip-hop-biggest-genre-9613422/.

xii   *with Drake and Kendrick Lamar*: John Lynch, "For the First Time in History, Hip-Hop Has Surpassed Rock to Become the Most Popular Music Genre, According to Nielsen," *Business Insider*, January 4, 2018, https://www.businessinsider.com/hip-hop-passes-rock-most-popular -music-genre-nielsen-2018-1.

xii   *some twenty-seven luxury brands*: A$AP Rocky, "Fashion Killa," Genius, accessed March 6, 2023, https://genius.com/A-ap-rocky-fashion-killa -lyrics.

xiii   *The custom titanium*: Kerry McDermott, "The Story Behind Kendrick Lamar's Crown of (Tiffany & Co.) Thorns," *Vogue*, June 27, 2022, https:// www.vogue.com/article/kendrick-lamar-crown-of-thorns-tiffany-co.

xiii   *8,000 cobblestone micro*: Conchita Widjojo, "Kendrick Lamar's Crown of Thorns by Tiffany & Co. Has Over 8,000 Diamonds," *Women's Wear Daily*, June 28, 2022, https://wwd.com/fashion-news/fashion-scoops /kendrick-lamar-crown-of-thorns-tiffanys-diamonds-1235236443/.

xiv   *"It wasn't protective"*: Dhani Mau, "How June Ambrose Changed the Relationship between Hip-Hop and Fashion Forever," *Fashionista*, April 18, 2022, https://fashionista.com/2022/04/june-ambrose-stylist-career -interview.

xiv   *"Hip-hop embraced"*: Sowmya Krishnamurthy, "A History of How Hip-Hop and Fashion Brands Started Working Together," *XXL*, February 7, 2019, https://www.xxlmag.com/history-rappers-and-fashion/.

xiv   *"When something is hot"*: Ibid.

xiv   *"The change [in branding]"*: Joel Dreyfuss, "Steve Stoute on Hip-Hop and Race Relations," *The Root*, September 4, 2011, https://www.the root.com/steve-stoute-on-hip-hop-and-race-relations-1790865666.

xv   *"The days of the gilded cage"*: Joelle Diderich, "EXCLUSIVE: Louis Vuitton CEO Talks Final Virgil Abloh Collection, Succession Plans," *Women's Wear Daily*, January 20, 2022, https://wwd.com/fashion-news/fashion-features/louis-vuitton-ceo-talks-final-virgil-abloh-collection-succession-plans-1235041087/.

xv   *"I now have a platform"*: Teo van den Broeke, "Virgil Abloh: 'I Now Have a Platform to Change the Industry . . . So I Should,'" British *GQ*, November 28, 2021, https://www.gq-magazine.co.uk/article/virgil-abloh-interview-2018/.

CHAPTER ONE: ACROSS 125TH STREET

1   *"I knocked them up"*: Daniel Day, *Dapper Dan: Made in Harlem* (New York: Random House, 2019), 189.

1   *in search of economic*: "The Great Migration (1910–1970)," National Archives, June 28, 2021, https://www.archives.gov/research/african-americans/migrations/great-migration#:~:text=The%20Great%20Migration%20was%20one,the%201910s%20until%20the%201970s.

1   *"In Harlem, Black was white"*: "The City of Refuge," *Atlantic Monthly*, February 1925, https://nationalhumanitiescenter.org/pds/maai3/migrations/text4/cityofrefuge.pdf.

1   *"sweet life"*: Aileen Jacobson, "Sugar Hill, Manhattan: The Sweet Life of Old New York," *New York Times*, January 30, 2020, https://www.nytimes.com/2020/01/29/realestate/sugar-hill-manhattan-the-sweet-life-of-old-new-york.html.

2   *notables like*: Strivers' Row, accessed March 6, 2023, https://www.striversrownyc.org.

2   *increased by over 40 percent*: "Black Capital: Harlem in the 1920s," New York State Museum, accessed March 6, 2023, http://www.nysm.nysed.gov/exhibitions/ongoing/black-capital-harlem-1920s-0.

2   *Black majority population*: Jonathan Gill, *Harlem: The Four Hundred Year History from Dutch Village to Capital of Black America* (New York: Grove Press, 2011), 184.

2   *Jamaica, Antigua, and Trinidad*: Erin Blakemore, "How the Harlem Renaissance Helped Forge a New Sense of Black Identity," *National Geographic*, February 24, 2022, https://www.nationalgeographic.com/history/article/how-the-harlem-renaissance-helped-forge-a-new-sense-of-black-identity.

2   *large numbers*: "In Spanish Harlem," Library of Congress, accessed March 6, 2023, https://www.loc.gov/classroom-materials/immigration/puerto-rican-cuban/in-spanish-harlem/.

2 *most significant*: Henry Louis Gates Jr. and Evelyn Brooks Higgin-
botham, *Harlem Renaissance Lives: From the African American National
Biography* (New York: Oxford University Press, 2009), vii.

2 *"whites only"*: "Black Capital: Harlem in the 1920s."

2 *literary luminaries like*: "A New African American Identity: The Harlem Renaissance," Smithsonian National Museum of African American
History and Culture, accessed March 6, 2023, https://nmaahc.si.edu
/explore/stories/new-african-american-identity-harlem-renaissance.

2 *"We younger Negro"*: Langston Hughes, "The Negro Artist and the
Racial Mountain," Poetry Foundation, October 13, 2009, https://www
.poetryfoundation.org/articles/69395/the-negro-artist-and-the-racial
-mountain.

3 *The supersized*: Alice Gregory, "A Brief History of the Zoot Suit,"
Smithsonian magazine, April 2016, https://www.smithsonianmag.com
/arts-culture/brief-history-zoot-suit-180958507/.

3 *when she popularized*: Leah Bourne, "History of the Miniskirt: How
Fashion's Most Daring Hemline Came to Be," *Stylecaster*, March 7,
2022, https://stylecaster.com/history-of-the-miniskirt/.

3 *"as one who elevates"*: Charles Baudelaire, "The Painter of Modern Life
and Other Essays," Columbia University, originally published 1863,
http://www.columbia.edu/itc/architecture/ockman/pdfs/dossier_4
/Baudelaire.pdf.

3 *"The Black dandy is this African diaspora"*: "Shantrelle P. Lewis on
'Dandy Lion: The Black Dandy and Street Style,'" *Aperture*, December
13, 2017, https://youtu.be/ErzwAfq3hoo.

3 *"In a society that sought"*: Richard J. Powell, *Cutting a Figure: Fashioning
Black Portraiture* (Chicago: University of Chicago Press, 2008), 63.

4 *oldest congregation*: Antwan Lewis, "Mother AME Zion Church Re-
opens After 2 Years," Fox News, April 14, 2022, https://www.fox5ny
.com/news/mother-ame-zion-church-the-black-church.

4 *had origins dating back*: *Fresh Dressed*, directed by Sacha Jenkins, CNN
Films, 2015.

4 *"Most of these designers"*: Teddy Tinson, "Honoring Willi Smith," CFDA,
February 2, 2020, https://cfda.com/news/honoring-willi-smith.

4 *"We [my grandmother and I]"*: Georgia Dullea, "Now and Always, Fashion Mad," *New York Times*, December 6, 1992, https://www.nytimes
.com/1992/12/06/style/now-and-always-fashion-mad.html.

5 *43 East 125th Street*: "25th Precinct Community Council Meeting,
Tonight," Harlem Neighborhood Block Association, April 20, 2022,
https://hnba.nyc/lost-church/.

5 *"When I opened"*: Day, *Dapper Dan: Made in Harlem*, 164.

5 *"I can't sew"*: Ibid., 176.

5 *"Were you fly?"*: Ibid., 31.

6 *"It was my first attempt at customization"*: Ibid., 168–170.

6 *the Ghetto Brothers and Savage Nomads: Fresh Dressed.*

6 *donned a denim jacket*: Rock Steady Crew, Facebook, June 17, 2019, https://www.facebook.com/129254899182/posts/this-is-truly-an-honor-repost-amhistorymuseumthis-customized-denim-jacket-was-wo/101 57298253529183/.

6 *"Custom apparel has"*: Elena Romero, *Free Stylin': How Hip Hop Changed the Fashion Industry* (Westport, CT: Praeger, 2012), 77.

6 *"It was a beautiful bag"*: Day, *Dapper Dan: Made in Harlem*, 178.

7 *"I was the only Black person"*: Ibid., 179.

7 *the oldest department store in America*: Jordan Valinsky, "Lord & Taylor Is Closing All of Its Stores after 194 Years in Business," CNN, August 27, 2020, https://www.cnn.com/2020/08/27/business/lord-and-taylor-store-closures-bankruptcy/index.html.

7 *first store to feature*: Steff Yotka, "'Barneys Started Our Career': Five New York Designers Remember the Department Store's Impact as Its Fate Hangs in Limbo," *Vogue*, November 1, 2019, https://www.vogue.com/article/barneys-new-york-bankruptcy-designer-memories.

7 *"Crests and logos"*: Day, *Dapper Dan: Made in Harlem*, 180.

8 *The quintessential Dapper Dan piece*: David Marchese, "Dapper Dan on Creating Style, Logomania and Working with Gucci," *New York Times Magazine*, July 1, 2019, https://www.nytimes.com/interactive/2019/07/01/magazine/dapper-dan-hip-hop-style.html.

8 *"My customers wanted to buy into that power"*: Day, *Dapper Dan: Made in Harlem*, 199.

8 *tens of thousands of dollars*: Bara Ndiaye, personal interview, September 2, 2022.

8 *"My clothes were expensive"*: Day, *Dapper Dan: Made in Harlem*, 203.

9 *"In the early days"*: Ibid., 268.

9 *red-and-white Gucci jacket*: LL Cool J (@llcoolj), Instagram, July 11, 2019, accessed December 1, 2022, https://www.instagram.com/p/Bzy7sgiJoua/?hl=en.

9 *"Sometimes you bang"*: Shawna Kenney, "The New York City Hip-Hop Shops That Kept People Fresh to Death," Rock the Bells, July 2, 2020, https://rockthebells.com/articles/80s-hip-hop-fashion/.

9 *"These were Gucci jackets"*: John Schaefer, "Designer Dapper Dan Remixed Hip Hop Fashion," *Soundcheck*, March 19, 2013, https://www.wnycstudios.org/podcasts/soundcheck/segments/276891-dapper-dan-remix.

9 *"A song like that"*: Brian Coleman, *Check the Technique: Liner Notes for Hip-Hop Junkies* (New York: Villard, 2009), 201.

10 *custom Louis Vuitton velour*: Detroit Griot (@JustCallmeBHunt), Twitter, November 8, 2017, https://twitter.com/JustCallmeBHunt/status/928318211245912064.

10 *designed by Christopher*: Liana Satenstein, "Salt-N-Pepa Are Back, Baby," *Vogue*, April 14, 2016, https://www.vogue.com/article/salt-n-pepa-push-it-jackets-90s-style.

10 *over one hundred hip-hop songs*: "Dapper Dan," Genius, accessed March 6, 2023, https://genius.com/search?q=dapper%20dan.

10 *"Luxury cars had always"*: Day, *Dapper Dan: Made in Harlem*, 193.

11 *In 1988, Big Daddy Kane*: "Dapper Dan," *Dazed*, accessed March 6, 2023, https://www.dazeddigital.com/artsandculture/gallery/18381/9/dapper-dan.

11 *In 1989, LL Cool J*: Day, *Dapper Dan: Made in Harlem*, 193.

11 *"Middle-class Blacks didn't"*: Marchese, "Dapper Dan on Creating Style, Logomania and Working with Gucci."

11 *"One day, a bunch"*: Day, *Dapper Dan: Made in Harlem*, 227.

12 *"In the fashion world"*: Arthur Zaczkiewicz, "Counterfeits, Knockoffs, Replicas: Parsing Legal Implications," *Women's Wear Daily*, June 2, 2016, https://wwd.com/business-news/retail/counterfeit-knockoff-replica-legal-10437109/.

12 *"Did I think I might"*: Day, *Dapper Dan: Made in Harlem*, 226.

12 *"very cordial"*: Ibid., 232.

12 *"Wow, this guy really"*: Ibid.

13 *"I was tired of fighting"*: Ibid., 241.

13 *He shut down Dapper Dan's Boutique in 1992*: Marchese, "Dapper Dan on Creating Style, Logomania and Working with Gucci."

CHAPTER TWO: LUXURY LAW

14 *hedonistic consumerism*: Andrea Migone, "Hedonistic Consumerism: Patterns of Consumption in Contemporary Capitalism," *Review of Radical Political Economics* 39, no. 2 (2007): 173–200.

14 *ancient Greece and Rome*: "What (Not) to Wear: Fashion and the Law: Sumptuous Origins," Harvard Law School, accessed March 7, 2023, https://exhibits.law.harvard.edu/sumptuous-origins.

15 *"cloth of gold"*: "What (Not) to Wear: Fashion and the Law: Purple Silk and Cloth of Gold," Harvard Law School, accessed March 7, 2023, https://exhibits.law.harvard.edu/purple-silk-and-cloth-gold.

15 *"Color's link to"*: Véronique Hyland, *Dress Code: Unlocking Fashion from the New Look to Millennial Pink* (New York: HarperCollins, 2022), 81.

15 *"excess of apparel"*: Maggie Secara, ed., "Who Wears What I," *Elizabethan Sumptuary Statues,* July 14, 2001, http://elizabethan.org/sumptuary/who-wears-what.html.

15 *"manifest decay of the whole realm"*: Ibid.

16 *"utter detestation and dislike"*: "What (Not) to Wear: Fashion and the Law: Colonial Massachusetts," Harvard Law School, accessed March 7, 2023, https://exhibits.law.harvard.edu/colonial-massachusetts.

16 *"Clothing was an important"*: Madelyn Shaw, "Slave Cloth and Clothing Slaves: Craftsmanship, Commerce, and Industry," *Journal of Early Southern Decorative Arts* 33 (2012), https://www.mesdajournal.org/2012/slave-cloth-clothing-slaves-craftsmanship-commerce-industry/.

16 osnaburg *or* osnabrigs . . . kersey . . . linsey-woolsey: Eulanda A. Sanders, "The Politics of Textiles Used in African American Slave Clothing," *Textile Society of America* 9 (2012), https://digitalcommons.unl.edu/cgi/viewcontent.cgi?article=1739&context=tsaconf.

16 *"Whites retained"*: Giorgio Riello and Ulinka Rublack, *The Right to Dress: Sumptuary Laws in a Global Perspective, c. 1200–1800* (Cambridge, UK: Cambridge University Press, 2019), 8.

16 *"slave codes"*: Nakia D. Parker, "Black Codes and Slave Codes," Oxford Bibliographies, March 25, 2020, https://www.oxfordbibliographies.com/display/document/obo-9780190280024/obo-9780190280024-0083.xml.

17 *"And whereas, many"*: "South Carolina's An Act for the Better Ordering and Governing Negroes and Other Slaves, South Carolina, 1740," accessed January 1, 2022, https://billofrightsinstitute.org/activities/an-act-for-the-better-ordering-and-governing-negroes-and-other-slaves-south-carolina-1740.

17 *"authorized, empowered and required . . . livery-men and boys"*: Robert S. DuPlessis, "Sartorial Sorting in the Colonial Caribbean and North America," Swarthmore College, 2019, https://works.swarthmore.edu/cgi/viewcontent.cgi?article=1507&context=fac-history.

17 *"The kind of negative stereotypes"*: Jonathan Michael Square, personal interview, February 25, 2021.

17 *"Fashion has always been"*: Max Berlinger, "How Hip-Hop Fashion Went from the Streets to High Fashion," *Los Angeles Times*, January 26, 2018, https://www.latimes.com/entertainment/la-et-ms-ig-hip-hop-fashion-streets-couture-20180125-htmlstory.html.

18 *"We make judgments"*: Carolyn Mair, *The Psychology of Fashion* (Routledge, 2018), 2.

18 *"Clothing is our second skin"*: Ibid., 5.

18 *"Many low-income Americans"*: Peter Ubel, "How the Psychology of Inequality Benefits Luxury Brands," *Forbes*, February 28, 2017, https://www.forbes.com/sites/peterubel/2017/02/28/do-luxury-brands-benefit-from-income-inequality/?sh=644a69b627b5.

18 *"Urban young people"*: André Leon Talley, *Fresh Dressed*, directed by Sacha Jenkins, CNN Films, 2015.

19 *"fashion at its most refined"*: "Couture by Numbers: What Does It Really Take to Make a Collection?," British *Vogue*, July 5, 2020, https://www.vogue.co.uk/fashion/article/couture-by-numbers.

19 *"the father of haute couture" and "the first couturier"*: Jessica Krick, "Charles Frederick Worth (1825–1895) and the House of Worth," The Costume Institute, The Metropolitan Museum of Art, October 2004, https://www.metmuseum.org/toah/hd/wrth/hd_wrth.htm.

19 *"Fashions were to France"*: Kimberly Chrisman-Campbell, "The King of Couture," *Atlantic Monthly*, September 1, 2015, https://www.theatlantic.com/entertainment/archive/2015/09/the-king-of-couture/402952/.

19 *The Fédération de la*: "Our History," Fédération de la Haute Couture et de la Mode, accessed January 1, 2021, https://www.fhcm.paris/en/our-history.

19 *A couture house is traditionally*: Harold Koda and Richard Martin, "Haute Couture," The Costume Institute, The Metropolitan Museum of Art, October 2004, https://www.metmuseum.org/toah/hd/haut/hd_haut.htm.

19 *Members must fulfill criteria*: "Everything You Need to Know about Haute Couture," Explore France, January 13, 2021, https://www.france.fr/en/news/article/everything-you-need-to-know-about-haute-couture.

20 *there were sixteen official haute couture designers*: "The Maisons," Fédération de la Haute Couture et de la Mode, accessed March 7, 2023, https://www.fhcm.paris/en/maisons?status=1.

20 vendeuses: Robin Givhan, *The Battle of Versailles: The Night American Fashion Stumbled into the Spotlight and Made History* (New York: Flatiron Books, 2015), 13.

20 *take over eight hundred hours*: "Haute Couture: What It Means, Who Buys It, and How Much It Actually Costs," *Stylecaster*, July 8, 2015, https://stylecaster.com/haute-couture-means-buys-costs/.

20 *"From a rudimentary muslin"*: Givhan, *The Battle of Versailles*, 13.

20 *"Couture is emotion"*: Katie Shillingford, "Exclusive Riccardo Tisci

Interview," *Dazed*, September 10, 2010, https://www.dazeddigital
.com/fashion/article/8302/1/exclusive-riccardo-tisci-interview.

CHAPTER THREE: EVERY DAY I'M HUSTLIN'

22 *"When you see these guys"*: LL Cool J, *Supreme Team*, directed by Nasir
"Nas" Jones and Peter J Scalettar, Showtime, 2022.

23 *"I remember going to some of them parties"*: Ibid.

23 *consisted of fourteen core members*: Ibid.

23 *street-level revenues exceeded $200,000*: Eastern District of New York,
U.S. Attorney's Office, "Kenneth 'Supreme' McGriff and 8 Leaders,
Members and Associates of McGriff's Enterprise Charged with Racketeering, Homicide and Drug Distribution," press release, January 26,
2005, https://www.justice.gov/archive/usao/nye/pr/2005/2005jan26.html.

23 *"The point of the game is"*: Supreme, *Supreme Team*.

24 *turkeys during Thanksgiving*: Nick Schonberger, "That's Gangster: Al
Capone, Birdman, and the Surprising History of the American Turkey
Drive," *First We Feast*, November 27, 2014, https://firstwefeast.com
/eat/2014/11/thanksgiving-gangster-traditions.

24 *"The Worst Year of Crime in City History"*: Leonard Buder, "1980 Called
Worst Year of Crime in City History," *New York Times*, February 25, 1981,
https://www.nytimes.com/1981/02/25/nyregion/1980-called-worst
-year-of-crime-in-city-history.html.

24 *robberies hit a record high*: George James, "New York Killings Set a
Record, While Other Crimes Fell in 1990," *New York Times*, April 23,
1991, https://www.nytimes.com/1991/04/23/nyregion/new-york-killings
-set-a-record-while-other-crimes-fell-in-1990.html.

24 *23.9 percent of the population*: Josh Barbanel, "New York City's
Economy Booms, and the Poor Begin to Profit," *New York Times*,
May 16, 1988, https://www.nytimes.com/1988/05/16/nyregion/new-york
-city-s-economy-booms-and-the-poor-begin-to-profit.html.

24 *Black unemployment rates*: "The Persistent Black-White Unemployment Gap Is Built into the Labor Market," Center for American Prog-
ress, September 28, 2020, https://www.americanprogress.org/article
/persistent-black-white-unemployment-gap-built-labor-market/.

24 *"I thought he was like"*: Pusha T, personal interview, March 1, 2021.

25 *more than ten thousand pairs*: Caroline Bula, "Inside DJ Khaled's Florida
Oasis and Plans to 'Own the Summer' with Superstar-Filled Single,"
Billboard, May 1, 2015, https://www.billboard.com/music/rb-hip-hop
/dj-khaled-music-florida-house-sneaker-collection-6546257/.

25 *"There was one question"*: Christopher "Kid" Reid, *Fresh Dressed*, directed by Sacha Jenkins, CNN Films, 2015.

25 *"If you were live"*: Ibid.

26 *The Puma Suede launched*: "The History of the Puma Suede," Puma, accessed March 1, 2023, https://about.puma.com/en/this-is-puma /archive-stories/history-of-suede.

26 *"I thought people would try"*: Rick Telander, "Senseless," *Sports Illus-trated*, May 14, 1990, https://vault.si.com/vault/1990/05/14/senseless -in-americas-cities-kids-are-killing-kids-over-sneakers-and-other -sports-apparel-favored-by-drug-dealers-whos-to-blame.

26 *"I had a friend who came"*: Bimmy Antney, personal interview, March 10, 2021.

27 *"Greed, for lack of a better word"*: *Wall Street*, directed by Oliver Stone, 20th Century Fox, 1987.

27 *"Bolivian Marching Powder"*: Jay McInerney, *Bright Lights, Big City* (New York: Knopf Doubleday, 1984), 2.

27 *"Your brain at this moment"*: Ibid.

27 *"reports abound of"*: Gregory Hywood, "Yuppies Flee in Horror from Drugs as Cocaine Spreads down the Line," *Australian Financial Review*, January 6, 1989, https://www.afr.com/politics/yuppies-flee-in-horror -from-drugs-as-cocaine-spreads-Down-the-line-19890106-jfsmp.

27 *"wouldn't do heroin"*: Nadine Brozan, "Women and Cocaine: A Grow-ing Problem," *New York Times*, February 18, 1985, https://www.nytimes .com/1985/02/18/style/women-and-cocaine-a-growing-problem.html.

28 *"Say hello to my little friend!"*: *Scarface*, directed by Brian De Palma, Universal Pictures, 1983.

28 *$5 to $20 for a vial*: "Special Report: Crack Wars," BBC, https://www .youtube.com/watch?v=b4243npZdDs.

28 *$16 to $125 per gram*: Carolyn Skorneck, "Price, Purity of Cocaine Vary Widely across Nation," *Los Angeles Times*, October 22, 1989, https:// www.latimes.com/archives/la-xpm-1989-10-22-mn-845-story.html.

28 *"Using it even once can"*: Eleanor Randolph, "Crack Use," *Washington Post*, September 14, 1989, https://www.washingtonpost.com/archive /lifestyle/1989/09/14/crack-use/38fbc038-a292-4935-827a-2a953 fe1ad43/.

28 *182,000 regular cocaine users*: Michal Marriott, "After 3 Years, Crack Plague in New York Only Gets Worse," *New York Times*, February 20, 1989, https://www.nytimes.com/1989/02/20/nyregion/after-3-years-crack -plague-in-new-york-only-gets-worse.html.

28 *increased to an estimated 600,000*: Ibid.

28 *"Without a steady supply"*: David Farber, *Crack: Rock Cocaine, Street*

Capitalism, and the Decade of Greed (Cambridge, UK: Cambridge University Press, 2019), 10.

28 *"The men who turned powder"*: Ibid., 3.

28 *"When people start to analyze"*: Eric Adams, *Supreme Team*.

29 *the homicide rate*: Roland G. Fryer Jr. et al., "Measuring Crack Cocaine and Its Impact," Harvard University, April 1006, https://scholar.harvard.edu/files/fryer/files/fhlm_crack_cocaine_0.pdf.

29 *"Crack poisoned bodies"*: Farber, *Crack*, 3–5.

29 *beepers, four-finger rings, and Nikes*: Michael Massing, "Crack's Destructive Sprint Across America," *New York Times*, October 1, 1989, https://www.nytimes.com/1989/10/01/magazine/crack-s-destructive-sprint-across-america.html.

29 *"Drugs are menacing our society"*: "President and Mrs. Reagan Address on Drug Abuse," C-Span, September 14, 1986, https://www.c-span.org/video/?406452-1/president-mrs-reagan-address-drug-abuse.

29 *"Any Questions?"*: "Partnership for a Drug-Free America: Any Questions?," Paley Center, accessed February 1, 2021, https://www.paleycenter.org/collection/item/?item=AT:23829.016.

29 *"celebration of cocaine"*: Bill Brewster and Frank Broughton, *Last Night a DJ Saved My Life: The History of the Disc Jockey* (New York: Grove Atlantic, 2014), 255.

30 *Possession of four ounces*: Madison Gray, "A Brief History of New York's Rockefeller Drug Laws," *Time*, April 2, 2009, https://content.time.com/time/nation/article/0,8599,1888864,00.html.

30 *"African Americans made up 88.3 percent"*: Elise Viebeck, "How an Early Biden Crime Bill Created the Sentencing Disparity for Crack and Cocaine Trafficking," *Washington Post*, July 28, 2019, https://www.washingtonpost.com/politics/how-an-early-biden-crime-bill-created-the-sentencing-disparity-for-crack-and-cocaine-trafficking/2019/07/28/5cbb4c98-9dcf-11e9-85d6-5211733f92c7_story.html.

30 *"We grew up with nothing"*: Bimmy Antney, personal interview, March 10, 2021.

31 *sentenced to twelve years of incarceration*: Eastern District of New York, U.S. Attorney's Office, "Notorious Queens Gang Leader Kenneth 'Supreme' McGriff Sentenced to Life Imprisonment for Racketeering, Double Murder-For-Hire Homicides, Narcotics Trafficking, and Laundering Drug Proceeds," press release, March 9, 2007, https://web.archive.org/web/20150215182843/http://www.justice.gov/usao/nye/pr/2007/2007Mar09b.html.

31 *"Yeah, we was known for that [fashion]"*: Bimmy Antney, personal interview, March 10, 2021.

31 *"Street guys and rap dudes"*: Nas, *Supreme Team.*

32 *who won't publicly confirm*: "Kareem 'Biggs' Burke," *Drink Champs*, Revolt, January 24, 2018, https://www.youtube.com/watch?v=g4m-vi VFLAg&t=1195s.

32 *"He's telling a story"*: Raekha Prasad, "My Boy Biggie," *Guardian*, December 6, 1999, https://www.theguardian.com/world/1999/dec/07 /gender.uk1.

32 *"He loved the respect"*: Martin A. Berrios, "Streets Is Talkin': Haitian Jack Speaks on Tupac, Suge Knight & Being Labeled a Snitch," *Hip-Hop Wired*, February 5, 2015, https://hiphopwired.com/443396/streets -talkin-haitian-jack-speaks-tupac-suge-jimmy-henchman-labeled -snitch/.

32 *Meanwhile, Tupac's childhood friends*: *Dear Mama*, directed by Allen Hughes, FX Networks, 2023.

33 *"Their style was a Queens"*: Bill Adler, personal interview, January 6, 2021.

33 *"Russell had an eye for fashion"*: Ibid.

33 *"Jay was cool enough"*: Stereo Williams, "How the Notorious Street Hustler Impacted Fashion," Rock the Bells, August 3, 2020, https://rock thebells.com/articles/who-started-hip-hop-fashion/.

33 *"The whole Adidas record"*: Zac Dubasik, "This History of Run-D.M.C. and Adidas as Told by D.M.C.," *Sole Collector*, March 11, 2014, https://solecollector.com/news/2014/03/this-history-of-run-d-m-c-and -adidas-as-told-by-d-m-c.

34 *"So, forty thousand people in"*: Gary Warnett, "How Run-DMC Earned Their Stripes," *Mr. Porter*, Mary 27, 2016, https://www.mrporter.com/en -us/journal/lifestyle/how-run-dmc-earned-their-adidas-stripes-826882.

34 *an extra half million pairs*: Barbara Smit, *Sneaker Wars: The Enemy Brothers Who Founded Adidas and Puma and the Family Feud That Forever Changed the Business of Sport* (New York: HarperCollins, 2008), 195.

34 *"It introduced hip-hop style"*: Bill Adler, personal interview, January 6, 2021.

CHAPTER FOUR: BURY THEM IN LO

35 *"When we would come back"*: *Very Ralph*, directed by Susan Lacy, HBO, 2019.

35 *two disparate boosting crews*: Jon Caramanica, "The Gang That Brought High Fashion to Hip-Hop," *New York Times*, June 28, 2016, https:// www.nytimes.com/2016/06/30/fashion/lo-lifes-fashion-hip-hop.html.

36 *"I was born when hip-hop"*: *Bury Me with the Lo On*, directed by Tom Gould, 2017.

36 *"I'm a hip-hop fiend"*: "Thirstin Howl The 3rd on Founding Lo Lifes, Rapping with Eminem, Battling Jay Z & Busta (Full Interview)," Vlad TV, September 18, 2021, https://www.youtube.com/watch?v=pywQ9 N1Mi6E.

36 *"We didn't start off with"*: Thirstin Howl The 3rd, personal interview, August 17, 2021.

36 *"As far as attending boosting"*: "How the Lo Lifes Met Up Everyday to Go Boostin (Life and Times of Rack-Lo) EP 8," Rack-Lo, April 11, 2021, https://www.youtube.com/watch?v=-fCUQYwAgL8.

37 *predominantly Jewish from the*: "History of Jewish Brownsville," Brownsville Jewish Community Center, accessed March 8, 2023, https://browns villejcc.com/history/.

37 *"When I was a child"*: Alfred Kazin, *A Walker in the City* (New York: Houghton Mifflin, 1969), 8.

37 *population in Brownsville had almost doubled*: Wendell E. Pritchett, *Brownsville, Brooklyn: Blacks, Jews, and the Changing Face of the Ghetto* (Chicago: University of Chicago Press, 2002), 84.

37 *highest concentration of public housing*: Feifei Sun, "Brownsville: Inside One of Brooklyn's Most Dangerous Neighborhoods," *Time*, January 31, 2012, https://time.com/3785609/brownsville-brooklyn.

37 *urban decay*: Jennifer Bleyer, "At Long Last, Developers Show an Interest," *New York Times*, June 17, 2007, https://www.nytimes.com /2007/06/17/realestate/17livi.html.

37 *The* New York Times *described*: Don Terry, "Growing Up Where Violence Wants to Come Play," *New York Times*, August 5, 1990, https://www.nytimes.com/1990/08/05/nyregion/growing-up-where -violence-wants-to-come-play.html.

37 *"We supported each other"*: Braydon Olson and Big Haz Uno, "Lo-Lifes Then and Now," *Vice*, June 30, 2011, https://www.vice.com/en/article /ppqy7n/lo-lifes-then-and-now-v18n7.

37 *"My family condoned it"*: Thirstin Howl The 3rd, personal interview, August 17, 2021.

37 *"How I felt having them"*: Thirstin Howl The 3rd, *"Bury Me with the Lo On* (Documentary Short for Book)," Facebook, January 18, 2018, https://www.facebook.com/watch/?v=1691905514201741.

38 *"My given name has"*: Oprah Winfrey, "Oprah Talks to Ralph," *O, The Oprah Magazine*, October 2002, https://www.oprah.com/omagazine /oprah-interviews-ralph-lauren/10.

38 *"The world was a little simpler"*: "Ralph Lauren," *Charlie Rose*, PBS, January 22, 1993, https://www.youtube.com/watch?v=fFil89MC7XA.

38 *"Then people said, 'Did you . . .'"* : Winfrey, "Oprah Talks to Ralph."

39 *from 1962 to 1964*: Christian Chensvold, "The Khaki Chronicles," Ralph Lauren, accessed March 5, 2023, https://www.ralphlauren.com /rlmag/the-history-of-khaki.html.

39 *took a job at Brooks Brothers*: "Ralph Lauren," *Business of Fashion*, accessed March 1, 2023, https://www.businessoffashion.com/community /people/ralph-lauren.

39 *"I didn't know how to make a tie"*: Kathleen Baird-Murray, *Vogue on Ralph Lauren* (New York: Abrams, 2013), 9.

39 *handmade ties made from high-quality materials*: "The Timeline," Ralph Lauren, accessed March 8, 2023, https://www.ralphlauren.com/rl-50 -timeline-feat.

39 *"We were exposed to fabulous things"*: "Bloomberg Game Changers: Ralph Lauren," *Bloomberg*, February 2, 2015, https://www.bloomberg .com/news/videos/2015-02-02/bloomberg-game-changers-ralph-lauren.

39 *"He closed his sample case"*: Ibid.

40 *Ralph Lauren had sold $500,000*: Ibid.

40 *"Had I changed that tie"*: Geoff Colvin, "Fashioning the Future: At 80, Ralph Lauren Is Facing His Namesake Company's Toughest Chapter Yet," *Fortune*, May 20, 2020, https://fortune.com/longform /ralph-lauren-company-founder-clothing-merchandise-sales-polo -fashion-business-rl-stock-fortune-500/.

40 *detail, down to the wood paneling*: "The Timeline," Ralph Lauren.

40 *"The business grew very rapidly"*: "Bloomberg Game Changers: Ralph Lauren."

40 *"The Polo shirt is to Ralph Lauren"*: "Ralph Lauren's Polo Shirt," Rizzoli, accessed March 8, 2023, https://www.rizzoliusa.com/book/978084 7866304/.

40 *"It's honest and"*: Ibid.

40 *to include multiple collections*: "The Timeline," Ralph Lauren.

41 *"He came from the trenches"*: Horse Power: Hip-Hop's Impact on Polo Ralph Lauren, Complex, February 13, 2018, https://www.youtube.com /watch?v=HQYEJGhIWbw.

41 *"He came from the dirt, just"*: Ibid.

41 *"It was a status symbol in the hood"*: Ibid.

41 *"When I seen that"*: "#TBT: Raekwon Talks Making the 'Snow Beach' Jacket Famous," *Complex*, June 25, 2015, https://www.complex.com /style/2015/06/raekwon-talks-ralph-lauren-polo-snow-beach-jacket.

42 "As far as clothing grails": Jake Woolf, "This 1992 Polo Sport Jacket Will Make You a Style God," *GQ*, October 28, 2016, https://www.gq.com /story/polo-sport-1992-snow-beach-jacket-buy.

42 "I wanted to wear something that": "#TBT: Raekwon Talks Making the 'Snow Beach' Jacket Famous."

42 "Every kid was like": Jian Deleon, "Interview: Just Blaze Breaks Down His Massive Polo Collection," *Complex*, May 9, 2012, https://www.complex .com/style/2012/05/interview-just-blaze-breaks-down-his-massive -polo-collection/.

42 "All-American": Hayley Phelan, "The Changing Face of the All-American Model," *Fashionista*, updated March 6, 2018, https://fashionista.com /2013/07/the-changing-face-of-the-all-american-model.

43 first hip-hop model: Robin Givhan, "A Hip Hop to the Runway," *Washington Post*, February 11, 1996, https://www.washingtonpost.com /archive/lifestyle/1996/02/11/a-hip-hop-to-the-runway/7420bb95 -f001-44bc-8e46-063c0c4851ba/.

43 Julia Chance and Sonya Magett, recognized: Jeff Chang, *Can't Stop Won't Stop: A History of the Hip-Hop Generation* (New York: Picador, 2015), 413.

43 "They were the first publication": "Tyson Beckford on Getting Discovered as a Model on the Street by *Source* Magazine," Vlad TV, August 19, 2021, https://youtu.be/3Hvn5YLI1Fc.

43 "Mr. Chin": "Tyson Beckford: Kids Teased Me, Called Me 'Mr. Chin' for My Chinese Eyes (Part 1)," Vlad TV, August 15, 2021, https://youtu.be /xAtwGS6qONk.

43 "Back then, it was survival of the fittest": "Tyson Beckford on Being Face of Polo, Dating Kim K, Kanye & Chris Brown Beef (Full Interview)," Vlad TV, September 11, 2021, https://youtu.be/Av7AuFjYsHo.

44 "Over the years, Weber": Herbert Muschamp, "Beefcake for the Masses," *New York Times*, November 14, 1999, https://www.nytimes .com/1999/11/14/magazine/beefcake-for-the-masses.html.

44 Ralph Lauren seeing his Polaroid: "Tyson Beckford on Being Face of Polo, Dating Kim K, Kanye & Chris Brown Beef (Full Interview)."

44 "Black, Male and, Yes, a Supermodel": Dan Shaw, "Black, Male and, Yes, a Supermodel," *New York Times*, November 20, 1994, https://www .nytimes.com/1994/11/20/style/black-male-and-yes-a-supermodel .html.

44 "Tyson is not, of course": Ibid.

44 Beckford signed: "History in the Making," Ralph Lauren, accessed March 8, 2023, https://www.ralphlauren.com/rlmag/ralph-lauren-polo

-black-models-icons.html?ab=en_US_rlmag_article_slotmore
_article1.

45 *"He's the great-looking guy"*: Givhan, "A Hip Hop to the Runway."

45 *"He always extended"*: "Thirstin Howl The 3rd on Founding Lo Lifes,
Rapping with Eminem, Battling Jay Z & Busta (Full Interview).

CHAPTER FIVE: 1991

46 *"These Boots Are Made for Walkin'"*: Cathryn Horn, "Hip-Happy Lagerfeld," *Washington Post*, July 24, 1991, https://www.washingtonpost
.com/archive/lifestyle/1991/07/24/hip-happy-lagerfeld/e4aa1777-4f4a
-4fc5-9503-e4fa94882e07/.

46 *"deafening rock and roll rhythms by Madonna"*: Laird Borrelli-Persson,
"Chanel Fall 1991: A Collection for Material Girls," *Vogue*, December 23, 2019, https://www.vogue.com/fashion-shows/fall-1991-ready-to
-wear/chanel.

47 *"It's the 'nouveau' rapper look"*: Roy H. Campbell, "Hip-Hop Is Getting
Haute," *Baltimore Sun*, May 9, 1991, https://www.baltimoresun.com
/news/bs-xpm-1991-05-09-1991129009-story.html.

47 *"I think what Lagerfeld has"*: Tim Blanks, "Throwback Thursdays with
Tim Blanks—Karl Lagerfeld's Hip-Hop-Inspired Fall 1991 Chanel
Show," Yahoo!, https://finance.yahoo.com/video/throwback-thursdays
-tim-blanks-karl-100000908.html.

47 *"Lagerfeld is deliberately provocative"*: Katherine Betts, "Runway Report,"
Vogue, January 1992, https://archive.vogue.com/article/1992/1/runway
-report-1992.

47 *"It's young, colorful, taken right from the street fashion scene"*: Mary
Rourke, "Chanel Shifts Gears: Karl Lagerfeld Puts His Signature on Ts,"
Los Angeles Times, March 20, 1991, https://www.latimes.com/archives
/la-xpm-1991-03-20-vw-564-story.html.

48 *"a little bit of girl and a little bit of boy"*: Michael Quintanilla, "'In Living
Color' Flygirls Start a Fashion Buzz," *Baltimore Sun*, August 7, 1991,
https://www.baltimoresun.com/news/bs-xpm-1991-08-07-1991219
151-story.html.

48 *"How many women are going to wear a silver catsuit?"*: Cathryn Horn,
"Fashion," *Washington Post*, March 18, 1991, https://www.washington
post.com/archive/lifestyle/1991/03/18/fashion/340d47bb-8bfb-4bb3
-bb7c-40716e32b9c4/.

48 *Her mother died*: Dana Thomas, *Deluxe: How Luxury Lost Its Luster*
(New York: Penguin Press, 2007), 145.

49 *in stained glass windows*: Susan Stamberg, "Coco Chanel: The Orphan

Who Transformed Fashion," NPR, September 18, 2009, https://www.npr.org/templates/story/story.php?storyId=112813709.

49 *not a very good one*: Ibid.

49 *"Without money, you are"*: Paul Morand, *The Allure of Chanel*, trans. Euan Cameron (London: Pushkin Press, 2013), 273, Kindle.

49 *Coco wanted something warm*: Susan Goldman Rubin, *Coco Chanel: Pearls, Perfume, and the Little Black Dress* (New York: Abrams, 2018).

49 *"My fortune is built"*: "Coco Chanel," *Biography*, December 10, 2021, https://www.biography.com/history-culture/coco-chanel.

49 *"By inventing the jersey"*: Morand, *The Allure of Chanel*, 350.

49 *"a canny little French woman and very exclusive"*: Jessica Vince and Justine Picardie, "La Grande Mademoiselle," *Harper's Bazaar*, September 11, 2017, https://www.harpersbazaar.com/uk/beauty/fragrance/a43647/gabrielle-chanel-fragrance/.

50 *She was a huge success*: Jessa Krick, "Gabrielle 'Coco' Chanel (1883–1971) and the House of Chanel," The Costume Institute, The Metropolitan Museum of Art, October 2004, https://www.metmuseum.org/toah/hd/chnl/hd_chnl.htm.

50 *"delighted guests squirting"*: Rhonda K. Garelick and Meryle Secrest, "Chanel vs. Schiaparelli," *Harper's Bazaar*, October 2, 2014, https://www.harpersbazaar.com/culture/features/a3781/chanel-schiaparelli-rivalry-1014/.

50 *"Look how ridiculous these"*: Alexander Fury, "Maria Grazia Chiuri and the History of Women at Dior," *New York Times*, October 3, 2016, https://www.nytimes.com/2016/10/03/t-magazine/fashion/maria-grazia-chiuri-dior-women-history-paris-fashion-week.html.

51 *She purchased a villa in the*: Hal Vaughan, *Sleeping with the Enemy: Coco Chanel's Secret War* (New York: Knopf Doubleday), 15.

51 *"I didn't go out"*: Jason Mangone et al., *Leaders: Myth and Reality* (New York: Penguin, 2018), 79.

51 *"The ability to wear her own clothes"*: Woody Hochswender, "Review/Television; The Chanel Who Created Fashions," *New York Times*, July 25, 1989, https://www.nytimes.com/1989/07/25/movies/review-television-the-chanel-who-created-the-fashions.html.

51 *"Luxury is a necessity"*: Anna Johnson, *Handbags: The Power of the Purse* (New York: Workman, 2002), 21.

51 *launched with perfumer Ernest Beaux*: Thomas, *Deluxe*, 146.

51 *"curled" or "ringed"*: Benjamin Reynaert and Mel Studach, "Bouclé Fabric Is Back," *Architectural Digest*, February 3, 2020, https://www.architecturaldigest.com/gallery/boucle-fabric-is-back.

52 *"I want them to see what"*: "Selections from Lady Bird's Diary on the

Assassination," PBS, November 22, 1963, https://www.pbs.org/ladybird/epicenter/epicenter_doc_diary.html.

52 *line-for-line copy*: Giovanna Osterman, "The History of Chez Ninon, the New York Couture Copycat," *CR Fashion Book*, January 28, 2020, https://crfashionbook.com/fashion-a30682069-chez-ninon-history-new-york-jacqueline-kennedy/.

52 *"It enables women to move with ease"*: "The Jacket—Inside Chanel," Chanel, March 13, 2013, https://www.youtube.com/watch?v=zx1R49B_tzw&t=15s.

52 *"The Chanel jacket . . . has definitely"*: Ibid.

52 *"The idea that Chanel should"*: Hochswender, "Review/Television; The Chanel Who Created Fashions."

53 *"There are things in fashion"*: "The Jacket—Inside Chanel."

53 *"It's called the classic for"*: Aleksija Vujicic, "These Are the 10 Most Iconic Chanel Bags of All Time," *Who What Wear*, December 2, 2022, https://www.whowhatwear.com/most-popular-chanel-bags/slide5.

54 *"It's the longest collaboration in fashion"*: J. J. Martin, "Fendi's Fairy Tale: Karl Lagerfeld Opens Up About His 50 Years with the Brand," *Harper's Bazaar*, October 17, 2016, https://www.harpersbazaar.com/fashion/designers/a17910/karl-lagerfeld-fendi-collaboration/.

54 *"We are not doing basic mink coats"*: Ibid.

54 *he was wearing a custom*: Yomi Adegoke, "'I Came up a Black Staircase': How Dapper Dan Went from Fashion Industry Pariah to Gucci God," *Guardian*, January 14, 2021, https://www.theguardian.com/society/2021/jan/14/i-came-up-a-black-staircase-how-dapper-dan-went-from-fashion-industry-pariah-to-gucci-god.

54 *The jacket made it onto Fendi's*: Kelefa Sanneh, "Harlem Chic," *New Yorker*, March 25, 2013, https://www.newyorker.com/magazine/2013/03/25/harlem-chic.

54 *one of the most name-checked*: Jacob Gallagher, "These Are the Fashion Brands That Rappers Name-Drop the Most," *Wall Street Journal*, April 22, 2019, https://www.wsj.com/articles/these-are-the-fashion-brands-rappers-namedrop-the-most-11555943601.

54 *"What I do, Coco would have hated"*: "Fashion: Backstage Pass Paris," CNN, July 14, 2012, https://www.youtube.com/watch?v=hJxRyEev8Ik.

55 *"$10 billion global fashion machine"*: Kim Bhasin and Benedikt Kammel, "How Chanel Became a $10 Billion Business under Karl Lagerfeld," *Bloomberg*, February 19, 2019, https://www.bloomberg.com/news/photo-essays/2019-02-19/how-chanel-became-a-10-billion-business-under-karl-lagerfeld.

55   *"I can Chanel-ize anything!"*: Bridget Foley, "In the Mind of King Karl," *Women's Wear Daily*, October 24, 2017, https://wwd.com/fashion-news /fashion-features/in-the-mind-of-king-karl-11033489/.

55   *"I think it's flattering"*: "Fashion: Backstage Pass Paris."

55   *"What I loved about Chanel"*: Aria Hughes, "Stylist Misa Hylton Breaks Down Lil' Kim's Iconic Chanel Looks," *Complex*, March 22, 2019, https://www.complex.com/style/2019/03/karl-lagerfeld-chanel-looks -lil-kim.

55   *first model to sign an exclusive*: "The History," Chanel, accessed March 8, 2023, https://www.chanel.com/lv/about-chanel/the-history/1980/.

56   *"Karl transformed me"*: Jessica Andrew, "12 Fashion People Reflect on Karl Lagerfeld's Legacy," *Teen Vogue*, February 19, 2019, https://www.teenvogue .com/story/karl-lagerfeld-legacy-prabal-gurung-kimora-lee-simmons.

56   *"He was the first"*: Foley, "In the Mind of King Karl."

57   *"The most stylish people are the homegirls"*: Venessa Lau, "Moment 73: Hip-Hop Stop," *Women's Wear Daily*, November 1, 2010, https://wwd.com /fashion-news/fashion-features/moment-73-hip-hop-stop-3346380/.

57   *In a black-and-white*: "29 Rare Archival Fashion Photos from Jackie Onassis to Lady Gaga," *Women's Wear Daily*, accessed February 1, 2022, https://wwd.com/fashion-news/fashion-features/gallery/29-rare -archival-fashion-photos-from-jackie-onassis-to-lady-gaga-10679284 /isaac-mizrahi-with-his-building-elevator-operator/.

57   *"Every era and every time has"*: Roy H. Campbell, "Hip-Hop Is Getting Haute," *Baltimore Sun*, May 9, 1991, https://www.baltimoresun.com /news/bs-xpm-1991-05-09-1991129009-story.html.

57   "So girl you know": "Where the Homegirls Are," *Newsweek*, June 16, 1991, https://www.newsweek.com/where-homegirls-are-204438.

57   *"We had to look to"*: Ibid.

58   *"There's a fine line between"*: Ibid.

58   *"The fun is to push that"*: Ibid.

58   *"It was really something that"*: Charlotte Neuville, personal interview, February 25, 2021.

58   *"The designers are way off"*: "Where the Homegirls Are," *Newsweek*.

58   *"When Black kids were wearing"*: Quintanilla, "'In Living Color' Flygirls Start a Fashion Buzz."

59   *"her style is closer"*: Mary Rourke, "A Suggestion of Nostalgia in New York: Fashion: World War II Looks, Pea Coats and Circle Skirts Pop Up in the Fall Collections. Designers Lose Interest in Loud Colors and Psychedelic Patterns," *Los Angeles Times*, April 10, 1991, https://www .latimes.com/archives/la-xpm-1991-04-10-vw-141-story.html.

59   *"It was a really big visual departure"*: Charlotte Neuville, personal interview, February 25, 2021.

59   *"Rap street style, with its jumble of jewelry"*: Woody Hochswender, "On the Road from Old Fashion to New, Hip-Hop," *New York Times*, April 10, 1991, https://www.nytimes.com/1991/04/10/garden/on-the -road-from-old-fashion-to-new-hip-hop.html.

59   *"It doesn't have to be overt"*: Charlotte Neuville, personal interview, February 25, 2021.

CHAPTER SIX: BROOKLYN'S FINEST

61   *when he was three years old*: "Interview with Karl Kani," Life and Lemonade TV, December 8, 2019, https://www.youtube.com/watch?app =desktop&v=V3wuAR03QCQ.

61   *grew the borough into the third-largest city in the United States*: "History of Brooklyn," PBS, accessed March 1, 2022, https://www.thirteen.org /brooklyn/history/history3.html.

62   *And by 1983*: Jen Hoyer, "West Indian Immigration and Carnival: Coming to Brooklyn," Brooklyn Public Library, August 31, 2017, https://www .bklynlibrary.org/blog/2017/08/31/west-indian-immigration.

62   *"My dad had vision"*: "Interview with Karl Kani," Life and Lemonade TV.

62   *"He was the first one that introduced"*: Karl Kani, personal interview, March 16, 2021.

62   *"Back in 1985"*: Ibid.

63   *"My dad was Panamanian"*: Ibid.

63   *"Back then, you gotta think, the choices"*: Ibid.

64   *"I'd never met a Black person"*: Daniel Day, *Dapper Dan: Made in Harlem* (New York: Random House, 2019), 126.

64   *"I actually had several tailors"*: Big Daddy Kane, personal interview, March 11, 2021.

65   *"I thought that it looked so royal"*: "Style Evolution: Big Daddy Kane," Rock the Bells, January 20, 2022, https://rockthebells.com/photo _galleries/big-daddy-kane-fashion-style/.

65   *"When I met Madonna"*: Big Daddy Kane, personal interview, March 11, 2021.

65   *"Me and my two dancers would get silk"*: Ibid.

65   *"I want you to make the pants baggier"*: Karl Kani, personal interview, March 16, 2021.

66   *"The neighborhood was very creative"*: "April Walker on Walker Wear, the Fashion Industry, Working with 2Pac & More," *Drink Champs*, Revolt, October, 9, 2021, https://www.youtube.com/watch?v=AsdA3Hm0ZFI.

67   *"I think I inherited a little bit of both"*: April Walker, personal interview, March 2, 2021.

67   *"Hip-hop was our rock and roll"*: Elena Romero, *Free Stylin': How Hip Hop Changed the Fashion Industry* (Westport, CT: Praeger, 2012), 71.

67   *"There was a lot going on"*: "April Walker on Walker Wear, the Fashion Industry, Working with 2Pac & More."

67   *"In school, I was always that"*: Romero, *Free Stylin'*, 71.

67   *"He was making mink coats"*: "April Walker on Walker Wear, the Fashion Industry, Working with 2Pac & More."

67   *"We have nothing like this in Brooklyn"*: April Walker, personal interview, March 2, 2021.

68   *"Brooklyn was very different"*: Ibid.

68   *and hired some of his tailors*: Romero, *Free Stylin'*, 72.

68   *"We bought the fabrics"*: "April Walker on Walker Wear, the Fashion Industry, Working with 2Pac & More."

68   *"There was no blueprint. I had no mentor"*: "Hip Hop Transformed Fashion Forever: April Walker," *Fashion Africa Now*, Soundcloud, February 24, 2021, https://soundcloud.com/user-356215593-634082463/hip-hop-transformed-fashion-forever.

68   *One time, the electricity got shut*: April Walker, *Walker Gems: Get Your A$% off the Couch* (self-pub., 2017), page 2.

68   *airbrushed shirt of Eric B.*: Marcus Gregory Blassingame, "Necessary Rebel," *In Black* magazine, July 6, 2021, https://issuu.com/inblackmagazinevol5/docs/0c1_cover_april_v6/s/12764271.

69   *"This airbrushed shirt"*: April Walker, personal interview, March 2, 2021.

69   *"We had three customers"*: Ibid.

69   *larger pockets, bigger sizes, longer crotch areas*: Romero, *Free Stylin'*, 73.

69   *"I wanted to get my clothes out there"*: "April Walker on Walker Wear, the Fashion Industry, Working with 2Pac & More."

70   *"He would be in the press a lot and"*: April Walker, personal interview, March 2, 2021.

70   *"I'd pick five stores in"*: Romero, *Free Stylin'*, 73.

70   *$300,000 in sales*: Ibid.

71   *"Come serve your sentence"*: Ibid., 74.

71   *"We sold nothing"*: Karl Kani, personal interview, March 16, 2021.

71   *"We did some really"*: Ibid.

72   *"Magazines were my reference"*: Tuma Basa, personal interview, May 27, 2002.

72   *"There was this image of a young"*: Romero, *Free Stylin'*, 70.

72   *"Puffy was the first business mogul"*: Angela Phillips, "Karl Kani: 'We Gave

the People What They Wanted,'" *The Face*, April 17, 2019, https://the face.com/style/the-godfather-of-streetwear.

73   *"Anything associated with Cross Colours"*: Fonda Marie Lloyd, "Kani Hip Hops to His Own Company," *Black Enterprise*, July 1994, 16.

73   *became Kani's majority owner*: Romero, *Free Stylin'*, 68.

74   *"Tupac used to wear my"*: Karl Kani, personal interview, March 16, 2021.

74   *"He just wanted to support"*: Ibid.

74   *he closed a $6 million order*: "Karl Kani on 2Pac Not Charging Him for Ad, Biggie Wearing Kani Jeans When He Died," Vlad TV, July 1, 2017, https://www.youtube.com/watch?v=NHk5Mm0sxjA.

74   *filed for Chapter 11 bankruptcy*: Romero, *Free Stylin'*, 57.

75   *"Our biggest retail"*: "History," Cross Colours, accessed March 9, 2023, https://crosscolours.com/pages/cross-colours-history.

75   *"They thought I was going to"*: Krisztina "Z" Holly, "Karl Kani: Godfather of Urban Streetwear," *The Art of Manufacturing*, July 25, 2016, https://podcasts.apple.com/au/podcast/karl-kani-godfather-of-urban-street wear/id1132427162.

75   *declared bankruptcy the day*: Romero, *Free Stylin'*, 74–75.

76   *"Being an independent company"*: Ibid., 73–76.

CHAPTER SEVEN: RED, WHITE, AND BLUES

77   "Yo, Andy. It's Snoop. I want to come check you out": Andy Hilfiger, personal interview, April 16, 2021.

77   *A basketball hoop entertained*: "Top Gear: The Oral History of Hip-Hop's Love Affair with Tommy Hilfiger," *Complex*, August 22, 2016, https://www.complex.com/style/2016/08/tommy-hilfiger-hiphop-oral-history.

78   *"It was by mistake in a way"*: "Insider Tommy Hilfiger's American Dream," The Business of Fashion, June 21, 2015, https://www.youtube.com /watch?v=OsSxNE4IH-g.

78   *"Music was my first love"*: Tommy Hilfiger, personal interview, April 12, 2021.

78   *"a certain something"*: Lisa Belkin, "Pushing Fashion in the Fast Lane," *New York Times*, November 9, 1986, https://www.nytimes.com/1986 /11/09/business/pushing-fashion-in-the-fast-lane.html.

79   *"My opening ad challenged the"*: "Tommy Hilfiger," George Lois, accessed March 9, 2023, http://www.georgelois.com/tommy-hilfiger.html.

79   *"My vision was always to reimagine classics"*: Tommy Hilfiger, personal interview, April 12, 2021.

79   *did $1 million in sales*: Lisa Belkin, "Pushing Fashion in the Fast Lane."

79   *"You have to have a great fit. You"*: Chris Black, "14 Lessons from Tommy

Hilfiger," *Highsnobiety*, accessed March 9, 2023, https://www.high
snobiety.com/p/tommy-hilfiger-interview-on-everything/.

80 *T-shirt was around $60*: David Rohde, "What Price Tommy Hilfiger,"
New York Times, March 23, 1997, https://www.nytimes.com/1997/03/23
/nyregion/what-price-tommy-hilfiger.html.

80 *"One pair of pants seems destined for stardom"*: Anne-Marie Schiro,
"Notes on Fashion," *New York Times*, June 18, 1985, https://www
.nytimes.com/1985/06/18/style/notes-on-fashions.html.

80 *"When I started, I was"*: Chris Black, "14 Lessons from Tommy Hilfiger."

81 *"Kidada has an innate sense of taste"*: Tommy Hilfiger, personal interview,
April 12, 2021.

81 *"I'm not gonna take the credit"*: Andy Hilfiger, personal interview, April
16, 2021.

81 *"Brands had beautiful advertising"*: Tommy Hilfiger, personal interview,
April 12, 2021.

82 *"The craziest thing about"*: "Top Gear: The Oral History of Hip-Hop's
Love Affair with Tommy Hilfiger."

82 "Hey. I'm back in town. We need some more gear": Andy Hilfiger, personal interview, April 16, 2021.

83 *"I gave Snoop some special stuff that"*: Ibid.

83 *"We are cutting back"*: Michel Marriott, "Out of the Woods," *New York
Times*, November 7, 1993, https://www.nytimes.com/1993/11/07/style
/out-of-the-woods.html.

83 *"Andy! Turn on Saturday"*: Andy Hilfiger, personal interview, April 16,
2021.

83 *"Having Snoop Dogg wearing"*: Tommy Hilfiger, personal interview,
April 12, 2021.

83 *"Snoop wearing this Tommy Hilfiger"*: Joe Walker, "Snoop Dogg
Responds to Kanye West Saying He Changed His Life as a Kid,"
HipHopDX, September 12, 2022, https://hiphopdx.com/news/id.73337
/title.snoop-dogg-kanye-west-snl-tommy-hilfiger.

83 *"Other designers didn't get it"*: Andy Hilfiger, personal interview, April
16, 2021.

84 *"I'm sure many of you"*: "Memorable Guest Follow-Ups," Oprah.com,
January 6, 2001, https://www.oprah.com/oprahshow/memorable-guests
-and-setting-it-straight/all.

84 *"Despite much investigation"*: Tommy Hilfiger, personal interview, April
12, 2021.

85 *which was confirmed by reps*: "Tommy Hilfiger Turns to Net to Combat
Rumors of Racism," *Wall Street Journal*, March 26, 1997, https://www
.wsj.com/articles/SB859409821829173500.

85 *"Why are they saying all those mean"*: Lakshmi Gopalkrishnan, "Dirty Linen," *Slate*, April 11, 1997, https://slate.com/culture/1997/04/dirty-linen.html.

85 *"people of all backgrounds"*: "Tommy Hilfiger Turns to Net to Combat Rumors of Racism."

85 *"Yet some of us keep"*: Leonard Pitts Jr., "Dissing Hilfiger," *Chicago Tribune*, January 12, 1999, https://www.chicagotribune.com/news/ct-xpm-1999-01-12-9901120113-story.html.

86 *"There are no easy"*: Yuniya Kawamura and Jung-Whan Marc de Jong, *Cultural Appropriation in Fashion and Entertainment* (London: Bloomsbury, 2022), Conclusion.

87 *"It definitely happened"*: Barbara Grizzuti Harrison, "Spike Lee Hates Your Cracker Ass," *Esquire*, March 20, 2013.

87 *"by means of chat rooms, bulletin"*: Abraham H. Foxman, "ADL Letter to Tommy Hilfiger," Anti-Defamation League, July 11, 2001, https://www.adl.org/resources/letter/adl-letter-tommy-hilfiger.

87 *"The next time somebody sends"*: "Memorable Guest Follow-Ups," Oprah.com.

88 *"It hurt my integrity"*: Ibid.

CHAPTER EIGHT: DON'T KILL MY VIBE

89 *"Over my dead body"*: Quincy Jones, *Q: The Autobiography of Quincy Jones* (New York: Broadway Books, 2002), 292.

90 *"urban Rolling Stone for the '90s"*: Ibid.

90 *"As I remember, no one knew"*: Carol Smith, personal interview, April 1, 2021.

90 *"It was weird. I had"*: Jonathan Van Meter, personal interview, March 18, 2021.

91 *"I was able to explain to"*: Ibid.

91 *with a budget of $1 million*: Dan Charnas, "'We Changed Culture': An Oral History of *Vibe* Magazine," *Billboard*, https://www.billboard.com/music/rb-hip-hop/vibe-magazine-oral-history-8477004/.

91 *"He, as a fashion person"*: Jonathan Van Meter, personal interview, March 18, 2021.

91 *"I put together all the things that"*: Stefan Campbell, personal interview, March 30, 2021.

92 *"The test issue sat on the newsstand"*: Jonathan Van Meter, personal interview, March 18, 2021.

92 *industry average of 40 percent*: David E. Sumner and Shirrel Rhoades,

Magazines: A Complete Guide to the Industry (New York: Peter Lang, 2006), 46.

92 "One of the questions": Jonathan Van Meter, personal interview, March 18, 2021.

92 "It was pretty quickly an": Carol Smith, personal interview, April 1, 2021.

92 "There was fashion from the very beginning": Keith Clinkscales, personal interview, April 1, 2021.

93 Smith wrote a $10 million business: Dan Charnas, "'We Changed Culture.'"

93 "My pitch to them": Jonathan Van Meter, personal interview, March 18, 2021.

93 left over from Life magazine: "Famed Photographer Dana Lixenberg and Patta to Host Pop-Up Shop for 'Tupac Biggie' Book," Vibe, September 25, 2021, https://www.vibe.com/news/entertainment/dana-lixenberg-pop-up-shop-vibe-magazine-photos-664621/.

93 "It should be beautiful to look at": Jonathan Van Meter, personal interview, March 18, 2021.

93 "We had deeper pockets than most": "Famed Photographer Dana Lixenberg and Patta to Host Pop-Up Shop for 'Tupac Biggie' Book."

94 "The way Snoop is photographed": Jonathan Van Meter, personal interview, March 18, 2021.

94 "It just emanated class": Keith Clinkscales, personal interview, April 1, 2021.

95 "Quincy Jones saw the cover and it was the": Jonathan Van Meter, personal interview, March 18, 2021.

95 "We all wanted Eddie [Murphy]": Dan Charnas, "'We Changed Culture.'"

96 "It wasn't about Madonna or Dennis": Jones, Q: The Autobiography of Quincy Jones, 292.

96 "I had moved heaven and earth": Jonathan Van Meter, personal interview, March 18, 2021.

96 "See you around, pal": Jones, Q: The Autobiography of Quincy Jones, 292.

96 "I'm talking to hip-hop fans": "Source Magazine Founder Dave Mays on the Rise & Fall of the Iconic Source!" Hip-Hop News Uncensored, October 14, 2021, https://www.youtube.com/watch?v=_PaR1M657pM.

96 "That was fine, people wanted": Robbie, "Jonathan Shecter aka Shecky Green—The Unkut Interview, Part 1," Unkut.com, January 29, 2013, https://www.unkut.com/2013/01/jonathan-shecter-aka-shecky-green-the-unkut-interview/.

97 "A few years in, we're": "Source Magazine Founder Dave Mays on the Rise & Fall of the Iconic Source!"

97 *"It was a fairly fast but gradual process"*: "Dave Mays on Launching & Losing *The Source*, Benzino, Eminem, Suge Knight, Snoop (Full Interview)," Vlad TV, January 16, 2022, https://www.youtube.com/watch?v=uqDrHKpLFrg.

97 The Source *had a circulation of forty thousand*: Jeff Chang, *Can't Stop Won't Stop: A History of the Hip-Hop Generation* (New York: Picador, 2015), 413.

98 *"Let me tell you, they were not"*: Julia Chance, personal interview, January 25, 2021.

98 *"I was raised in a Black"*: Ibid.

99 *"ghetto gentlemen swag"*: Slick Rick, personal interview, May 3, 2021.

99 *"Britain represented that preppy"*: Angela Phillips, "'We Had a High Society Way of Dressing All Year Round': Slick Rick's Great British Childhood," *Bonafide*, November 20, 2016, http://www.bonafidemag.com/high-society-way-dressing-year-round-slick-rick-british-heritage-returning-uk/.

99 *"Everything was guerilla style"*: Julia Chance, personal interview, January 25, 2021.

100 *"She was a native New Yorker"*: Ibid.

100 *"I basically went to her"*: Sonya Magett, personal interview, January 20, 2021.

100 Hip-hop brands like: Dan Charnas, *The Big Payback: The History of the Business of Hip-Hop* (New York: New American Library, 2010), 456.

100 *"I would always"*: Sonya Magett, personal interview, January 20, 2021.

100 *"I was able to pull for"*: Julia Chance, personal interview, January 25, 2021.

101 *"No one ever verbally"*: Sonya Magett, personal interview, January 20, 2021.

101 *"I was pulling Timberland"*: Julia Chance, personal interview, January 25, 2021.

101 *"Timberland is wrestling"*: Michael Marriott, "Out of the Woods," *New York Times*, November 7, 1993, https://www.nytimes.com/1993/11/07/style/out-of-the-woods.html.

101 *"If you hear that hip-hop kids are wearing"*: Ibid.

102 *"The youth market came"*: Ibid.

102 *"I think that they think"*: Ibid.

102 *"This was my opinion. I wasn't"*: Julia Chance, personal interview, January 25, 2021.

102 that The Source *had provided*: Charnas, *The Big Payback*, 457.

CHAPTER NINE: GHETTO FABULOUS

103   *ghet·to-fab·u·lous*: *Oxford English Dictionary*, online ed.

103   *"This dude's gonna be a problem"*: "Music Talks: Andre Harrell Speaks with Sean 'Diddy' Combs (Full Episode)," Revolt, August 30, 2017, https://www.youtube.com/watch?v=vFfbbADgxwo.

104   *"I ran there and I ran back"*: Ibid.

104   *"My goal is to bring real"*: Chuck Philips, "The $50 Million Rap Master," *Los Angeles Times*, June 11, 1992, https://www.latimes.com/archives/la-xpm-1992-06-11-ca-247-story.html.

104   *"I grew up thinking"*: Lynn Hirschberg, "Living Large," *Vanity Fair*, September 1993, https://www.vanityfair.com/hollywood/1993/09/andre-harrell-uptown-entertainment/.

104   *"I think it's something"*: O'Neal McKnight, personal interview, May 27, 2022.

104   *"the sound of young America"*: Mick Brown, "Barry Gordy: The Man Who Built Motown," *Telegraph*, January 23, 2016, https://s.telegraph.co.uk/graphics/projects/berry-gordy-motown/index.html.

104   *mandatory etiquette coaching*: Gary Graff, "Motown Etiquette Coach Maxine Powell Dies at 98," *Oakland Press*, October 14, 2013, https://www.theoaklandpress.com/2013/10/14/motown-etiquette-coach-maxine-powell-dies-at-98/.

105   *"Motown is the first thing"*: Danyel Smith, "Ghetto-Fabulous," *New Yorker*, April 21, 1996, https://www.newyorker.com/magazine/1996/04/29/ghetto-fabulous.

105   *"ghetto fabulous"*: Dream Hampton, "The Originator," *Life and Times*, October 5, 2011, https://lifeandtimes.com/the-originator.

105   *"I was sitting on"*: Nerisha Penrose, "Mary J. Blige on Navigating Self-Acceptance Through Beauty," *ELLE*, January 26, 2022, https://www.elle.com/beauty/a38830509/mary-j-blige-the-state-of-black-beauty-super-bowl/.

105   *"It was the champagne lifestyle"*: "Music Talks: Andre Harrell Speaks with Sean 'Diddy' Combs (Full Episode)."

105   *"I knew it was the right move"*: Ibid.

105   *"They wanted to see Andre"*: O'Neal McKnight, personal interview, May 27, 2022.

106   *"Ghetto fabulous is just"*: Penrose, "Mary J. Blige on Navigating Self-Acceptance Through Beauty."

106   *"Fifty percent of fabulous"*: Smith, "Ghetto-Fabulous."

106   *"Russell and Andre were the only two"*: O'Neal McKnight, personal interview, May 27, 2022.

107 *"But just slipping into designer"*: Robin Givhan, "Rapper Attitude in Designer Diamonds and Furs: Ghetto Fabulous Goes Global," *New York Times*, October 9, 1999, https://www.nytimes.com/1999/10/09/news/rapper-attitude-in-designer-diamonds-and-furs-ghetto-fabulous-goes.html.

107 *"Middle-class girls can't be"*: Smith, "Ghetto-Fabulous."

107 *"For me, pulling clothes"*: Sowmya Krishnamurthy, "A History of How Hip-Hop and Fashion Brands Started Working Together," *XXL*, February 7, 2019, https://www.xxlmag.com/history-rappers-and-fashion/.

108 *"We would just brainstorm"*: "Misa Talks Being a Stylist for Mary J. Blige, Missy Elliott, and the 1999 MTV Music Awards," Premium Pete Show, April 20, 2018, https://www.youtube.com/watch?v=z69hpRZ4rBk.

108 *"Ghetto fabulous now refers"*: Givhan, "Rapper Attitude in Designer Diamonds and Furs."

108 *"My full-time job"*: "Andre Harrell Reveals Why He Fired Sean Combs," *Wall Street Journal* Live, September 19, 2014, https://www.youtube.com/watch?v=vkyKkHfqzbE.

108 *"Puffy wanted me to fight"*: Kiki Mason, "Pop Goes the Ghetto," *New York* magazine, October 23, 1995, 42.

108 *"Dre created a monster"*: Ibid.

109 *"They wanted me to"*: "Andre Harrell Reveals Why He Fired Sean Combs," *Wall Street Journal* Live.

109 *"It was like leaving home"*: Mason, "Pop Goes the Ghetto."

109 *"I told [Puffy], 'I'm really letting you go so you can get rich'"*: "Andre Harrell Reveals Why He Fired Sean Combs," *Wall Street Journal* Live.

109 *"The energy felt like"*: Sean "Diddy" Combs as told to Janelle Okwodu, "Diddy at 50: The Hip-Hop Legend on His Groundbreaking Fashion Career," *Vogue*, November 4, 2019, https://www.vogue.com/article/sean-diddy-combs-interview-fashion-legacy-puffy-takes-paris-anniversary.

110 *"huffing and puffing"*: Shawn Setaro, "The Definitive History of Puff Daddy's Name Changes," *Complex*, November 6, 2017, https://www.complex.com/music/2017/11/definitive-history-puff-daddy-name-changes.

110 *connection to his heroin dealings*: Arnold H. Lubuasch, "Ten Found Guilty of Heroin Charge," *New York Times*, February 24, 1973, https://www.nytimes.com/1973/02/24/archives/ten-found-guilty-of-heroin-charge-convicted-of-taking-part-in.html.

110 *"I don't have a lot of"*: "Confessions: Diddy Opens Up About His Father, Melvin Combs," Revolt, October 23, 2013, https://www.youtube.com/watch?v=S9HNZwUiuM8.

110   *worked multiple jobs*: Soraya Nadia McDonald, "Can Diddy Outrun His Demons," *Washington Post*, June 24, 2015, https://www.washington post.com/news/arts-and-entertainment/wp/2015/06/24/can-diddy-out run-his-demons/.

110   *"I wasn't going to be homeless"*: Katherine E. Finkelstein, "These Days, Even Puff Needs a Mommy; Star's Devoted Mother Is There, with Lunch," *New York Times*, January 31, 2001, https://www.nytimes .com/2001/01/31/nyregion/these-days-even-puff-needs-a-mommy-star -s-devoted-mother-is-there-with-lunch.html.

110   *Puffy modeled in* Essence: Dan Charnas, *The Big Payback: The History of the Business of Hip-Hop* (New York: New American Library, 2010), 459.

111   *"We used to just all hang"*: Groovey Lew, personal interview, September 14, 2021.

111   *"He was just regular. He's just basic"*: Ibid.

111   *"thousand-dollar blazers"*: Ibid.

111   *From the age of twelve*: Lindsay Lavine, "Sean Combs' Advice for Aspiring Entrepreneurs," *Fast Company*, October 20, 2014, https:// www.fastcompany.com/3037263/sean-combs-advice-for-aspiring -entrepreneurs.

111   *"If you want beautiful"*: Groovey Lew, personal interview, September 14, 2021.

112   *"I wanna dress like a skinny"*: Sean Combs, Twitter Spaces, May 20, 2022

112   *specialty tailors 5001 Flavors*: Ibid.

113   *"I know I ain't no pretty"*: Justin Tinsley, *It Was All a Dream: Biggie and the World That Made Him* (New York: Abrams, 2022), 237.

113   *"He was playing on all that"*: "The Notorious B.I.G.," *Behind the Music*, VH1, July 8, 2001.

113   *"'We need a sexy record'"*: The Notorious B.I.G., "One More Chance/ Stay with Me (Remix)," Genius, accessed March 10, 2023, https:// genius.com/The-notorious-big-one-more-chance-stay-with-me-remix -lyrics.

113   *Italian size 60 (or XXXL in U.S. sizing)*: Godfrey Deeny, "Dolce & Gab- bana Linkup with DJ Khaled for a Unisex Collection," *Fashion Network*, March 11, 2011, https://us.fashionnetwork.com/news/Dolce-gabbana -linkup-with-dj-khaled-for-a-unisex-collection,1286850.html.

114   *"maudlin 'tribute'"*: Tom Sinclair, "I'll Be Missing You," *Entertainment Weekly*, May 30, 1997, https://ew.com/article/1997/05/30/ill-be-missing -you/.

114   *"somewhat turgid"*: Jeremy Simmonds, *The Encyclopedia of Dead Rock Stars: Heroin, Handguns, and Ham Sandwiches* (Chicago: Chicago Review Press, 2012), 369.

114   *"That was one way of me"*: Lakin Starling, "June Ambrose Explains How Bad Boy's Shiny Suits Changed High Fashion Forever," *Fader*, May 20, 2016, https://www.thefader.com/2016/05/20/june-ambrose-bad-boy -style-mo-money-video.

115   *one of the most expensive*: Jennifer Michalski, "The Most Expensive Music Videos of All Time," *Business Insider*, January 20, 2014, https:// www.businessinsider.com/most-expensive-music-videos-2014-1.

115   *"We were just stepping"*: Jackie Willis, "EXCLUSIVE: Diddy Says He Knew Jennifer Lopez's Iconic GRAMMYs Dress Was Going to 'Change the Game,'" *ET Online*, June 20, 2017, https://www.etonline.com /fashion/219962_diddy_says_he_knew_jennifer_lopez_iconic _grammy_dress_was_going_to_change_the_game.

115   *"After all, people wanted"*: Eric Schmidt, "The Tinkerer's Apprentice," *Project Syndicate*, January 19, 2015, https://www.project-syndicate .org/magazine/google-european-commission-and-disruptive -technological-change-by-eric-schmidt-2015-01.

115   *"modern-day Gatsby"*: Chris Gardner and Lindsay Weinberg, "The Hamptons' 'Modern-Day Gatsby': Diddy's White Party Turns 20," *Hollywood Reporter*, April 16, 2018, https://www.hollywoodreporter.com /movies/movie-news/hamptons-modern-day-gatsby-diddys-white -party-turns-20-1100974/.

116   *"I remember the first party"*: Ibid.

116   *"Having an entire party all"*: Ibid.

116   *the majority of the audience*: Geoff Boucher, "Hip-Hop Takes a Dip," *Chicago Tribune*, June 24, 2002, https://www.chicagotribune.com /news/ct-xpm-2002-06-24-0206240117-story.html.

116   *"hypermaterialistic theme of ghetto fabulousness"*: Marcus Reeves, *Somebody Scream!: Rap Music's Rise to Prominence in the Aftershock of Black Power* (New York: Faber and Faber, 2009), 219.

116   *"With a reduced concern for shouting"*: Ibid., 219–220.

117   *"We couldn't compete with"*: Ahmir "Questlove" Thompson, personal interview, November 2, 2022.

118   *"It's a line that you had to learn"*: Pharoahe Monch, personal interview, August 21, 2021.

119   *"I fought like hell for that"*: Selwyn Seyfu Hinds, personal interview, June 7, 2021.

119   *"Q-Tip's articulation doesn't necessarily"*: Ibid.

CHAPTER TEN: LADIES FIRST

120 *"Versace as a kid playing"*: Robert Klara, "Versace's Logo," *Adweek*, accessed March 10, 2023, https://www.adweek.com/brand-marketing/versaces-medusa-logo-breaks-every-design-rule-so-why-does-it-work/.

120 *"When I asked Gianni"*: Ibid.

120 *"I think it's the responsibility"*: Amy S. Spindler, "Gianni Versace, 50, the Designer Who Infused Fashion with Life and Art," *New York Times*, July 16, 1997, https://www.nytimes.com/1997/07/16/style/gianni-versace-50-the-designer-who-infused-fashion-with-life-and-art.html.

121 *"Before [Gianni], I don't think"*: Hannah Marriott, "Fashion, Unfiltered: How 2017 Became the Year of Versace," *Guardian*, December 5, 2017, https://www.theguardian.com/fashion/2017/dec/05/fashion-how-2017-became-the-year-of-donatella-versace.

121 *"He was the first to realize"*: Spindler, "Gianni Versace, 50, the Designer Who Infused Fashion with Life and Art."

121 *conflicting reports as to whether the two men*: Julie Miller, "The Truth About Gianni Versace and Andrew Cunanan's Relationship," *Vanity Fair*, August 1, 2018, https://www.vanityfair.com/hollywood/2018/01/versace-american-crime-story-andrew-cunanan.

121 *No motive was proven*: Amy Mackelden, "Why Did Andrew Cunanan Go on a Killing Spree? American Crime Story Explores His Motives," *Harper's Bazaar*, https://www.harpersbazaar.com/culture/film-tv/a15924270/why-did-andrew-cunanan-kill-gianni-versace/.

121 *50 percent of his company to his eleven-year-old niece, Allegra*: Stephen M. Silverman, "Versace's Teen Niece to Take Over Company," *People*, June 15, 2004, https://people.com/celebrity/versaces-teen-niece-to-take-over-company/.

122 *$807 million with 130 stores*: Spindler, "Gianni Versace, 50, the Designer Who Infused Fashion with Life and Art."

122 *"In my dream, Gianni . . ."*: Sven Michelson, "The Epic of Donatella," SSense, accessed March 10, 2023, https://www.ssense.com/en-us/editorial/fashion/the-epic-of-donatella.

122 *"I was the new face of Versace"*: Ibid.

122 *"What is comfortable fashion?"*: Nicki Minaj, "Donatella Versace," *Interview*, November 28, 2011, https://www.interviewmagazine.com/fashion/donatella-versace-nicki-minaj.

123 *"The poster is vulgar"*: "Is Lil' Kim sexualizing our children?," *Rolanda* (clip), posted by @Nastiestone, Twitter, November 13, 2022, https://twitter.com/NASTIESTONE/status/1591910273879015424?s=20&t=jHDlRjQTlZoB3q1SYhK6QQ.

123 *"Lil' Kim is what I use to get"*: Kristal Brent Zook, "The Mask of Lil' Kim," *Washington Post*, September 3, 2000, https://www.washingtonpost.com /archive/lifestyle/style/2000/09/03/the-mask-of-lil-kim/b9a06fe7-adde -49fa-9259-aa1dbf71e655/.

123 *"If he hadn't said what he said to me"*: Ibid.

123 *while rapping in their neighborhood*: "#TBT Lil' Kim Reveals Her First and Last Conversation with Biggie, *106 & Park*," BET, December 26, 2019, https://youtu.be/yfZi_pBQQDI.

123 *"As far as the neighborhood"*: Ibid.

124 *He coached her*: Clover Hope, "The Meaning of Lil' Kim," Pitchfork, January 25, 2001, https://pitchfork.com/thepitch/the-meaning-of-lil -kim-motherlode-book/.

124 *"He threw the negatives on the table"*: Georgette Cline, "Respect Me," *XXL*, November 10, 2016, https://www.xxlmag.com/lil-kim-interview -hard-core-album/.

124 *Kim refuted those claims*: Shamika Sanders, "Lil' Kim Talks Biggie Writing Her Rhymes & Says She Still Feels His Spirit in the Studio [EXCLUSIVE]," *Hello Beautiful*, September 23, 2014, https://hello beautiful.com/2744959/lil-kim-talks-biggie-new-mixtape-exclusive/.

124 *"What makes me any different from a model?"*: "Lil' Kim on Tavis Smiley Talk Show (BET)," Martina Watkins, February 25, 2021, https://www .youtube.com/watch?v=iEni4yP7UbM.

124 *"I have low self-esteem"*: Allison Samuels, "A Whole Lotta Lil' Kim," *Newsweek*, June 25, 2000, https://www.newsweek.com/whole-lotta-lil -kim-160903.

124 *multiple plastic surgery*: "Lil Kim Plastic Surgeries—Surgeon Reacts," Dr. Gary Linkov, October 27, 2021, https://www.youtube.com/watch?v= ovuJph5xhBE.

125 *"Donatella is my girl"*: Janelle Okwodu, "Lil' Kim Shares the Story Behind Her Iconic '90s Met Gala Looks," *Vogue*, May 4, 2020, https://www .vogue.com/article/met-gala-lil-kim-1999-versace-iconic-outfit.

125 *"it helped to kickstart the trend"*: Ibid.

125 *"By wearing African clothes"*: Alexa Tietjen, "Queen Latifah Talks Wearing African Clothing in This Amazing Throwback Interview," July 10, 2016, VH1, https://www.vh1.com/news/kbdbu4/queen-latifah-style.

126 *"When I did that image"*: Nadja Sayej, "The Story Behind Lil' Kim's Iconic Louis Vuitton Logo-Print Portrait," *Vice*, November 6, 2018, https://www.vice.com/en/article/qvqde3/lil-kim-louis-vuitton-david -lachapelle.

127 *"If I was Kim I would"*: Liz Raiss, "How the Most Iconic VMAs Look

of All Time Came Together," *Fader*, August 26, 2016, https://www
.thefader.com/2016/08/26/vma-lil-kim-purple-misa-hylton.

127   *"I loved the idea of feeling"*: Landon Peoples, "Ten Years Later, Missy
Elliott Still Knows Her Plastic Bag Suit Was Fly as Hell," May 11,
2017, *Refinery29*, https://www.refinery29.com/en-us/2017/05/154034
/missy-elliott-marc-jacobs-fall-2017-collection.

127   *The look by June Ambrose*: Vincent Boucher, "Music's 'Secretary of
Style': June Ambrose Reflects on 30-Year Career, Creating Iconic Looks
for Missy Elliott, Diddy and Others," *Hollywood Reporter*, June 8,
2021, https://www.hollywoodreporter.com/lifestyle/style/june-ambrose
-stylist-jay-z-puma-1234961092/.

127   *used Indian bridal fabric*: Raiss, "How the Most Iconic VMAs Look of
All Time Came Together."

127   *"I think it was more of a friendly"*: "Lil' Kim Remembers the VMA Boob
Encounter with Diana Ross," MTV, August 24, 2013, https://www.mtv
.com/video-clips/gzut1e/lil-kim-remembers-the-vma-boob-encounter
-with-diana-ross.

127   *started her brand with bedazzled logo*: Allison P. Davis, "Lady Kimora:
The Baby Phat Designer Returns," *The Cut*, August 20, 2019, https://
www.thecut.com/2019/08/kimora-lee-simmons-baby-phat-relaunch
.html.

127   *"I would never wear this"*: Giovanna Osterman, "The Enduring Impact
of Baby Phat," *CR Fashion Book*, May 4, 2020, https://crfashionbook
.com/fashion-a32339202-baby-phat-kimora-lee-simmons-streetwear/.

128   *"I was paying homage"*: Lakin Starling, "Kimora Lee Simmons Turned
Her Culture into a Billion-Dollar Fashion Brand. Now She Says a
Little Credit Is Due," *Fader*, October 11, 2016, https://www.thefader
.com/2016/10/11/kimora-lee-simmons-baby-phat-black-fashion
-interview.

128   *"I had the best jeans in the world"*: Ibid.

128   *"never-ending whirlwind"*: Mary Tannen, "She's Like a Rainbow," *New
York Times Magazine*, July 7, 2006, https://www.nytimes.com/2006
/07/02/magazine/02beauty.html.

128   *"a flamboyant ex-model"*: Ibid.

129   *"I want to be a role model"*: "Ryan Meets the Fabulous Kimora Lee
Simmons!" Mix, November 8, 2011, https://www.youtube.com/watch
?v=Z0VwEfqXiV0.

129   *"It's stylish. It's sexy"*: "Aaliyah & Damon Dash at Baby Phat Lingerie
Fashion Show 2000 (Rare)," Aaliyah Archives, accessed June 2, 2021,
https://www.youtube.com/watch?v=YzIycHbE30Y.

129　*And they did*: Cam'ron, personal interview, August 3, 2021.

129　*"principal creative arbiter"*: Tracie Rozhon, "Phat Fashions Is Being Sold to Kellwood for $140 Million," *New York Times*, January 9, 2004, https://www.nytimes.com/2004/01/09/business/phat-fashions-is-being-sold-to-kellwood-for-140-million.html.

CHAPTER ELEVEN: THUG LIFE ALTA MODA

130　*"Some people just have"*: Dominique Sisley, "Some People Just Have an Aura": David McLean on His Unseen Tupac Photos," *AnOther* magazine, August 3, 2021, https://www.anothermag.com/art-photography/13479/some-people-just-have-an-aura-david-mclean-on-his-unseen-tupac-photos.

130　*From his walk, he seemed*: Alexandre Marain, "Do You Remember When 2Pac Walked for Versace Back in 1995?," *Vogue*, June 18, 2018, https://www.vogue.fr/vogue-hommes/culture/articles/tupac-2pac-versace-runway-performance/65397.

131　*"I was one of the only kids in Italy"*: Ricardo Tisci, *Fresh Dressed*, directed by Sacha Jenkins, CNN Films, 2015.

131　*"Nobody in fashion was working with Black artists"*: Rob Nowill, "Donatella Versace Has the Formula for a 'Pandemic-Proof' Brand," *Hypebeast*, March 4, 2021, https://hypebeast.com/2021/3/donatella-versace-ss21-fw21-menswear-interview.

131　*"the most beautiful man in the world"*: Taylor Ford, "12 Celebrity Runway Cameos You Might Have Missed," i-D, *Vice*, July 9, 2016, https://i-d.vice.com/en/article/bjz94d/12-celebrity-catwalk-cameos-you-might-have-missed.

131　*"It gave me an eerie feeling"*: Frank Alexander and Heidi Siegmund Cuda, *Got Your Back: Protecting Tupac in the World of Gangsta Rap* (New York: St. Martin's Press, 2000), 105.

131　*"I always loved rap music"*: Nowill, "Donatella Versace Has the Formula for a 'Pandemic-Proof' Brand."

131　*"He walked to our table"*: Alexander and Cuda, *Got Your Back*, 105.

132　*"We put him in the show"*: Keith Clinkscales, personal interview, April 1, 2021.

132　*"Tupac had never been out"*: "2pac Was Nervous & Didn't Want to Go to Versace Fashion Show in Italy," The Art of Dialogue, May 7, 2018, https://youtu/1cuQI1DLC9Y.

132　*"I wanted him to have the name of revolutionary"*: "Tupac Shakur and Tupac Amaru," Chuck Walker, February 16, 2014, https://charlesfwalker.com/tupac-shakur-tupac-amaru/.

132 *"The empathy, the mimetic instinct"*: Wesley Case, "Tupac Shakur in Baltimore: Friends, Teachers Remember the Birth of an Artist," *Baltimore Sun*, March 31, 2017, https://www.baltimoresun.com/food-drink /bal-tupac-shakur-baltimore-school-for-arts-hall-of-fame-induction -story.html.

132 *As a teenager wearing ripped jeans*: *Dear Mama*, directed by Allen Hughes, FX Networks, 2023.

133 *"His eyes opened to a world he had"*: "2pac Was Nervous & Didn't Want to Go to Versace Fashion Show in Italy."

133 *He partied and did Ecstasy*: Alexander and Cuda, *Got Your Back*, 107, 109–111.

133 *"You couldn't help but notice how"*: Ibid., 111.

133 *"This shit is cool. I could do this all day long"*: Ibid.

134 *"Kids today are dressing for death"*: Bob Baker, "Dressing for Death: Officers Help Parents Understand What Gangs Are All About," *Los Angeles Times*, May 11, 1988, https://www.latimes.com/archives/la-xpm-1988 -05-11-me-2379-story.html.

134 *"The brown people were generally"*: Keith Estiller, "The Influence of Chicano Culture in Fashion as Told by Leading Latino Pioneers in the Industry," *Hypebeast*, February 20, 2017, https://hypebeast.com/2017/2 /chicano-influence-in-fashion.

135 *"It was about what level of money"*: Crooked I, personal interview, September 6, 2021.

135 *"Swap meets is where you would go to get Dickies work pants"*: Ibid.

135 *In 1990, San Francisco designer Michael Hoban*: Abby Ellin, "Back to the '60s (and Fringe) in Brazil," *New York Times*, June 25, 2012, https://www.nytimes.com/2012/07/26/fashion/north-beach-leathers -is-in-business-again.html.

135 *"eight ball"*: Gary Buiso, "8-Ball Jacket Creator Praises Subway Slapper's Style, *New York Post*, November 23, 2014, https://nypost .com/2014/11/23/8-ball-jacket-creator-praises-subway-brawlers -style/.

135 *"It had a connotation in the dope world"*: Ibid.

136 *"As fast as you could make them"*: Ibid.

136 *"I used to get my hair done"*: Eric Spitznage, "Q&A: Ice-T on Pimping and the Pope," *Esquire*, July 19, 2013, https://www.esquire.com/entertain ment/interviews/a23972/ice-t-interview/.

136 *"The game is this, though"*: Deidre Dyer, "Snoop Dogg on How the Pimp Game Shaped His Style," *Fader*, October 16, 2014, https://www.the fader.com/2014/10/16/snoop-dogg-style-happy-socks-collab.

136 *"As males we all have feminine ways"*: Ibid.

136 *out M-O-B (likely a reference to the Bloods)*: Lynn Hirschberg, "Does a Sugar Bear Bite?," *New York Times*, January 14, 1996, https://www.nytimes.com/1996/01/14/magazine/does-a-sugar-bear-bite.html.

136 *"Suge could get whatever"*: Sheldon Pearce, *Changes: An Oral History of Tupac Shakur* (New York: Simon & Schuster, 2022), 202.

137 *It was Snoop Dogg's idea*: Sheldon Pearce, "The Devil's Bargain: The Inside Story of Tupac Shakur and Suge Knight," *Los Angeles* magazine, July 9, 2021, https://www.lamag.com/culturefiles/tupac-changes-suge-knight/.

137 *"Whether the odds are in your favor"*: Malcolm Gladwell, "Shakur Goes Free Pending Appeal," *Washington Post*, October 14, 1995, https://www.washingtonpost.com/archive/lifestyle/1995/10/14/shakur-goes-free-pending-appeal/efa795fb-b278-409d-9cd5-236999a88623/.

137 *"I had a shirt to wear under here"*: Damian Lillard, personal interview, March 15, 2021.

137 *"He slowly transitioned away from the gangster"*: Darralynn Hutson, "'All Eyez On Me' Costume Buyer Reveals What It Was Like to Style Tupac in the '90s," *Complex*, June 12, 2017, https://www.complex.com/style/2017/06/tupac-all-eyez-on-me-costume-designer-reveals-what-it-was-like-working-with-the-rapper.

138 *"How you like this Versace hookup?"*: "Tupac Introduces Kiss at the 1996 Grammy Awards," Alright, Still, https://www.youtube.com/watch?v=mMqwTU83Pc8.

138 *shouted out the brand in the campus newspaper*: Shonda L Huery, "Alumni Exchange Ideas and Styles at Brunch at Fashion Show," Howard *Hilltop*, November 5, 1993, https://dh.howard.edu/cgi/viewcontent.cgi?article=1097&context=hilltop_902000.

138 *"People gravitate to a gangster"*: *Hip Hop Uncovered*, season 1, episode 3, "Sh*ts Real," directed by Rashidi Natara Harper, FX Networks, 2021.

139 *the rapper's last words to him were*: Devon Maloney, "Tupac's Last Words: 'F**k You,' Says First Responder Cop (Report)," *Billboard*, May 25, 2014, https://www.billboard.com/music/rb-hip-hop/tupac-shakur-2pac-last-words-says-first-responder-cop-chris-caroll-6099260/.

CHAPTER TWELVE: POPPIN' TAGS

141 *"goal of building a premium brand"*: Jean E. Palmieri, "EXCLUSIVE: Sean Combs Regains Control of Sean John Brand," *Women's Wear Daily*, December 2021, https://wwd.com/business-news/mergers-acquisitions

/exclusive-sean-combs-regains-control-of-sean-john-brand-12350
22144/.

141 *"Puff is the ultimate producer"*: Dao-Yi Chow, personal interview,
November 17, 2022.

142 *"The energy was high"*: Ibid.

142 *which Sean John employees were told*: Ibid.

142 *"Make sure the music is at that level"*: "Sean Jean Collection 2000 New
York Fashion Week Debut," Video Fashion, August 25, 2016, https://
www.youtube.com/watch?v=lWgLqkLpWd8.

143 *"Puff was always about big moments"*: Dao-Yi Chow, personal interview,
November 17, 2022.

143 *runaway success*: Suzanne Kapner, "Puffy's Unforgivable Hits Winning
Formula," *New York Post*, April 3, 2006, https://nypost.com/2006/04/03
/puffys-unforgivable-hits-winning-formula/.

143 *$150 million globally*: Julie Naughton, "Unforgivable: Combs' Passion
Play," *Women's Wear Daily*, April 20, 2007, https://wwd.com/fashion
-news/fashion-features/unforgivable-combs-passion-play-498999/.

143 *1,200 stores and had sales of $200 million*: Palmieri, "EXCLUSIVE:
Sean Combs Regains Control of Sean John Brand."

143 *2016, the annual retail sales were $450 million*: Jean E. Palmieri,
"Global Brands Acquires Majority Stake in Sean John," *Women's Wear
Daily*, November 30, 2016, https://wwd.com/menswear-news/mens
-retail-business/sean-combs-puffy-global-brands-sean-john-10714373/.

143 *"Sean John really pushed fashion"*: Deirdre Maloney, personal interview,
May 12, 2022.

144 *"I am living the American dream"*: Associated Press, "P. Diddy Bags Top
Fashion Award," CBS News, June 8, 2004, https://www.cbsnews.com
/news/p-diddy-bags-top-fashion-award/.

144 *"I'm putting them outta business"*: Damon "Dame" Dash, personal interview, May 5, 2022.

144 *"They were really, really rude"*: Ibid.

144 *"When three young Black men"*: Sowmya Krishnamurthy, "How the
Roc-A-Fella Chain Became a Symbol of Hip Hop Royalty," *Time*, February 21, 2022, https://time.com/6149657/jean-yuhs-kanye-west-roc-a
-fella-chain/.

145 *"They ain't want nothing to do with it"*: "Kareem 'Biggs' Burke," *Drink
Champs*, Revolt, January 24, 2018, https://www.youtube.com/watch
?v=g4m-viVFLAg&t=1195s.

145 *"I've always been fresh"*: Damon "Dame" Dash, personal interview, May
5, 2022.

145 *"Every sketch, every sample of clothing"*: James Sherwood, "Hip-Hop on a Roll," *New York Times*, October 10, 2003, https://www.nytimes.com/2003/10/10/news/hiphop-on-a-roll.html.

145 *"I remember one time I ran into Ralph Lauren"*: Damon "Dame" Dash, personal interview, May 5, 2022.

146 *"We was just doin' it"*: "Juelz Santana on Dipset Being Major Fashion Trendsetters, Cam'ron Wearing Pink First (Part 14)," Vlad TV, November 8, 2022, https://youtu.be/XDlefCSR8j8.

146 *One 2004 promo photo*: "Cam'ron & Juelz Santana," Rocawear ad, posted by Altan Akbay, Pinterest, accessed March 12, 2023, https://www.pinterest.com/pin/368380444519722581/.

146 *"colorless and accessible to everyone"*: Sherwood, "Hip-Hop on a Roll."

147 *"People look at Victoria Beckham"*: Ibid.

147 *hip-hop album with Roc-A-Fella that was shelved*: Rebecca Merriman, "Victoria Beckham Made a Hip Hop Album in 2003 and It's Been Leaked Online," *Mirror*, May 26, 2016, https://www.mirror.co.uk/3am/celebrity-news/victoria-beckham-made-hip-hop-8048123.

147 *"plug"*: Damon "Dame" Dash, personal interview, May 5, 2022.

147 *"Bloomingdale's wields big"*: Deirdre Maloney, personal interview, May 12, 2022.

147 *"Buying for Bloomingdale's"*: Ibid.

147 *"It's a lot more analytical"*: Deric Humphrey, personal interview, May 6, 2022.

148 *surpassed $300 million in sales*: "Dashing to Growth: Rocawear Projects Sales of $500 Million," *Women's Wear Daily*, May 8, 2003, https://wwd.com/fashion-news/fashion-features/dashing-to-growth-rocawear-projects-sales-of-500-million-731941/.

148 *"Yeah, I ain't gonna lie. I got killed once"*: Lenny "Lenny S" Santiago, personal interview, August 17, 2021.

148 *"I'm gonna smash this outfit"*: LaTrice Burnette, personal interview, August 5, 2021.

148 *"It don't matter how much your clothes cost"*: Cam'ron, personal interview, August 3, 2021.

149 *"Tommy Hilfiger and Ralph Lauren capitalized"*: Sherwood, "Hip-Hop on a Roll."

149 *"The fact of the matter is they're not living it"*: Ibid.

149 *"How easy is this?"*: "LL Cool J—Gap Commercial—1997," Mark Seliger, April 29, 2019, https://www.youtube.com/watch?v=JRK5pgfD_z0.

149 *"They spent $30 million basically"*: "LL Cool J Took FUBU to the Next Level in a GAP Commercial, Ep. 48, Club Shay Shay," Club Shay Shay, April 14, 2022, https://youtu.be/tvYs4ay-90s.

150 *"I was a partner in [FUBU]"*: "Exclusive: LL Cool J's Commercial Controversy, Oprah's Next Chapter, Oprah Winfrey Network," OWN, January 18, 2013, https://www.youtube.com/watch?v=Lqf14C9cQi4.

150 *FUBU into a $350 to $400 million*: "LL Cool J Took FUBU to the Next Level in a GAP Commercial," Club Shay Shay.

151 *"We blur logos in every video"*: Teresa Wiltz, "'Whole Brand Thing' Leaves MTV Blurry," *Chicago Tribune*, March 7, 1996, https://www.chicago tribune.com/news/ct-xpm-1996-03-07-9603070268-story.html.

151 *"We don't (blur)"*: Ibid.

152 *production and delivery problems*: Julee Greenberg, "Eve Gives Fetish Another Try," *Women's Wear Daily*, June 14, 2007, https://wwd.com /feature/eve-gives-fetish-another-try-493443-2035432/.

152 *shifted her focus to acting*: "Eve's Ends Her Clothing Fetish," *Vibe*, September 8, 2009, https://www.vibe.com/news/entertainment/eves-ends -her-clothing-fetish-46666/.

152 *became the biggest rapper of all time*: Eminem, Guinness World Records, accessed March 12, 2023, https://www.guinnessworldrecords .com/search?term=eminem.

153 *over $240 million worldwide*: "8 Mile," *Box Office Mojo*, accessed March 12, 2023, https://www.boxofficemojo.com/release/rl3326182913/.

154 *the average annual cost to create*: "The Cost of Starting Out," *Women's Wear Daily*, February 7, 2003, https://wwd.com/fashion-news/fashion -features/the-cost-of-starting-out-756688/.

154 *"That means designers with sales"*: Ibid.

154 *"To get into the fashion business"*: Dao-Yi Chow, personal interview, November 17, 2022.

154 *he shared that Tommy Hilfiger*: "Dame Dash On Starting Rocawear, His Football League, NFTs & More, Assets Over Liabilities," Revolt, June 1, 2022, https://youtu.be/Jnnmb5oiQNU.

154 *had purchased button-down shirts*: Ibid.

154 *"So now, [the company]"*: Ibid.

154 *Jay-Z bought out Dame's 25 percent share of Rocawear*: Lauren DeCarlo, "Dash Cashes Out of Rocawear," *Women's Wear Daily*, September 26, 2005, https://wwd.com/business-news/financial/dash-cashes-out-of-roca wear-561123/.

154 *a reported $204 million in cash*: "Jay-Z Cashes In with Rocawear Deal," Dealbook, *New York Times*, March 3, 2007, https://archive.nytimes .com/dealbook.nytimes.com/2007/03/06/jay-z-cashes-in-with-200 -million-rocawear-deal/.

154 *"Rocawear was my idea, it was my baby"*: "Dame Dash on Starting Rocawear, His Football League, NFTs & More, Assets Over Liabilities."

155   *"When we started our own brand, it was less"*: Dao-Yi Chow, personal interview, November 17, 2022.

155   *"When I think about the whole"*: Robin Givhan, "They Laughed When Diddy Launched a Fashion Line. Then He Changed the Industry," *Washington Post*, April 21, 2016, https://www.washingtonpost.com/sf /style/2016/04/21/they-laughed-when-diddy-launched-a-fashion-line -then-he-changed-the-industry/.

CHAPTER THIRTEEN: LOUIS VUITTON DON

157   *"We knew that we weren't"*: Derek "Fonzworth Bentley" Watkins, personal interview, January 17, 2023.

157   *"I remember Kanye saying"*: Thom Bettridge, "Group Chat: The Oral History of Virgil Abloh," *GQ*, March 4, 2019, https://www.gq.com /story/virgil-abloh-cover-story-spring-2019.

158   *"He looked at me with eyes that spoke"*: Donda West and Karen Hunter, *Raising Kanye: Life Lessons from the Mother of a Hip-Hop Superstar* (New York: Gallery, 2007), 181.

158   *"'old soul'"*: Ibid.

158   *"The one thing your child must know is that he is loved"*: Ibid., 57.

158   *"This love is eternal"*: Ibid., 58.

158   *"My mama's my best friend"*: Ibid., 59.

159   *"Kanye wore a pink shirt with the collar sticking"*: Josh Tyrangiel, "Why You Can't Ignore Kanye," *Time*, August 21, 2005, https://content.time .com/time/subscriber/article/0,33009,1096499,00.html.

159   *"We all grew up street guys"*: Ibid.

159   *"I played them 'Jesus Walks' and they didn't sign me"*: Kanye West, "Last Call," Genius, accessed March 12, 2023, https://genius.com/Kanye -west-last-call-lyrics.

160   *Kanye was desperately vying*: Jeen-Yuhs: A Kanye Trilogy, directed by Coodie Simmons and Chike Ozah, Netflix, 2022.

160   *"I just wanted to create a chain"*: Sowmya Krishnamurthy, "How the Roc-A-Fella Chain Became a Symbol of Hip Hop Royalty," *Time*, February 21, 2022, https://time.com/6149657/jean-yuhs-kanye-west-roc-a-fella -chain/.

160   *Burke remembered 1997 or 1998*: Ibid.

160   *"jewelry can make it look like you have a lot more than you do"*: Ibid.

161   *"I'm the only person who ever gave Roc-A-Fella artists a chain"*: Ibid.

161   *"When* College Dropout *dropped"*: West and Hunter, *Raising Kanye*, 175.

162   *"I'm a Polo head and I knew Kanye"*: Trace William Cowen, "Designer

Sam Hansen Shares Backstory on Kanye West's 'The College Drop-out' Bear in New Interview," *Complex*, October 20, 2021, https://www.complex.com/style/sam-hansen-backstory-kanye-west-the-college-dropout-bear.

162 *Hansen admitted to me*: Sam Hansen, personal interview, January 20, 2023.

162 *"They got random people to be in the suit for different"*: Ibid.

162 *"revolution"*: Elva Aguilar and Rob Kenner, "Music Critics Review Their Reviews of Kanye West's 'The College Dropout,'" *Complex*, February 11, 2014, https://www.complex.com/music/2014/02/kanye-west-college dropout-reviews.

162 *philosopher*: Ibid.

162 *"full-service hip-hop artiste"*: Ibid.

163 *"It was definitely a risk"*: Kim Osorio, personal interview, February 24, 2021.

163 *"It was totally different"*: Ibid.

164 *"Some may think that this is the ultimate street style"*: Brooke Bobb, "Remember When Kanye West Carried a Goyard Briefcase to Paris Fashion Week?," *Vogue*, February 28, 2017, https://www.vogue.com/article/fashion-runway-kanye-went-paris-fashion-week-ready-to-wear-2017.

164 *Coco Chanel, Jeanne Lanvin, Pablo Picasso, the Rockefellers, and the Maharaja of Kapurthala*: "A Heritage of Excellence," Goyard, accessed March 12, 2023, https://www.goyard.com/eu_en/goyard-history.

164 *sold for over $90,000 on eBay*: Heba Hasan, "Kanye West's $245 Air Yeezy II Sneakers Sell Online for $90,000," *Time*, June 8, 2012, https://newsfeed.time.com/2012/06/08/kanye-wests-245-air-yeezy-ii-sneakers-sell-online-for-90000/.

164 *"The anaconda-textured side panel"*: John Gotty, "How the Air Yeezy 2 Led to Kanye West's Greatest Success—and Nike's Biggest Failure," *Complex*, June 9, 2017, https://www.complex.com/sneakers/2017/06/nike-air-yeezy-2-five-year-anniversary.

165 *and sold out in ten minutes*: Tyler Brooke, "Nike Air Yeezy 2 Sells Out in 10 Minutes after Surprise Release," *Bleacher Report*, February 9, 2014, https://bleacherreport.com/articles/1954115-nike-air-yeezy-2-sells-out-in-10-minutes-after-surprise-release.

165 *"The inspiration came from a jacket"*: Armand Limander, "Kanye West's Louis Vuitton Kicks," *New York Times*, https://archive.nytimes.com/tmagazine.blogs.nytimes.com/2009/01/22/mens-fashion-kanye-wests-vuitton-kicks/.

165 *"For people who can't afford to buy $2,000 trousers"*: Kin Woo, "Kanye West for Louis Vuitton," *Dazed*, January 23, 2009, https://www.dazed digital.com/fashion/article/1699/1/kanye-west-for-louis-vuitton.

165 *"This Yeezy right now, speaking to y'all!"*: "Kanye West's Epic Rant at Pusha T's Listening," *The Source*, September 12, 2013, https://www .youtube.com/watch?v=7BxCDysoSxg.

166 *"Mascotte was supposed to be the high-end brand for Rocawear"*: Sam Hansen, personal interview, January 20, 2023.

166 *"After the split between Jay and Dame"*: Ibid.

166 *"the X-Men coming together"*: Karizza Sanchez, "The Untold Story of Pastelle, Kanye West's First Clothing Line," *Complex*, July 10, 2018, https://www.complex.com/style/2018/07/kanye-west-pastelle-first -clothing-line-untold-story.

166 *"Wow. Now we are the kings of street fashion"*: Ibid.

167 *"I swear to you guys all I do is"*: "Pastelle Jacket!" Kanye University, November 26, 2008, http://web.archive.org/web/20091029132533/http://www .kanyeuniversecity.com/blog/?e3106=214698_-1__0_~0_-1_10 _2009_0_0&content=&month=11_2008&page=14&em3298=&em32 82=&em3281=&em3161=.

167 *"Pastelle feels more down-to-earth"*: Thomas Chou, "What Ever Happened to Kanye West's 'Pastelle'?," *VMan*, July 12, 2018, https://vman .com/article/what-ever-happened-to-kanye-wests-pastelle/.

167 *Justin Reed sold one version for $10,000*: "Kanye West," Justin Reed, accessed March 13, 2023, https://justinreed.com/products/kanye-west -pastelle-varsity-jacket-2008.

167 *"The guy wanted to know every little detail, and he came in super-early"*: Sanchez, "The Untold Story of Pastelle, Kanye West's First Clothing Line."

167 *"He was very energetic about [Pastelle]"*: Ibid.

167 *"We worked on the project a lot, but no money and no glory"*: Ibid.

168 *"I have to sit around Big Sean, Kanye West"*: Pusha T, personal interview, March 1, 2021.

168 *"Ye was like, 'I listen to you. You're a lyricist'"*: Ibid.

168 *He likened Kardashian to a modern-day*: Khariun Hamid, "Kanye West Calls Kim Kardashian the Modern Marilyn Monroe," *Acclaim*, accessed March 13, 2023, https://acclaimmag.com/music/kanye-west-calls-kim -kardashian-modern-marilyn-monroe/.

169 *"It's literally like"*: Jon Caramanica, "The Agony and Ecstasy of Kanye West," *New York Times*, April 10, 2015, https://www.nytimes .com/2015/04/10/t-magazine/kanye-west-adidas-yeezy-fashion -interview.html.

169 *had to remove their uncomfortable shoes*: Bennett Marcus, "Amina Blue and Chanel Iman on What Really Happened at Yeezy Season 4," *The Cut*, September 9, 2016, https://www.thecut.com/2016/09/models -amina-blue-and-chanel-iman-talk-yeezy-season-4.html.

169 *"This second round of drab"*: Cathryn Horn, "Kanye West Is Fooling the Fashion World," *The Cut*, September 17, 2015, https://www.thecut .com/2015/09/cathy-horyn-kanye-west-dkny-proenza-michael-kors .html.

169 *"I'm kind of over Kanye"*: Dana Schuster, "Fashion Week Creator Fern Mallis Is Unimpressed by Kanye," *New York Post*, February 18, 2015, https://nypost.com/2015/02/18/fashion-week-creator-fern-mallis-is -unimpressed-by-kanye/.

169 *"I think he's fine as a rapper"*: Derrick Bryson Taylor, "Kelly Cutrone Slams Kanye: 'He's a Joke as a Fashion Designer,'" Page Six, February 19, 2015, https://pagesix.com/2015/02/19/kelly-cutrone-slams-kanye -hes-a-joke-as-a-fashion-designer/.

170 *"attempting to do clothing has been difficult"*: Dana Schuster, "Kanye Goes on Rant after Fashion Week Creator Slams Him," *New York Post*, February 20, 2015, https://nypost.com/2015/02/20/kanye-west-goes -on-twitter-rant-after-fern-mallis-slams-him/?_ga=1.197756071.92802 047.1438822646.

170 *"too famous"*: Ibid.

170 *"He went crazy on me—tweeting"*: Fern Mallis, personal interview, March 9, 2021.

170 *"Designers have a tougher skin"*: Ibid.

170 *"He pissed off as many people as he pleased"*: Ibid.

CHAPTER FOURTEEN: BILLIONAIRE BOYS CLUB

171 *the most sacred Shinto*: Mark Cartwright, "Ise Grand Shrine," World History, April 6, 2017, https://www.worldhistory.org/Ise_Grand_Shrine/.

171 *"Soul of Japan"*: "About Ise Jingu," Ise Jingu, accessed March 14, 2023, https://www.isejingu.or.jp/en/about/index.html.

171 *Millions of devotees*: "Ise Grand Shrine: Everything You Need to Know about Japan's Most Sacred Shinto Shrine," JR Pass, accessed March 14, 2023, https://www.jrpass.com/blog/ise-grand-shrine-everything-you -need-to-know-about-japans-most-sacret-shinto-shrine.

171 *godfather of streetwear*: "Hiroshi Fujiwara," *Highsnobiety*, accessed March 14, 2023, https://www.highsnobiety.com/tag/hiroshi-fujiwara/.

171 *"The first impact was punk rock"*: Tiffany Godoy, "Tiffany Godoy Speaks with the Godfather of Streetwear in Tokyo," Ssense, accessed

March 14, 2023, https://www.ssense.com/en-us/editorial/fashion/hiroshi -fujiwara-is-the-living-internet.

172   *"If you want to know what's going on, ask Hiroshi"*: Fraser Cooke, "Hiroshi Fujiwara," *Interview*, March 23, 2010, https://www.interviewmagazine .com/fashion/hiroshi-fujiwara.

172   *"fashionable casual clothes"*: "Streetwear," *Collins Dictionary*, accessed March 14, 2023, https://www.collinsdictionary.com/us/dictionary/english /streetwear.

172   *"In essence, streetwear involves the"*: "Defining Streetwear," *Hypebeast*, accessed March 14, 2023, https://strategyand.hypebeast.com/street wear-report-history-definition.

172   *"We were just making stuff for ourselves"*: Molly Long, "How to Build a Streetwear Brand and Influence People," *Design Week*, January 17, 2020, https://www.designweek.co.uk/issues/13-19-january-2020/street wear-branding/.

172   *"Neptunes sound" of sparse beats*: Ryan Bassil, "The Evolution of the Neptunes," *Vice*, September 16, 2013, https://www.vice.com/en/article /rnvgxb/youneedtohearthis-the-evolution-of-the-neptunes.

172   *"They looked like dorks to me"*: Sowmya Krishnamurthy, "N.O.R.E. on Returning to '5E' and His 20 Years in the Rap Game: 'I Ain't Making Old Guy Music. I'm Making Music,'" *Billboard*, August 1, 2018, https://www.billboard.com/music/rb-hip-hop/nore-5e-album-interview -pharrell-superthug-8467933/.

173   *"I think growing up and being a skater kid"*: Loïc Villepontoux, personal interview, July 22, 2022.

173   *"We were shopping with Jacob the Jeweler"*: Pusha T, personal interview, March 1, 2021.

173   *Pharrell made his first trip to Japan in 2003*: "Nigo + Pharrell: The Culture's Best Duo," Billionaire Boys Club, December 23, 2021, https://www.bbcicecream.com/blogs/news/nigo.

173   *"He's got a clothing line and"*: Pusha T, personal interview, March 1, 2021.

173   *"We started getting boxes upon boxes"*: Ibid.

173   *"I was getting the clothes for so long"*: Joshua Hunt, "Everybody Wishes They Knew Nigo," *GQ*, March 25, 2022, https://www.gq.com/story /nigo-interview-pharrell-pusha-t.

173   *The first rapper to wear BAPE*: History Vault (@historyvlt), Instagram, March 31, 2019, https://www.instagram.com/p/BvrnMbapZPg/?hl=en.

173   *worn by photographer Shawn Mortensen*: Maureen Hilbun, personal interview, March 16, 2023.

174   *"Shawn asked Biggie if he could"*: Ibid.

174   *was exhibited at the BAPE Gallery*: "The Photography of Shawn Mortensen," accessed March 16, 2023, https://shawnmortensenphotography.com/Exhibitions.php.

174   *Biggie was rumored to have requested bespoke BAPE*: Ben McKimm, "Actually, Biggie Was the First Rapper to Wear Bape," *Man of Many*, July 29, 2021, https://manofmany.com/fashion/first-rapper-to-wear-bape-biggie.

174   *"He loved it so much"*: Kevin Le, personal interview, March 17, 2023.

174   *when he opened for them on tour*: Sheldon Pearce, "Exploring Hip-Hop's Love Affair With Bape," Pitchfork, January 24, 2019, https://pitchfork.com/thepitch/exploring-hip-hops-love-affair-with-bape/.

174   *spotted in a mustard*: Martin Goodacre, *Beastie Boys Portugal 1998*, photo, Getty Images, accessed March 17, 2023, https://www.gettyimages.com/detail/news-photo/ad-rock-mca-and-mike-d-of-the-beastie-boys-group-portrait-news-photo/991866302.

174   *and then on tour*: Lauren Zoric, "Two Turntables and a Microphone," accessed March 17, 2023, https://www.angelfire.com/fl2/beastie/beastie16.html.

174   *in custom Bape took*: "Action Figures," *Beastie Mania*, 2001, https://www.beastiemania.com/qa/action-figures/actionfigures2.php.

175   *"Who the fuck is Pharrell?"*: Shawn Setaro and Kiana Fitzgerald, "From Bape to Babies: A Timeline of Pusha-T and Drake's Stormy Relationship," *Complex*, October 17, 2018, https://www.complex.com/music/2018/10/a-timeline-of-drake-and-pusha-t-beef/i-dont-see-no-clipse.

175   *"I mess with Pharrell"*: "Soulja Boy on Being the First to Wear 'BAPE,'" Bootleg Kev, April 30, 2021, https://www.youtube.com/watch?v=z6F1SJakXLA.

175   *"Nigo is just as important and"*: Karizza Sanchez, "Kid Cudi & Nigo: The Originators," *Complex*, September 9, 2019, https://www.complex.com/style/kid-cudi-nigo-2019-cover-story.

175   *"BAPE is like my generation's Chanel"*: Gaby Wilson, "Watch Pusha T And Virgil Abloh Reflect on 10 Years of BAPE NYC," MTV, April 28, 2015, https://www.mtv.com/news/hf4uvz/pusha-t-virgil-abloh-bape-nyc.

175   *"Wealth is of the heart and mind"*: "About," Billionaire Boys Club, accessed March 14, 2023, https://www.bbcicecream.com/pages/about-new.

175   *"It was crowded, and we knew that"*: Loïc Villepontoux, personal interview, July 22, 2022.

175   *"They all had Bathing Ape tags"*: Ibid.

176   *"Yeah, that ['Frontin'' video debut] was calculated"*: Kadia Blagrove

et al., "The Oral History of Billionaire Boys Club and Ice Cream," *Complex*, December 3, 2013, https://www.complex.com/style/2013/12/oral-history-bbc-icecream.

176   *The pricing*: Loïc Villepontoux, personal interview, July 22, 2022.

176   *"elevated the brand"*: Ibid.

176   *generated $25 million to $30 million*: David Lipke, "New Strategy for Billionaire Boys Club," *Women's Wear Daily*, June 6, 2013, https://wwd.com/feature/new-strategy-for-billionaire-boys-club-6972229-316958/.

176   *"It's a hard business, especially"*: Loïc Villepontoux, personal interview, July 22, 2022.

177   *"Every five years, music completely changes"*: Pharrell Williams, "MTV's Hip-Hop POV," MTV, April 6, 2012.

177   *Buffalo Hat, Jelly Mould Hat, and Mountain Hat*: Sophia Chabbott, "The Story Behind Pharrell's Grammy Hat—and Where You Can Buy It," *Glamour*, January 27, 2014, https://www.glamour.com/story/the-story-behind-pharrells-gra.

177   *"We interned at Fendi but we ain't do shit"*: Fabian Gorsler, "Here's How Much Kanye West & Virgil Abloh Earned While Interning at Fendi," *Highsnobiety*, March 27, 2018, https://www.highsnobiety.com/p/kanye-west-virgil-abloh-fendi-internship/.

177   *"I paid them $500 a month!"*: Vanessa Friedman and Elizabeth Patron, "Louis Vuitton Names Virgil Abloh as Its New Men's Wear Designer," *New York Times*, March 26, 2018, https://www.nytimes.com/2018/03/26/business/louis-vuitton-virgil-abloh.html.

177   *"Me and Virgil are in Rome"*: Parry Ernsberger, "8 GIF Reactions to Kanye's BBC Radio 1 Interview Fashion Quotes," MTV, September 24, 2013, https://www.mtv.com/news/5opk8l/kanye-west-bbc-interview.

178   *"We couldn't figure out how to"*: Graeme Campbell, "Looking Back on Virgil Abloh's Best Career Moments," *Highsnobiety*, November 28, 2001, https://www.highsnobiety.com/p/virgil-abloh-career-biography/.

178   *phrase Pyrex 23*: Steff Yotka, "A Brief History of Virgil Abloh's Meteoric Rise," *Vogue*, March 28, 2018, https://www.vogue.com/article/virgil-abloh-biography-career-timeline.

179   *at least twenty-six partnerships*: Héloïse Salessy and Alexandre Marain, "Off-White: 26 Collaborations That Brought Virgil Abloh to the Forefront of the Fashion Scene," trans. Isabel Nield, French *Vogue*, November 29, 2001, https://www.vogue.fr/fashion/fashion-inspiration/story/off-white-the-18-collabs-that-cemented-virgil-ablohs-career/1635.

179   *"From day one, I said I wanted Virgil"*: Alexandra Macon, "Inside Hailey Bieber's Final Wedding Dress Fitting," *Vogue*, October 28, 2019,

https://www.vogue.com/article/inside-hailey-bieber-wedding-dress
-fitting-off-white-virgil-abloh.

179 *"Kids' fervor for the stripe patterns"*: Takashi Murakami, "Virgil Abloh,"
Time, 2018, https://time.com/collection/most-influential-people-2018
/5238167/virgil-abloh/.

180 *"I'm here; I want to show"*: Sarah Mower, "Virgil Abloh Talks Louis
Vuitton: 'I Want a Young Generation to Know, Hey, There's Someone
Here Who's Listening,'" *Vogue*, June 28, 2018, https://www.vogue.com
/article/louis-vuitton-virgil-abloh-debut-interview.

180 *"Laying a foundation, that's what this season"*: Ibid.

180 *"I felt like it was supposed to be me"*: Kyle Munzenrieder, "Kanye West
Thinks He Should Have Virgil Abloh's Job at Louis Vuitton," *W* magazine, October 24, 2019, https://www.wmagazine.com/story/kanye-west
-virgil-abloh-louis-vuitton.

181 *"the biggest fashion movement in recent history"*: Emily Farra, "Which
Street Style Tribe Did You Join in 2017?," *Vogue*, December 18, 2017,
https://www.vogue.com/article/street-style-tribes-of-2017-top-trends
-streetwear-demna-gvasalia-suits.

181 *"the once humble aesthetic has successfully"*: Elinor Block, "The History
of Streetwear: From Stüssy to Vetements," *Women's Wear Daily*, October 27, 2017, https://www.whowhatwear.com/streetwear.

181 *valued at $2.1 billion two years later*: "Carlyle to Flip Streetwear Icon
Supreme in $2.1B Deal," *PitchBook*, November 10, 2020, https://
pitchbook.com/newsletter/carlyle-to-flip-streetwear-icon-supreme-in
-21b-deal-nZW.

181 *"Streetwear is never a trend. It was always a movement"*: Jian DeLeon,
personal interview, April 29, 2021.

181 *"Back then, it just felt so fresh and"*: Jessica Schiffer, "HLZBLZ's Lanie
Alabanza-Barcena: 'Streetwear Today Is about Making as Much
Money as Possible,'" *Glossy*, November 14, 2017, https://www.glossy
.co/fashion/hlzblzs-lanie-alibanza-streetwear-today-is-about-making
-as-much-money-as-possible/.

182 *expanded his brand to twenty-five countries in Europe and thirteen stores*:
"About Us," Karl Kani, accessed March 15, 2023, https://karlkani.com
/pages/about-us.

182 *"I know this"*: Jessica Defino, "Kimora Lee Simmons Is Positioning
Baby Phat as Chanel for a New Generation," *Fashionista*, June 13,
2019, https://fashionista.com/2019/06/kimora-lee-simmons-baby-phat
-relaunch.

182 *"As women, we are special, exotic"*: Ibid.

CHAPTER FIFTEEN: DEVIL IN A NEW DRESS

183   *"In my world, you could be a gangsta"*: "I Young Thug in #mycalvins—Calvin Klein Fall 2016 Global Campaign," Calvin Klein, July 6, 2016, https://youtu.be/-ymE6dUF98Y.

183   *"I think he is going to have a major"*: Cameron Wolf, "VFILES Founder on Why It Was So Important to Put Young Thug on Its Mentor Panel," *Complex*, August 17, 2016, https://www.complex.com/style/2016/08/vfiles-founder-important-young-thug-mentor-panel.

184   *"This is the cover for my album"*: "This is THE Moment Young Thug Chose the Dress—What Rox," *VFiles*, September 1, 2016, https://youtu.be/qaitCRnqsdY.

184   *"When we got on set, it definitely"*: Ben Dandridge-Lemco, "How Young Thug's *JEFFERY* Album Cover Came Together," *Fader*, August 26, 2016, https://www.thefader.com/2016/08/26/young-thug-my-name-is-jeffery-album-cover-photographer.

184   *"I was literally shocked"*: Erica Euse, "Designer Behind Young Thug's 'JEFFERY' Dress Says He Wants to Design for Macklemore Next," *Complex*, September 18, 2016, https://www.complex.com/style/2016/09/alessandro-trincone-on-young-thug-jeffery-cover.

184   *"It was worse than struggle"*: Will Stephenson, "Young Thug: Came from Nothing," *Fader*, February 11, 2014, https://www.thefader.com/2014/02/11/young-thug-came-from-nothing.

184   *"I was in the streets at eight"*: Simon Vozick-Levinson, "Perma-Stoned Oddball Young Thug Is the Hottest Voice in Rap," *Rolling Stone*, December 4, 2014, https://www.rollingstone.com/music/music-features/perma-stoned-oddball-young-thug-is-the-hottest-voice-in-rap-66515/.

184   *"I didn't do it for people"*: Vanessa Satten, "Watch Young Thug's XXL Cover Story Interview," *XXL*, October 10, 2016, https://www.xxlmag.com/young-thug-interview-xxl-cover-story/.

185   *"Ninety percent of my clothes are women's"*: Mark-Anthony Green, "Young Thug Did Not Try to Kill Lil Wayne, Does Wear Women's Clothes," *GQ*, September 28, 2015, https://www.gq.com/story/young-thug-hyun35-album-interview.

185   *"the closest music style icon"*: Emma Hope Allwood, "Young Thug Is the Closest Music Style Icon We Have to Bowie," *Dazed*, August 26, 2016, https://www.dazeddigital.com/fashion/article/32579/1/young-thug-is-the-closest-style-icon-we-have-to-bowie.

185   *femme style*: Chioma Nnadi, "This Was the Decade That Hip-Hop Style

Got Femme," *Vogue*, July 18, 2019, https://www.vogue.com/article /young-thug-jeffrey-lil-uzi-vert-kanye-west-lil-nas-x-hip-hop-style.

185 *"You look hot in a dress"*: "I Young Thug in #mycalvins—Calvin Klein Fall 2016 Global Campaign," Calvin Klein, https://www.youtube.com /watch?v=-ymE6dUF98Y.

185 *"He's a hip-hop cross-dresser"*: "Charlamagne: Young Thug's Not Gay, He Just Cross-Dresses," Vlad TV, October 22, 2015, https://www.you tube.com/watch?v=cPvJmGSLemE.

186 *"He's not gay. There's nothing gay"*: "Young Thug's Fiancée Jerrika: We Laugh at Gay Rumors," VladTV, May 15, 2015, https://www.youtube .com/watch?v=Eea7TqrY4MA.

186 *"I like everything that people say"*: Sam Wolfson, "Young Thug: 'I Like Everything People Say about Me—You Gay, You a Punk, You Can't Rap, You're the Hardest,'" *Guardian*, October 8, 2015, https://www .theguardian.com/music/2015/oct/08/young-thug-hits-bring-money-lil -wayne.

186 *There's footage of the rapper*: "YOUNG THUG, Before They Were Famous, Biography," Before They Were Famous, November 27, 2016, https://www.youtube.com/watch?v=id8cO4HC1iU.

187 *"There is a merging of intellectualism"*: Crystal Belle, "From Jay-Z to Dead Prez: Examining Representations of Black Masculinity in Mainstream Versus Underground Hip-Hop Music," *Journal of Black Studies* 45, no. 4 (March 28, 2014): 289.

187 *"R&B is very much about spending"*: Touré, personal interview, January 12, 2023.

187 *gay, bisexual, and omnisexual*: Myles E. Johnson, "Little Richard's Queer Triumph," *New York Times*, May 10, 2020, https://www.nytimes .com/2020/05/10/opinion/little-richard-queer.html.

187 *"A third degree of gender"*: Dr. Jonathan Michael Square, personal interview, February 25, 2021.

187 *"What separates hip-hop in that regard is its relationship"*: Touré, personal interview, January 12, 2023.

188 *"drug dealer screw face"*: Ibid.

188 *"The South got something to say!"*: "The South Got Something to Say," Solomon Summers, June 24, 2017, https://www.youtube.com /watch?v=VJu40C0vE3g.

189 *"Man, TV ain't got no temperature"*: "Bun B: Pimp C Told Jay Z the TV Ain't Got No Temperature, Jay Looked at Me and Said . . . Big Pimpin $1M," B High Atl, October 13, 2021, https://www.youtube .com/watch?v=Oz2CuVf1MGo.

189 *"Future long ago mastered"*: Shiona Turini, "Future's Instinctive, Unassailable Style," *The Cut*, March 31, 2017, https://www.thecut.com/2017/03/futures-instinctive-unassailable-style.html.

190 *$10,000 head-to-toe designer look*: Amir Vera, "Rappers Gucci Mane and Jeezy Verzuz Battle Ends Peacefully, Despite Some Jabs, Drawing at Least 1.8M People," CNN, November 19, 2020, https://www.cnn.com/2020/11/19/entertainment/gucci-mane-jeezy-verzuz-trnd/index.html.

190 *"OutKast really broke the mold"*: Derek "Fonzworth Bentley" Watkins, personal interview, January 17, 2023.

190 *"André was beloved, his masculinity was unquestionable"*: Touré, personal interview, January 12, 2023.

190 the *"Black Mecca of the South"*: Phyl Garland, "Atlanta: Black Mecca of the South," *Ebony*, August 1971, 12.

191 *long timeline of bawdy*: Scott Henry, "Timeline: The Long, Risqué History of Atlanta's Nightlife," *Atlanta* magazine, September 19, 2019, https://www.atlantamagazine.com/news-culture-articles/timeline-the-long-risque-history-of-atlantas-nightlife/.

191 *turned the streets into a party with hundreds*: Errin Haines Whack and Rebecca Burns, "Freaknik: The Rise and Fall of Atlanta's Most Infamous Street Party," *Atlanta* magazine, March 18, 2015, https://www.atlantamagazine.com/90s/freaknik-the-rise-and-fall-of-atlantas-most-infamous-street-party/.

191 *"Atlanta specifically has always"*: Derek "Fonzworth Bentley" Watkins, personal interview, January 17, 2023.

191 *"Rat Pack"*: Ibid.

191 *"Good day, good sir"*: Ibid.

191 *"you had rough guys who played football"*: Meredith Bryan, "Andre 3000: 'Just Because You Like to Dress Well . . . That Don't Mean You're Gay!'" *Observer*, September 5, 2008, https://observer.com/2008/09/andre-3000-just-because-you-like-to-dress-well-that-dont-mean-youre-gay/.

192 *"I was like, 'Let me take this. Let me not'"*: Marissa G. Muller, "André 3000 Says He Understands Kanye West's Fashion Rants Because He Lost Millions with Benjamin Bixby Line," *W* magazine, November 6, 2017, https://www.wmagazine.com/story/andre-3000-kanye-west-fashion-rants.

192 *"He's a great bridge between them"*: Touré, personal interview, January 12, 2023.

192 *"I can't rap you two Andre 3000 songs"*: Will Lavin, "Young Thug on OutKast's Andre 3000: 'I Ain't Never Paid Attention to Him,'" *NME*,

November 28, 2020, https://www.nme.com/news/music/young-thug
-on-outkasts-andre-3000-i-aint-never-paid-attention-to-him-282
7199.

192   *The term "metrosexual" is widely credited*: "Metrosexuals," Encyclopedia
.com, accessed March 17, 2023, https://www.encyclopedia.com/social
-sciences/encyclopedias-almanacs-transcripts-and-maps/metrosexuals.

192   *"Nevertheless, the metrosexual man"*: Mark Simpson, "Here Come the
Mirror Men: Why the Future is Metrosexual," Mark Simpson.com,
accessed March 17, 2023, https://www.marksimpson.com/here-come
-the-mirror-men/.

193   *"For some time now, old-fashioned"*: Mark Simpson, "Meet the Metrosexual," Salon, July 22, 2002, https://www.salon.com/2002/07/22/metro
sexual/.

193   *"With me, 'no homo' is basically"*: "Camron Speaks about 'No Homo,'"
Hot 97, March 23, 2007, https://www.youtube.com/watch?v=WUx
Muk-T0gk.

194   *spending $5,000 on a signature custom*: Calum Gordon, "How
Cam'ron's Baby-Pink Outfit Predicted Fashion's Future," *Dazed*, November 8, 2017, https://www.dazeddigital.com/fashion/article/37999/1
/how-camrons-baby-pink-outfit-predicted-fashions-future.

194   *"I'd never seen anybody like Cam"*: Wayne "Wayno" Clark, personal interview, August 3, 2021.

194   *"You'll never tell what a dude"*: Ibid.

194   *"Cam was the first hard-core"*: Jon Caramanica, "It's Not Easy Being
Pink," *New York Times*, October 17, 2004, https://www.nytimes.com
/2004/10/17/fashion/its-not-easy-being-pink.html.

195   *"secure in [his] manhood"*: Sean Michaels, "Kanye West: I'm Confident with My Manhood," *Guardian*, February 10, 2009, https://www
.theguardian.com/music/2009/feb/10/kanye-west-hip-hop-fashion.

195   *"go to Paris [and] have conversations"*: Ibid.

195   *"I think this is one of the strongest things"*: "I Am Cait, Kanye West Shares
Empowering Words with Caitlyn, E!," E! Entertainment, July 26, 2015,
https://youtu.be/NB9hIzE2QJg.

195   *"I know from the meeting that Ricardo"*: "Kanye West; Story Behind
Kanye's Givenchy Kilt," Emmanuel Omale, December 29, 2012,
https://www.youtube.com/watch?v=uTdmlOIBf-c.

195   *"I just love this . . . I just like the silhouette"*: Ibid.

195   *"In the criteria of the small state"*: "ASAP Rocky Talks Interracial Dating,
Homeless Shelters, Homophobia + More," Hard Knock TV, November
2, 2012, https://www.youtube.com/watch?v=xjQBzfLA9MA.

196   *"I did a magazine cover with a gay designer"*: Ibid.

196   *variants a total of 213 times*: Daniel Martin, "Tyler, The Creator: 'My Gay Fans Don't Find My Language Offensive,'" *NME*, June 16, 2011, https://www.nme.com/news/music/odd-future-82-1278567.

196   *"My gay fans don't find my language"*: Ibid.

196   *"Is Tyler, the Creator coming"*: Benjamin Lee, "Is Tyler, the Creator Coming Out as a Gay Man or Just a Queer-Baiting Provocateur?," *Guardian*, July 25, 2017, https://www.theguardian.com/music/2017/jul/25/tyler -the-creator-flower-boy-gay-man-or-queer-baiting-provocateur.

197   *"Ideas about gender identity are rapidly"*: "On the Cusp of Adulthood and Facing an Uncertain Future: What We Know About Gen Z So Far," Pew Research Center, May 14, 2020, https://www.pewresearch .org/social-trends/2020/05/14/on-the-cusp-of-adulthood-and-facing-an -uncertain-future-what-we-know-about-gen-z-so-far-2/.

197   *a record 7.1 percent of U.S. adults*: Julianne McShane, "A Record Number of US Adults Identify as LGBTQ. Gen Z Is Driving the Increase," *Washington Post*, February 17, 2022, https://www.washingtonpost.com /lifestyle/2022/02/17/adults-identifying-lgbt-gen-z/.

197   *most prominent openly gay rapper*: Kris Ex, "Modern Day," *XXL*, September 28, 2021, https://www.xxlmag.com/lil-nas-x-interview/.

197   *"Honestly, I don't feel as"*: Ibid.

198   *"You know what? Yeah"*: Jeremy O. Harris, "Lil Nas X Is in the Right Place at the Right Time," *GQ*, November 15, 2021, https://www.gq.com /story/lil-nas-x-musician-of-the-year-2021.

198   *"It's gonna rub people"*: Jonathan Michael Square, personal interview, February 25, 2021.

198   *"You don't want to do something"*: Touré, personal interview, January 12, 2023.

CHAPTER SIXTEEN: DRIP GODS

199   *"'Bish' stole my look!"*: Diane Dixon (@dianedixon), Instagram, May 30, 2017, https://www.instagram.com/p/BUuXDUbjueP/?hl=en.

199   *"They ain't let me in the"*: Dapper Dan, in conversation with Kenza Fourati, Dumbo House, Brooklyn, New York, August 11, 2021.

199   *"I didn't expect nothing but"*: Daniel Day, *Dapper Dan: Made in Harlem* (New York: Random House, 2019), 269.

200   *"We still struggle to garner"*: Faith Cummings, "Gucci, Dapper Dan, and How the Fashion Industry Fails Black People," *Teen Vogue*, June 1, 2017, https://www.teenvogue.com/story/gucci-dapper-dan-cultural -appropriation.

200   *"I was shocked like everybody"*: Dapper Dan, in converstaion with Kenza Fourati.

200   *"Anybody I do any collaborations"*: Ibid.

200   *"A 'dream deferred'"*: Dapper Dan (@dapperdanharlem), Instagram, December 20, 2017, https://www.instagram.com/p/Bc75ameH-lB/%3Futm_source=ig_embed&ig_rid=e285a608-986e-47cc-b5ef-372853655b73/.

200   *"Let the fashion industry take note"*: Faith Cummings, "Dapper Dan's Gucci-Backed Atelier Opens in Harlem," *Teen Vogue*, January 10, 2018, https://www.teenvogue.com/story/dapper-dan-gucci-atelier-harlem.

200   *"innovator"*: Janelle Okwodu, "Behind the Moment: Dapper Dan's Ascent from Hustler to Fashion Innovator," *Vogue*, September 17, 2020, https://www.vogue.com/article/dapper-dan-behind-the-moment-video-hustler-to-fashion-innovator.

201   *"Gabrielle Coco Chanel didn't see"*: Alice Newbold, "An Exclusive Look at the Making of the Chanel-Pharrell Capsule Collection," British *Vogue*, March 25, 2019, https://www.vogue.co.uk/article/chanel-pharrell.

201   *"Maybe it's a Japanese thing"*: Miles Socha, "Nigo Wants to Revive 'Fun' in Fashion at Kenzo," *Women's Wear Daily*, January 19, 2022, https://wwd.com/fashion-news/designer-luxury/nigo-kenzo-interview-debut-1235032937/.

202   *"He was always someone"*: Véronique Hyland, "Nicki Minaj Puts Her Fendi Prints On," *ELLE*, September 17, 2019, https://www.elle.com/fashion/a29021576/nicki-minaj-fendi-prints-on-collection/.

202   *"They really got close during"*: Véronique Hyland, personal interview, April 29, 2021.

202   *"I just wish he'd gotten a chance"*: Hyland, "Nicki Minaj Puts Her Fendi Prints On."

203   *"fashion's last rebel"*: William Van Meter, "Jeremy Scott, Fashion's Last Rebel," *New York Times*, November 3, 2011, https://www.nytimes.com/2011/12/01/fashion/jeremy-scott-fashions-last-rebel.html.

203   *"When you see my look"*: Rachel Hahn, "Cardi B and Jeremy Scott Reminisce on Their First Met Gala Together," *Vogue*, May 5, 2020, https://www.vogue.com/article/cardi-b-oral-history-met-gala.

203   *took approximately 33,600 hours*: Ibid.

204   *"Can you believe"*: Cardi B (@iamcardib), Twitter, November 22, 2021, https://twitter.com/iamcardib/status/1462886668344692751.

204   *"Blackface is white supremacy"*: Robin Givhan, "Blackface Is White Supremacy in Fashion—and It's Always Been in Season," *Washington*

Post, February 7, 2019, https://www.washingtonpost.com/lifestyle/black face-is-white-supremacy-as-fashion-and-its-always-been-in-season /2019/02/07/fdb60c06-2b1e-11e9-b2fc-721718903bfc_story.html.

204   *"People have realized you cannot pretend"*: Jason Dike, "Have Fashion Brands Stuck to Their BLM Commitments?," *Popular Times*, January 7, 2021.

205   *"I want to say this especially"*: Sara Nathan, "Anna Wintour Admits to 'Hurtful and Intolerant' Behavior at Vogue," Page Six, June 9, 2020, https://pagesix.com/2020/06/09/anna-wintour-admits-to-hurtful-and -intolerant-behavior-at-vogue/.

205   *"Firms stating what is basic political"*: Scott Galloway, "A Somber Instagram Post Is Meaningless When It Comes from a Multi-Billion Dollar Company with the Power to Do Much More," *Business Insider*, June 5, 2020, https://www.businessinsider.com/scott-galloway -for-brands-actions-stronger-than-words-for-blm-2020-6.

206   *"The whole journey I've been"*: Dapper Dan, in conversation with Kenza Fourati.

207   *including British designers Grace*: Elizabeth Paton and Guy Trebay, "Pharrell Williams Is Louis Vuitton's Next Men's Designer," *New York Times*, February 14, 2023, https://www.nytimes.com/2023/02/14/style /pharrell-williams-louis-vuitton-mens-creative-director.html.

207   *"Make sure you come get the next Dapper Dan"*: "Dapper Dan on Hip-Hop Fashion, Harlem History and Constant Reinvention, *The Limits* (podcast), NPR, July 5, 2022, https://www.youtube.com/watch?v=670 46jn8010.

Index

About the Author

Sowmya Krishnamurthy's work has been featured in *XXL*, *Rolling Stone*, *Vibe*, *Essence*, *Complex*, *Billboard*, *Playboy*, the *Village Voice*, and *Time*. As an on-air expert, she's appeared on NPR, CNN, MSNBC, BBC, MTV, and SiriusXM. *Fashion Killa* is the culmination of Sowmya's expertise in music, fashion, and pop culture. Sowmya was born in India and raised in Michigan, and graduated from the University of Michigan's Stephen M. Ross School of Business. This is her first book.